The Urbana Free Library

To renew: call **217-367-4057**
or go to **urbanafreelibrary.org**
and select **My Account**

THE ETHICAL CARNIVORE

THE ETHICAL CARNIVORE

My Year Killing to Eat

Louise Gray

BLOOMSBURY

LONDON · OXFORD · NEW YORK · NEW DELHI · SYDNEY

Bloomsbury Natural History
An imprint of Bloomsbury Publishing Plc

50 Bedford Square
London
WC1B 3DP
UK

1385 Broadway
New York
NY 10018
USA

www.bloomsbury.com

BLOOMSBURY and the Diana logo are trademarks of Bloomsbury Publishing Plc

First published 2016

British Library Cataloguing-in-Publication Data
A catalogue record for this book is available from the British Library.

Library of Congress Cataloguing-in-Publication data has been applied for.

ISBN (hardback) 978-1-4729-3839-8
ISBN (trade paperback) 978-1-4729-3554-0
ISBN (ebook) 978-1-4729-3840-4

2 4 6 8 10 9 7 5 3 1

Illustrations by Samantha Goodlet

Typeset in Bembo Std by Deanta Global Publishing Services, Chennai, India
Printed and bound in Great Britain by CPI Group (UK) Ltd, Croydon CR0 4YY

To find out more about our authors and books visit www.bloomsbury.com.
Here you will find extracts, author interviews, details of forthcoming events
and the option to sign up for our newsletters.

For Dad

Contents

We are healthy only to the extent that our ideas are humane.
Kurt Vonnegut

Prologue

My first kill is a disaster. Either that, or some kind of totemic message sent from the animal spirit world to teach me a lesson.

It starts well enough, on a perfect English summer's afternoon, the day before my birthday. I had decided to spend a year only eating animals I had killed myself. I was an environmental journalist, only too aware of the impact factory farming was having on the planet and the need to cut down on meat. But every time I tried to switch to being vegetarian, I was offered meat from the wild or a local farm. As a farmers' daughter, I had no problem with meat sourced in this way. But I had no desire to be one of those ungracious people who turns up at dinner parties and only eats the food after asking a series of irritating questions.

The only logical thing to do seemed to be to only eat animals I had killed myself. From the moment I said it, not entirely seriously, I realised I had touched a raw nerve. My friends and colleagues were fascinated. They had no idea how animals were killed or processed. How would it feel to kill an animal? How would you catch it? How would you butcher it? They were hungry: hungry for a connection to the meat they were eating and the wider natural world. I realised I would actually have to do it.

I set off a little trepidatious about shooting a gun, but confident I am in safe hands with 'a proper old-school gamekeeper'. It is as if the Essex countryside has put on her best clothes for the occasion. Bunting hangs from the thatched cottages and the fields shine gold in the late afternoon sun. It is only when I pass the pub offering a discount for those wearing yellow jerseys that I remember the Tour de France passed through earlier that day. I roll down the windows to let in the smell of cut hay and turn up the radio. The song of the summer comes on, high and breezy. By the time I arrive at Hamel's Park in Hertfordshire I am windblown and smiling.

Steve Reynolds stands in the yard as I drive in, hands on his hips, squinting into the sun. I see with relief that he looks like the archetypal gamekeeper, with his ginger muttonchops and checked shirt open almost to the waist. He is surrounded by barking dogs, too, though on closer inspection I realise they are poodles wearing diamante collars rather than the spaniels and labradors you would traditionally find at an estate cottage.

I stretch out a hand, but he is suspicious at first. He wants to know if I am a 'sab' or 'saboteur' who disrupted shoots in the 1990s in protest against fox hunting and other blood sports. I laugh to put him at his ease. 'No, no,' I say, and explain my mission. 'I just want to find out what it's really like to kill an animal. I think it will make people appreciate food more, so they eat less meat.'

'Hmmm.' He seems unsure. His wife, Christine, appears in the doorway, arms folded. 'Not realistic,' she says. 'People want cheap stuff in packets nowadays; most of the pheasants we shoot are sent to Belgium.' Then, remembering herself, 'Come in, come in.'

I am ushered inside to stand awkwardly in the front room waiting for a glass of water. To distract from further discussion of my idea, which seems rather silly now under the down-to-earth gaze of Steve and his wife – rather than my middle-class friends – I admire the decor. 'Wow, is that a barn owl?' Taxidermy lines the walls, among them a fox, hare and a peregrine falcon. Steve is keen to tell me they are all roadkill or picked up from under electricity lines, especially the birds of prey, which would be illegal to kill. His most prized specimens are animals with unusual markings or features, such as the woodcock with the short beak, the white partridge and albino stoat. I wander into another room to see even more glassy eyes staring out at me alongside pictures of Steve receiving various prizes for conservation, looking uncomfortable in a suit. 'It's how a countryman's house should look!' he says.

As we sail off in an open-sided jeep, a gun rattling away on the dashboard, boxes of bullets at our feet, I ask what a countryman is. 'Well, there's a boy in the country and a countryboy, if you know what I mean?'

'And which are you?'

'I'm a countryman, mate!'

We rumble across the busy A10 to a field where we can sight the gun and continue to chat as Steve sets up the targets and lets down his guard. He wasn't born into this sort of life, he explains. His father was a shopkeeper back in the days when everyone knew how to shoot, and of course he taught his son. Steve loved crawling about in the early morning dew more than anything else and when a job came up on an estate he jumped at it. He's pretty much been here ever since. 'We all look after each other, see? I keep the predators down, and the songbirds, the pheasants and other wildlife can flourish.'

I ask lots of questions about the rifle but only understand the answers because of research on the internet the night before, knowing that Steve – like most shooting men – will presume I know what he is on about. I know a rifle has grooves inside the barrel, so-called 'rifling' to spin a bullet and deliver a more deadly accurate shot. It is used for killing ground game. A shotgun, which fires a spray of pellets, is used to kill birds. We use a .22 calibre rifle, referring to the diameter of the bore or inside of the barrel, with a wooden stock. Steve handles the gun with ease, never pointing the barrel at me and handing it over only when I sit on a stool with a rest for the gun in front of me. There is no ceremony in coming face to face with a deadly weapon, though it feels strange. I press my cheek against the cool wood and smell gunpowder and oil, like the gun room at home where Dad used to keep his antique guns and my late mother's jewellery box. Being so close to the metal sets my teeth on edge.

The gun is heavy and wobbles at first, making black rings appear around the edge of the telescopic sight. I breathe in and as I breathe out relax, as I have been taught, until the gun is steady and I can get my eye the right distance from the sight. The view clears, the cross hair appears and I gently squeeze the trigger.

Steve is impressed with my aim and after just a few shots we drive into a valley where cows graze a lush water meadow. Steve has set up a makeshift hide by covering a gate in hazel branches and setting out a chair and support for the gun. Almost as soon as I get in position a rabbit – or vermin, as gamekeepers call them – hops into view. I am waiting for Steve's order since he can identify the younger rabbits that won't be breeding yet by their sleek fur and relatively smaller size. 'Go on, he's perfect, shoot him.' There is no black rim, the cross hair hovers over his shoulder, my heart is pumping; I can't afford to think about this too much. I pull the trigger.

The rabbit somersaults into the air, lands and impossibly dashes forward. 'Again!' But I can't, my hands are shaking. Steve takes the gun but it is too late – the rabbit is gone. He lifts his face from the sight and holds out his hand. 'Well done, your first kill.'

'But … But it's still alive.'

'No it's not, it's just in the thistles there.' I take his huge, warm hand. I don't feel pleased, I feel like I have done something horribly, horribly wrong. We hurry over the field to where the rabbit should be, but there is no blood. 'He'll just be over the fence,' says Steve. We struggle over the barbed wire and start bashing away at the undergrowth. There is no sign of the rabbit. I am beginning to panic. I pick up a stick and thrash at the nettles and poke in among the thistles. At one point I hesitate – I'll be stung if I go in there – and then curse myself: how could I put a few stings above the suffering of an animal? My mind is racing. What if we don't find the rabbit? Why didn't Steve bring a dog, even if it was a bloody poodle?

'He's gone,' he says.

'Really?' I want to keep searching.

'They have a massive surge of adrenaline when they are injured; they can get quite far. He could have run as far as the burrow.' Now I am cursing myself for being so egotistical. Why did I embark on this stupid project? What was I trying to prove? I am a bad person. A bad person who has caused terrible suffering just to try and make a point at a dinner party. I whip the nettles so hard my stick breaks. I can't speak or I'll cry. I'm trying to keep calm. 'Come on,' says Steve. 'We're not going to find him now.'

As I struggle to get my shaking legs back over the fence he laughs at me. 'See what I mean? The difference between a countrygirl and a girl in the country.' As soon as we sit down back at the hide I want to go over and over it again, searching for comfort.

'Could he still be alive? Could he survive?'

'No, no he's dead, you hit him alright.'

'Then … then he's bleeding to death?'

Steve doesn't answer for a moment. Then, 'He's dead. He will have died quick,' he says. 'He just got to some cover and we can't find him.'

'Oh my God, could he be bleeding to death in the burrow?' I think about the babies; they call them kittens.

Steve doesn't answer immediately. 'I'm not going to lie to you. This is reality. I've missed before. I've injured an animal twice in my life. Deer, big animals. It's what happens.'

I am trying to listen, trying to block out flashbacks to childhood. Why didn't I think of *Watership Down* before? I hated that film as a child. It only took my sister singing a few lines of 'Bright Eyes', the Art Garfunkel song on the soundtrack, and I would burst into tears. I remember the rabbits hiding terrified in the burrows. I remember the blood sliding over the screen. The saddest sequence of all comes back to me now, the moment of death, the sooty spirit rabbit dancing around the sun: 'All the world will be your enemy, Prince with a Thousand Enemies, and whenever they catch you, they will kill you …'

Steve can see I am distressed and is desperately trying to make me feel better. 'Why is there a rubber on the end of a pencil?' he says.

'So you can rub things out?'

'Because we all make mistakes.' So we can't rub things out then, I think, not once they are done. Steve tries another tack. 'You know fishing? Think of all those fish. Do you know what they do? They don't bash them over the head and kill them quick. No, they suffocate to death; that's agony, that is.' I still can't respond. 'What about pheasant shooting?' he says. 'Pheasant shooting is not perfect.' I am momentarily pulled out of my *Watership Down* moment. This is unusual for a gamekeeper. 'Yes, shotguns aren't that accurate, not like rifles. Shot gets in the birds all the time and they fly on; they're not always killed outright. That's why we have dogs, to pick them up quick.'

I am grateful. It's true. I'm not so bad, am I? I was trying to do something good – to make people think about killing. This is easy to justify; we are all indirectly letting animals die every day. OK, the slaughterhouse might be a more accurate shot than me but it must go wrong. All attempts to kill humanely can go wrong. At least I went out and tried to do it myself. At least I know that now ...

'You had this smile when you turned up in my yard,' says Steve. 'But it's gone now.' I do feel different. I feel like a killer. I try to smile. 'C'mon, you've got to get back on the horse.' It has started spitting with rain, the evening has cooled, and what with us crashing about in the undergrowth the rabbits nearby have all gone. But there are a few coming out again now, further away. Steve gets out another rifle, a high-performance .17 calibre that is more accurate and powerful. It looks more like an American gun, with a green stock and huge telescopic sight. I don't feel comfortable with it, preferring the familiar wood and iron. 'Come on, this'll get you one of those bunnies over there.' He sets me up again and, although my heart is racing and my breathing is shallow, I take the gun.

At first the sight wobbles around, I need to calm down, but I bring it under control. Steve looks down the barrel as well, his eye behind the sight, his breath against my cheek. I know he wants to make up for the disastrous start to the evening. 'I'd just love you to get a rabbit, Louise. I would.' I just want to go home and curl up and cry, I want this to be over, but I also want to please Steve. 'Look, under the yellow flowers, two bunnies.' I can see the rabbits in the sights. My heart is beating in my chest and I have to concentrate to breathe. I swing the barrel back and forth; they are both about the same size, small – they must be young. But can Steve really tell? Is it a doe? Do I really want to kill again? What good would that do? It would just make things worse, more suffering for my stupid ego. What if I miss again?

The rabbits hop away. 'It's OK,' says Steve. 'Take a deep breath, try again.' I know he has to be finished by 7 pm and it is much later now, but he also desperately wants me to go home with a 'something in the bag'. More kits come into view. I can see them through the sight, nibbling the grass, turning towards me, standing on their hind legs to check for predators ... 'but first they have to catch you digger, listener, runner, prince with the swift warning'. I have the cross hair over the shoulder again, I have to get it right. I don't know why I am doing this.

'Come on.' I can feel Steve willing me to pull the trigger. I stare and stare, my thoughts galloping, trying to think of a reason why I am doing this, until another rabbit hops out of sight. Steve sees I have lost my confidence and thinks it's because I don't trust the gun. We swap places and he takes a shot. I jump at the sound of the gun and realise I am shaking, my nerves still on edge. I wonder how these people, mostly men, do this so casually. 'Well, it went over the rabbit's head,' he laughs. 'Come on, we'll try another spot but we'll have to be quick.'

'It's OK Steve,' I say. 'Maybe I could come back another day?' I am trying to smile like I did earlier, to put him at his ease, but really I want to be alone.

'OK.' He looks disappointed for me. 'Well, you know you can come back anytime you like.'

'Yes, of course.'

We drive back through the meadows; the rabbits are still coming out and the cattle are undisturbed, like nothing has happened, but I feel completely different. Back at Steve's house, I hurry to get away and let him get to the pub. I thank him and shake his hand and get back in my car. I know exactly where I am going. The countryside seems darker now, although it is still light. A muntjac deer crosses in front of the car. The hedgerows, so pretty before, are full of shadows. I drive straight back across the busy A10, look left and right, look again. I can't get close to where we were shooting so I park the car in the middle of the lane and just hope no one needs to get past; there don't seem to be many houses down here. I grab a birch walking stick I won in a raffle and set off at a run. I feel desperate now to try and make amends for what I have done. My breath comes in gasps and I am glad; at last I can express the panic I feel. It makes me light-headed but it's a release.

Back at the barbed wire fence I rip my sweatshirt but I don't care. I start searching where Steve and I were looking, but perhaps we were wrong? I realise my legs are still shaking. Why is there no blood? I crouch down to get further into the trees. I think about where rabbit burrows are. By the riverbank? I wade through the brambles to where I can see glimpses of a stream and jump down into the water; there are no signs of burrows but are they rabbit droppings? They can't be. I see there is a hole, too big for a rabbit. A fox perhaps. I get down on my hands and knees and sniff. It is musty – it must be a fox – or a badger. Why don't I know? I feel crazed, like an animal, like part of this wood. I scramble back up and continue searching, lying down to look under the nettles. It smells dank, like autumn.

It is getting dark under the canopy and I can hear the rain on the leaves. Something primeval tells me I shouldn't be here, alone in the forest at night. As my breathing calms down and my heart slows I realise this is fruitless; the rabbit is nowhere to be seen. I am going to have to give up this search and this idea of killing animals – even if it was well intentioned. What was I thinking anyway, setting out on this silly quest? I will have to become a vegetarian of course, maybe a vegan. I can't forget what this feels like.

As I walk back towards the fence I half-heartedly thrash around with my stick again. I poke a thick clump of thistles right by the fence and feel something soft. It can't be. But even from the end of the stick I can feel it is a body; a soft, warm, dead body. I look down and there he is, sleek brown fur. I pick him up and see his face; his eyes are open and down his muzzle is a beautiful white blaze. I can feel his shoulder blades under my fingers, his dead weight. I ought to say something. 'Thank you?' I whisper. 'I mean, sorry.' I realise I don't know what to say. I should have looked up some Native American prayer for this moment, something appropriate, but really I have nothing useful to say, nothing that will bring life back. The rabbit also has a white chest. They are the most extraordinary markings: the blaze is the shape of Harry Potter's scar, like he's a wizard of Farthing Wood. How is anyone meant to be able to kill their supper when we have been brought up on a literary diet of talking woodland animals?

But I'm glad I've found him; at least I know the suffering is over. I see where the bullet has entered near his spine. I broke his neck; he didn't get far, we just didn't search close to the fence. He is warm and a desperate thought comes into my head: perhaps he is still alive? Perhaps I can take him to a vet? I struggle through the fence and start to run; I want to make this better. I go past a dog walker, but he doesn't turn a hair at a girl running down the field with a half-white rabbit. 'Come on Coco,' he says to a fat chocolate labrador.

I lay the rabbit in the footwell of the passenger seat and drive back to Steve's house. He has gone and Christine pops her head over the stable-style door to the kitchen. 'Hi,' I say. I want to ask her if she will check the rabbit is dead, perhaps give me the name of a vet, some kind of rabbit resuscitation technique? But she just looks surprised. 'Sorry, is Steve here?'

'He's in the pub, The Crown, in Buntingford.' She gives me directions and I rush back to the car, hardly thinking how I must look in my ripped top, covered in sticky willy, with red-rimmed eyes.

The Crown is a red brick pub, warmed by the sun, and I find Steve in the bar, his back to me, though I know him by the curly hair and the yellow braces. I tap his shoulder and he turns. 'I've got something to show you, you have to come now.' His drinking companions laugh in shock – who is this mad woman?

'You haven't …?'

I know the rabbit is dead now. 'Yes, I found him, come on, you have to see.' We hurry out into the street where I have parked my battered Ford Fiesta on a double yellow line. I reach into the passenger side and bring out the rabbit with the white blaze. Steve takes him with more than a little reverence.

'Well I never, I've never seen anything like this before.' He looks me straight in the eye. 'You're special, Louise. You are. You went in there and you crawled around in the nettles till you found him. You're passionate, aren't you? About what you are doing?'

'Well of course I am, I had to.' How could I explain what this meant? To feel responsible. 'I had to find him.' I realise Steve's blue eyes are brighter than before; they have gone turquoise. 'Steve, are you crying?'

'I've got a big heart, Louise, that's all. Just a big heart. I'm kind, I care, that's all.' We hug, a tight squeeze from a total stranger who a few hours before I had never met. He admires the rabbit again. 'You flinched, didn't you?'

'Yes.' I curse myself once again. I had been told to breathe in, breathe out, stay calm, squeeze the trigger, but it must have been nerves. I hadn't realised I would be so scared. I hadn't realised how it would make me feel. A small flinch and the bullet went high, into the neck, not the heart. 'I need a drink.'

'I'm bloody buying you one.'

We go inside and I order a glass of the cheapest brandy. Steve's drinking companions are quite taken with this strange girl in a damp sweatshirt, with muddy knees and leaves in her hair. 'Darling, stay and have another drink with us,' says Mick the window cleaner. 'Let's see this rabbit then.'

'No, no,' protests Steve. 'People are eating.' He motions to the others to keep their voices down as commuters come in for their evening drink.

'That's kind of the whole point,' I say, thinking of my mission statement for the first time that evening. Here they are probably dining on local 'wild rabbit' but none of them want to see the body.

'You'll have to stuff him, of course,' says Steve. 'He's so handsome.'

'I'm not sure. Does that mean I can eat him too?' His death cannot be for display.

'Course!' Steve replies.

'Oh, OK, but I want to take him home just now, I want to show my dad.'

'That's fine, just put him in a brown paper bag and put him in the freezer and send him to me when you're ready. And come back, do you hear? We have more vermin to kill – signal crayfish and squirrels.' I have met a proper countryman and I'm grateful.

I thank Steve and his companions and get back into my car. Driving back it is raining, the bunting has been taken down and the light of the day is sinking into the earth. I leave the radio off, wanting to think about the experience and the rabbit still lying in my footwell, bleeding onto an old tax disc.

When I get back to my brother's house, I am still pumped on adrenaline and tell them all the story in the doorway. 'I made a gamekeeper cry!' They all laugh and although I tell them how awful I feel, how I missed, no one focuses on the suffering; they seem to be able to brush over it, just like we do every day. They all want to see the rabbit. My sister-in-law screams. 'You've killed someone's pet rabbit!' He is so pretty, but certainly wild.

My dad is amazed. 'Well I've shot hundreds of rabbits but I've never seen one like this …' He also seems a little hurt by my adventure. 'Darling, didn't I ever teach you how to shoot a rabbit? Surely I must have …' No Daddy, you didn't, I think. And not for the first time, I wonder why. I guess I never showed an interest. I sat in the back of the truck, I covered my ears and looked away. But then did my brothers really want to do it? Is it because I'm a girl? A coward?

It's too much to think about tonight. Instead I sit up late looking at an almost full moon and going over everything that just happened. I don't want to forget the rabbit with the white blaze. He has taught me what it feels like to get it wrong. That is the risk we take when we kill an animal. Is this the price for being a carnivore? I also wonder about how I feel now, now I have found him. I do feel better, but should I? It doesn't make anything any different, unless I believe he died straight away with no suffering or that this is some kind of sign – and that is ridiculous.

Steve phones, although it is near midnight. I presume he is checking I got home OK after the brandy. 'No, I wasn't worried about the journey, I was worried about your head,' he says. 'You've had quite an evening.' I realise that I was acting quite strangely, clearly a little traumatised, quite manic.

'My head? Well yes, I do feel a little different.' My heart, too, I think; it still feels constricted, a little bruised by loss, by what I have done. 'I'm just trying to work it out actually, think about it.'

'Yes, you think about it my dear.' Despite the fact he does it every day, Steve seems to understand the impact of killing an animal.

'I feel I owe it to the rabbit,' I say. 'It sounds stupid but I don't want him to die for nothing. He's special, right?'

I put down the phone and look at the waxing moon. 'OK Buster, "Prince with a Thousand Enemies", whatever you are or will become, here's your prayer: I will make your death worthwhile. I won't give up my "silly quest". I will go out and I will find out what it means to kill, to eat. And then, I'll write a book about it.'

CHAPTER ONE

Pearls

'I weep for you,' the Walrus said:
'I deeply sympathize.'
With sobs and tears he sorted out
Those of the largest size,
Holding his pocket-handkerchief
Before his streaming eyes …
                    'The Walrus and the Carpenter',
                                by Lewis Carroll

There is a little pot of pearls I keep on losing. I have been trying to fill it up since I was a child. Every time we eat hand-picked mussels in Torridon, in north-west Scotland, where my family goes on holiday, I carefully collect the tiny pearls under my nails: they are the shape of Rice Krispies and shades of purple, green and grey – but pearls nevertheless. I drop them into a shot glass and vow that one day it will be full. Of course the glass is always missing by the time I return and I have to start again. But one day, I am sure, it will start filling up, and I will be able to make a brooch with those misshapen pearls.

It is in Torridon where I first start thinking about the ethics of eating animals. As the Environment Correspondent on the *Daily Telegraph* for five years, I reported on the rising levels of greenhouse gases in the atmosphere that are warming the globe. I was well aware that animal agriculture was one of the main contributors to the problem. I also wrote about the welfare issues, the overuse of antibiotics and the pollution of water. Look beneath the surface and the statistics are pretty scary. We are already eating 60 billion animals a year and by 2050 the figure is expected to rise to 100 billion. In the rich world we eat three or four times as much animal protein as we need. Yet despite all the articles I wrote about the consequences of rising temperatures – the floods, droughts and species extinctions – eating fewer animals was rarely considered as a solution.

When I left the newspaper, a little burnt out and depressed by the state of the environment, I went to live alone in Torridon for a few months. For the first time in my life I was miles away from any shops or other people. I had time to think and get back in touch with nature. The stonechats and greylag geese came to sit outside my window and every morning stags would be grazing. I got to know them: one with a black chest, one with a pale coat and another with wide, wide antlers, always the last to turn and run. It was as if he was challenging me: this was his patch, what was I doing here? I often went walking in the gloaming, as the light was fading to a blue dusk. One dreich evening the stag was standing in the path, a silhouette, his wide-beam antlers holding up the sky. We stared at each other for a moment, then I turned and walked away.

Torridon means place of transference in Gaelic. I was certainly shifting my thought patterns, asking important questions for the first time: what makes us any different to the animals outside the window? Is it our ability to think? If so, shouldn't we think about the animals we eat? Despite all those tortured conversations with my vegan friends, I did not believe the answer was to give up meat completely. Perhaps it was my background as a farmer's daughter, albeit a largely arable farmer. Or perhaps because I was so immersed in a natural environment where everything relied on each other. The salmon eat the flies, the eagles eat the voles, the wolves – if they were still here – would eat the deer. Eating animals felt like part of the cycle of life and death that I was caught up in myself.

Ethics is the effort to live a moral life. To me that meant understanding fully the consequences of my actions. To be an ethical carnivore for a year, I decided to be vegetarian most of the time and only eat animals I had caught, killed and butchered myself.

After the shock of the rabbit, shellfish seemed the easiest place to start. I do my research, beginning with the godfather of animal rights, Peter Singer. In his book *Animal Liberation*, published in 1975, he used the word 'speciesism' to refer to the attitude of certain humans towards other species. It is the extreme end of animal rights, a belief that taking any life on the basis of species is wrong. He argued that the development of civilised society would mean all species are considered equally, just as we have come to respect people of different sexes and nations.

However, on shellfish he is a little more relenting. In the first editions of *Animal Liberation*, he sanctioned oyster eating, but later reversed the decision. He justified the U-turn by saying it was as yet unclear whether oysters suffer. Even PETA (People for the Ethical Treatment of Animals) admits it is unclear whether oysters suffer. The bivalves do not move, suggesting there is no evolutionary reason to feel pain, as they cannot escape what is causing such discomfort anyway. Also the nervous system is very simple; there is nothing like a brain to process pain. I can't help thinking about the pearls, though – why do molluscs coat an irritating microscopic object in pearl, other than because it causes pain?

While it is so uncertain, PETA and Singer argue against eating animals. But 'ostrovegans' in California – where else? – eat no animal products other than molluscs. They argue that in the case of uncertainty you might as well take advantage of natural proteins and minerals. In fact, you have a duty to eat oysters and mussels because growing the shellfish can be good for the environment.

I agree the question of ethics should take in not only pain perception, but also the impact the animal has on the wider environment. In the UK, shellfish and how we eat them have shaped our coastline for centuries. I decide to find out how oysters are harvested where I grew up in Essex.

Oyster fishing seemed like the perfect birthday treat, the day after the rabbit, especially with my father in tow. We seldom spend time together and it's another glorious summer's day. Dad tuts about the state of the crops and my overtaking skills as we drive east towards the sea. I count the ash trees as we pass Eight Ash Green – one, two, three, four, five – wondering if they will survive the latest onslaught of disease. As we cross the Orwell Bridge, the land flattens out and a salt crust forms on anything green, washing the leaves silver. We sink, fields turning to mud flats, houses to bungalows, brightly coloured and tatty from the sea breeze. In Brightlingsea the yachts chink in the wind and day trippers bob up and down on the waves. Like most of the coastal towns in Essex, it used to be a thriving fishing port, but the industry collapsed with the arrival of 'factory boats' further out in the North Sea hoovering up what was left of a once thriving fishery. In a sign of the times only one fishing vessel in the harbour now goes out commercially for cod, while another is used to service the local wind farm.

Dad and I are in treat mode, sipping cappuccinos as we wander down the jetty to board the *Jacqueline Anne*. It is not difficult to find our host for the day. Bram Haward, an eighth generation oysterman, is already loading buckets and barrels of fuel into the hold of a battered little oyster dredger. With his earrings and baseball cap, he doesn't look like a yachtie, not even an Essex yachtie – he looks like a pirate.

I take a proffered hand and clamber on board. As we cast off, I wonder what it used to look like, when a summer's morning in this harbour meant shouts and clanging chains and the smell of fish, rather than the muffled sound of Radio 4 and the smell of coffee, but Bram doesn't remember fishing boats ever being here. 'It's always been just us and tourists,' he says, nodding at my camera.

'Shifting Baseline Syndrome' they call it, when a generation can't remember the abundance of wildlife in the past, so they think things are OK – improving, even – when really they are far from what they could be. I suffer from it myself. I grew up on a farm in the 1980s and I thought things had improved until one day I was chatting to Graham Madge, the press officer for the RSPB (Royal Society for the Protection of Birds) and possibly one of the most knowledgeable people on birds I know. It was the charity's annual farmland bird count and I was telling him that as far as I was concerned, birdlife on farms had increased – hadn't it? I certainly saw more birds.

'And where did you grow up, Louise?'

'Essex.'

'And have you ever seen a lapwing?'

'No.' I don't want to admit I'm not even sure what a lapwing looks like. Doesn't it have a back-to-front kiss curl sitting on top of its head?

'There used to be whole flocks of them you know, just where you grew up …' I try to imagine what a flock of lapwings looks like but can't, so I look up the collective noun instead. A 'deceit' of lapwings, Google tells me. I do feel deceived, to have grown up without this beautiful bird. To have lost so much, to still be losing …

Bram has noticed one big change in his environment, though: the increase in the number of Pacific rock oysters. This non-native species was introduced from the Pacific forty years ago to be cultivated for fancy restaurants. No one bothered with biosecurity in the swinging sixties, and anyway it was assumed it was impossible for the species to survive our cold winters. Of course they did more than survive – they thrived, and now encrust the south coast. Bram calls them 'gigas' after their scientific name, *Crassostrea gigas*, and they are indeed gigantic, reaching the width of a man's hand in five years and a hand like Bram's in nine.

As we chug around the harbour in the little oyster dredger our skipper lowers what looks like a net on skis, around the size of a fruit crate, to scrape oysters from the bottom. It takes only a few seconds to fill the contraption before it is hauled up on to deck and we can take the huge muddy great oysters in both hands. 'You see, you are actually doing the environment a favour by eating these,' says Bram, tossing another enormous oyster into the bucket. 'Though don't know how you'll eat this many …'

Every so often we find one of the rare native oysters. The fan-shaped shells with pretty purple and green markings seem delicate in comparison to the gnarly old rock oysters and are much smaller – though they can grow just as big, given enough time. We throw the native oysters back as they are not allowed to be eaten when they are spawning during the summer – or when there is not an 'r' in the month.

In the past oysters surrounded this part of Britain, fluttering their shells like so many stationary Pac-Men. Like all bivalves they filter feed by drawing in water over tiny hairs or 'cilia', the Latin word for eyelashes. Sediments, nutrients and phytoplankton are absorbed and clean water spat out, thereby cleaning the surrounding environment. Each oyster filters up to 5 litres (8.8 pints) of water per hour. At the same time, the seabed is stabilised by growing shells that over generations create rock-like reefs. Oyster beds used to surround most of northern Europe, perhaps making the grey North Sea crystal clear. Can you imagine it? It is the kind of image that makes me want to dive back in time, into those crystalline waters, to see what there once was before we replaced molluscs with mud. To see the Romans, who made their colonial capital in Colchester, Essex because it was close to an easy source of protein, march in and feast on local fare. Indeed, according to Sallust, writing on Caesar's invasion, the oyster was the only good thing those 'poor Britons' could produce.

And it was always the food of the poor. In Victorian times, the poorer you were the more oysters you packed into your pie to make up for the lack of meat. Oyster and stout was the snack of the masses. In 1864 more than 700 million oysters were consumed in London alone. As Sam Weller in Charles Dickens' *The Pickwick Papers* notes: 'It's a very remarkable circumstance that poverty and oysters always seem to go together.' They were a cheap and easy form of protein but the bounty couldn't last. Industrial dredging was invented and before long we had scraped the bowl clean.

Oysters became rare and therefore a delicacy, especially the native oysters, not only struggling to bounce back after centuries of overfishing but also now competing with an invasive species: *gigas*. Off East Anglia, Bram and his father have been trying to give the native oysters a helping hand by gently taking the young spats and planting them in lanes out on the marshes where the best feeding is available. This ancient art of cultivating oysters is being practised around the British Isles, often supported by government or European money. In some areas, like Scotland and South Wales, native oyster seeds have had to be brought in from elsewhere to try and re-establish oyster beds long destroyed and only identified by ancient maps, the remains of some shells or old place names like 'Oyster Mouth' and 'Oyster Bay'. The hope is that one day these new oyster beds will not only provide food once again but also filter the water and provide protection against erosion and storms.

In New York, a scheme to reintroduce oysters, the 'Billion Oyster Project' or BOP, has become even more urgent after Hurricane Sandy. Like in London, oysters were once the food of the masses, the original pizza slice. But pollution and overfishing pushed the species out. Now new oyster beds are being created using the shells recycled from fancy hotels. Eating oysters is not only fashionable – it's also ethical.

My oysters need time to filter themselves by sitting in clean water for at least 48 hours, before I can eat them. In the meantime I celebrate my birthday with my family. My present from Dad? A string of cultivated pearls.

By the time I get around to eating the oysters it is a week or so later, in mid-July, and raining. I pick up two girlfriends, Jenna and Harriet, at Colchester train station. They skip up the platform dressed in skinny jeans and anoraks. It's the kind of day trip they recommend in weekend supplements. 'West Mersea, the place to see and be seen – and eat local seafood …' We can't see anything since the haar rolling in from the sea is so thick, but eventually locate my oysters in a wooden shack on the harbour front.

The Company Shed may look scruffy but it is the height of foodie fashion. The waitresses wear wellies and carry fresh fish to the tables, where diners are given a chopping board and a roll of kitchen paper and expected to get on with it.

Nowadays the place is full of trendy Londoners cracking open shellfish. The proprietress Heather does not have time for yet another food blogger poking around. She irritably sends us through some shower curtains to the garage out back, full of tanks, where we find Phil, a handsome oysterman, to show us where my catch might be. He hands me a vicious-looking instrument, called a 'shucking' knife, that looks like a cross between a knife and a screwdriver, then demonstrates how to insert the knife into the 'mouth' of the oyster and wiggle it around until it opens. It is then just a case of cutting the 'feet' still attached to the shell and dinner is served.

Apparently the best oystermen can shuck 1,000 oysters in a day. I struggle with one. This oyster may not have a brain but he positively does not want to let go of life. It's hard work, the rock oyster not yielding until I bash away at the calcite, and finally relenting with a satisfying 'pop'.

'Go on, down in one,' says Phil.

'So what's it like?' ask the girls.

And without thinking, I say it: 'You know that moment? When you just can't swallow?' The shed is silent but for the gurgling of the tanks and the rising giggle in Jenna's throat. 'Umm …' I feel my own discomfort creeping up my neck, burning my cheeks. The hot oysterman flushes pink, and Jenna snorts and careens backwards on her long legs to pretend to look interested in a tank of lobsters. Harriet, dear Harriet, as usual feels terrible for someone else. She just looks at the oysterman with her huge blue eyes as if to say 'sorry, I am sorry for my friends'.

We are disgraced and sit in the corner of the cafe, ignored, like the back seat of the school bus. 'So, c'mon, "Ethical Carnivore": what does it feel like killing and eating your first living creature?' asks Jenna, aware I am going to write a blog about the whole experience. I squirt lemon on the quivering muscle sitting before me, which I am about to eat alive. It does look more sentient than broccoli. But like the Walrus in the famous Lewis Carroll poem 'The Walrus and the

Carpenter', who wolfs down all the baby oysters with lashings of bread and butter, I would be lying if I said I felt sad.

'It's like floating over the lid of a jewel box – you swim down through the kelp forest and then down again into life encrusted upon life; complex, colourful and delicate.' Guy Grieve, the founder of The Ethical Shellfish Company, is describing to me what it is like to go scallop diving off the Isle of Mull. 'Then you hear the most nightmarish sound in the world,' he continues. 'A grating, tinkling sound, like the swinging of chains, like a Dickensian ghost approaching. Next time you come to the scallop beds, it is all gone. Rubblised, a scree slope. The whole water column is full of silt, the undersea world blanketed in detritus.'

Three times a day Guy goes where no one else goes. He sees what no one else sees and hears what no one else hears. He hears the scallop dredgers. 'It is the sound of pure, rampant, meaningless greed,' he says. Scallop dredging is one of the most controversial fishing methods in the world, yet it is widely used inshore around the British Isles. It uses a large rake that scrapes along the seabed, flipping the scallops into a net.

Guy, an adventurer who set up his company after sailing around the world and living alone in Alaska, still can't quite believe that it is allowed in a country like the UK. He points out that scallops will live again quite happily on a 'rubblised' dead zone, feeding on the phytoplankton that passes overhead. But what about everything else? The greater biodiversity supported by seaweed and corals? Could this be one of the reasons for the continued decline in the other fisheries for cod and haddock around the west coast?

Guy argues that there is an alternative: putting on a dry suit and 70kg (154lb) of weights and diving to the bottom of the ocean to carefully pick out only the larger scallops, leaving the coral, ferns and other 'life encrusted upon life' unharmed. 'I want to go into the garden and pick the apples – without trampling the flowers,' he says. 'We don't need this total war approach. We don't need to destroy everything to make food, because we can do it a bit more sustainably.'

Later I pop open one of Guy's hand-dived scallops at a restaurant in Edinburgh and tear away the stomach or 'black frill', leaving only the white flesh and a coral sac of roe. It is quickly grilled and placed back in the shell, like Botticelli's *Venus*. Food of the gods. Of course it costs more than a dredged scallop, 150 per cent more, but I consider it a treat. As Guy says: 'How would you like your scallop? With or without marine destruction?'

As far as the scallop divers and creel fishermen of the British Isles are concerned, the ethics of eating shellfish are very much about how the animals are harvested. Dredged scallops and trawled prawns are blamed for ripping up the seabed, leaving a dead zone where other fish can no longer find food. In contrast, langoustines or lobsters caught in creels do not damage the seabed and they support more fishermen. The Scottish Creel Fishermen's Federation was set up recently with the purpose of promoting this way of fishing. Soon labels in the supermarket will show 'creel caught' prawns to go with your 'hand-dived scallops'.

At Shieldaig Harbour on Loch Torridon I pick up a crate of prawns and take them back for my supper. The pink langoustines poke out of the crate, waving their razor sharp claws and making the plastic cardboard squeak like a huge living creature. I pop them in the freezer first to 'put them to sleep' and later as I throw them into the pot I can't stop myself muttering 'sorry, sorry, sorry …'

We tend to be more sentimental about crustaceans than molluscs. I blame Phoebe from *Friends*. There is a famous scene from the US series where she describes Ross as Rachel's 'lobster', meaning they will mate for life. Like most things in Hollywood, it's total bullshit – lobsters are actually rather promiscuous creatures – but still, it's a nice idea.

My granny hated killing shellfish. I remember bringing her back a fresh lobster from Seacliff beach once, many years ago. My cousin Jack Dale, who works creels off the East Lothian coast, had given it to me as a gift to 'take back to London'. 'Ach, just put him on the seat next to you and you'll get the whole carriage!' But Granny – who would normally refuse me nothing – refused to cook it. This was a surprise. My Granny was a farmer's wife, capable of gutting pheasants and cutting up rabbits, but she was being squeamish about a shellfish? 'Oh, it's horrible,' she said. 'Tell me when you are going to do it, I don't want to be in the room.' I'm ashamed to say I threw the lobster in a pan of boiling water and then ran out of the kitchen so I didn't hear the 'screams' – or the whistle of air escaping the body cavity. Jack was right – I got the whole carriage – and that night when I arrived back in London I had great fun sharing out the cooked lobster in a beer garden in Camden.

A few years later I go back to Seacliff and find Jack's son Robbie still hauling in creels from Seacliff, one of the smallest harbours in Scotland, hewn from the same red sandstone as Tantallon Castle above. As their wee boat *Keyte* backs out of the harbour a seal dives down by the rocks, the eider ducks flap out of the water and a fulmar circles overhead. It is a classic and glorious British seaside scene and, perhaps surprisingly for a couple of 20-somethings, Robbie and his fellow creel fisherman Sam Lowe do not take it for granted. It is hard physical work hauling in five creels at a time, going out in all weathers, but they love their job and that is partly because of the wildlife they see.

We have a glorious day puttering around the East Lothian coast. Cormorants dry their wings on the rocks and gannets whizz past carrying seaweed back to their nests on the Bass

Rock. Smaller lobsters, which have not reached the legal landing size, are thrown back, as well as any other species. We find red kelp cod, spiky sea urchins and a strange sea scorpion that sits on your palm and vibrates like a mobile phone.

The lobsters that are big enough have plastic bands put around their huge claws. While they are safe to handle, I take time to examine the delicate hem of blue around the fanned tail, the huge robotic claws, the antennae tentatively feeling their way through their underwater world. Sometimes they walk hand in hand, the older lobsters leading the young ones. They can live up to 100 years. Perhaps they do fall in love?

I am told the most humane way to kill a lobster is to stun it first. This can be done by stabbing the animal correctly or by using an extraordinary kitchen gadget called a 'Crustastun'. From the pictures on the internet this looks like an enormous toastie machine in which the crab or lobster is placed. When the lid is closed an electric stun is passed through the animal that will kill it instantly. Before you laugh, it is used in all the top restaurants to ensure the meat is never ruined by stress and to 'create a good feeling in the kitchen'. A scaled-up version is used in crab processing plants in Britain.

Unfortunately, I have to learn to kill the hard way. Ewan MacMichael, otherwise known as 'The Lobinator', a kitchen porter at the Nether Abbey Hotel in North Berwick, shows me how to do it correctly. We take a cooled lobster, which has been kept at low temperature for a few hours to make it 'unconscious', and lay it on the block. The 'Lobinator' gives me a large, heavy knife and instructs me to stab down quickly and cut forwards through the head, then backwards, splitting the whole body and disabling the nervous system or ganglia that runs down the centre of the animal. It is over so fast and the lobster is so cold and unmoving, I don't have time to think too much about what a beautiful creature it is, but I notice the chefs don't do the killing, not if they can help it.

I take my fresh lobster back down to the sea, to the Lobster Shack, a trendy pop-up restaurant on North Berwick harbour. There was a time when such a thing would be unheard of. The Scots famously eat junk food more often than their own renowned seafood. This not only means the animals are exported, often long distances, alive, but also the locals are not getting the delicious healthy meat they deserve. However, thanks to places like this – and the hard work of the creel fishermen – things are changing.

With a grant from the Coastal Communities Fund, Jack and his fellow creel fishermen have set up the Firth of Forth Lobster Hatchery in North Berwick. 'Berried hens', or female lobsters carrying eggs, are brought back by the fishermen so the eggs can be reared in tanks. Nine to 12 months later tiny baby lobsters, the size of a fingernail, hatch. In the wild only 0.05 per cent would survive predation, but in the tanks most survive and at 12 weeks old they are returned to the sea.

In other countries the lobster population has collapsed due to overfishing and it has been impossible to bring the species back. This 'lobster ranching' is a kind of insurance policy to ensure a healthy population can be sustained. It also engages the people who are eating the lobster with where their food comes from. Tourists are invited to view the hatchery and even go out for a trip on Jack's boat before coming back to eat a lobster. I have mine grilled. Just like when you boil the crustacean, air escapes the body cavity, making a ghostly whistle, and the claws move. But like with the oysters, I think I'm over that superstitious nonsense now; I'm more concerned about the ethics of how these animals were fished and the wider community this supports.

I sit and enjoy my lobster with garlic butter and chips, gazing out to the Bass Rock, thinking about the whole experience. My phone vibrates like a sea scorpion: it's a message from the boys on the creel boat. I laugh – there's a picture of Sam with an octopus on his head and an electric blue lobster they kept one summer as a pet: a glimpse of all the wondrous things that happen beneath the waves, that we will never normally see.

I decide to take Steve up on his offer of catching some invasive shellfish. The Hertfordshire countryside is lovely as ever, the cricket bat willows rustling silver, the stubble peachy in the fields as I drive the familiar road to Hamel's Park.

Steve takes me down to the pond to lift the signal crayfish traps. He made the pond himself to attract wildlife and it has worked – the water is thick with reeds where moorhens and coots nest. As we walk down we snap the buds of Himalayan balsam and laugh as they explode. 'Another invasive species you can't do anything about,' says Steve. The purple flowers, or 'policeman's helmets' as they are known, were imported from India and now clog waterways. 'But they also feed the bees all year round,' says Steve. 'I'm pretty relaxed about these things,' he says, as he fishes creels out of the pond with a pitchfork. 'You can't hold back nature.'

The signal crayfish wave their red claws like mini lobsters. They are the same greeny blue as the pond until we throw them into a pan of rollicking hot water – then the whole body turns pinky prawn red. Steve traps them all year, but he doesn't think he'll get rid of them. 'They're here to stay now.' We tip them into a colander and start peeling the armour off. It's a slow, fiddly job and you don't get much flesh. But it's worth it. The white tails taste like Torridonian langoustines.

'Why don't more people eat them?' I ask with my mouth full.

'Too much work,' says Steve.

'Then why do you do it?' I ask.

'Because when I was a kid, I had to,' he says. His mother was ill. He learnt the skills needed to live off the land. Catching animals to kill and eat wasn't a game, and certainly wasn't a sport – it was about survival and providing for the people you love.

I carefully peel another crayfish tail. I want to get back on the horse. Not just because I have fully recovered from what happened with the rabbit, but because I am beginning to learn how important food is to your natural environment. Unlike climate change, where everyone ignores you when you start talking about it, everyone is interested in food, just take a look at the TV schedules. If I learn about where food comes from, I can make the best decisions to protect what I love. I want to be like Steve, a country person, able to live off our beautiful countryside.

Steve just shakes his head and smiles, and tells me I had better start practising.

CHAPTER TWO

Novice Macnab

No man is born an artist, nor an angler.

Izaak Walton

In the 17th century classic *The Compleat Angler*, a young man is taught how to fish by his tutor. It is a charming tale, full of flowers and gentle philosophy, and ranks second only to the King James Bible as the most frequently reprinted book in the English language. As soon as I pick it up I can see why. The language is arcane but the message is timeless. It promises peace, reconnection with nature and communion with God if we would all just 'go a-angling'. I'm hooked.

Fishing seems a good place to start learning how to source my own food in the countryside. The participants are gentle and they are everywhere – four million people in the UK fish. My first tutor is, unexpectedly, the journalist and author George Monbiot. We meet to talk about rewilding, his idea of bringing back extinct species, even wolves, to the Highlands. But the evening is too beautiful to sit around chatting so we go fishing instead on Loch Dughaill near Shieldaig. It is late April and the cuckoos have just returned from Africa. The dog violets wink through squashed orange bracken, and creamy primroses soften the moss burnt bronze by another hard winter, anything green nibbled down by the hungry deer.

George explains what is happening in the environment as he selects a fly. The chironomid midges are coming up to hatch and the trout should not be too far behind. He pauses and considers his box of hand-tied flies. I have always loved the jewel-like nature of the flies in their little box. All the pretty colours and ridiculous names: a Wickham's Fancy or a Grouse & Claret? A March Brown or a Half Hog? In the end he chooses a little brown job; to me it looks rather dowdy.

Above us the last remnant of Caledonian pine forest this far west, Coille Creag-Loch, the wood by the crag on the loch, clings on between the mountains and the sea lochs beyond. The 250-year-old 'granny pines', descended from trees that have been here continuously for 8,000 years, are enjoying the twilight. It is another world, almost Mediterranean, compared to the scrubby knee-high forest over most of the mountains around here. It is what George is fighting to recreate, a world where you might find wood ants, crossbills, red squirrels or a lynx padding down the mountain looking for prey.

'The thing I like about fishing,' says George, 'is that it is as close as you'll get to Paleolithic hunting, especially if you can see the fish. You are the same distance away as you would be with a spear. It is about spotting the fish and stalking it, about coming up very carefully behind it, tuning in to the ecology, being aware of what the fish is doing,

what it is thinking and what is happening around it; what
flies are coming off the water, what stage the fly is at. It is
not you spearing the fish, but the fish spearing itself which
is another level of engagement.' Also, it is silent, I think.
Shooting blows the world apart. With fishing you cast that
line, throw the spear, and even if you have success, death
comes quietly.

Trout feed on the vertical, swimming upwards to strike
their prey, and within minutes George has tricked one,
made it 'spear itself'. He reels it in, laughing in excitement.
It's a brown trout. Brown does not mean dull, not in this
case; it means gold, spotted with red. A brownie, the same
word for a magical creature, a fairy. George is using
barbless hooks, to make it easier to release the fish. He lets
it go immediately. I think of one of my favourite quotes
from *The Compleat Angler*: 'You can't lose what you
never had.'

Brownies are magical: in an act of alchemy a brown trout
can go to sea and 'smolt' or turn silver, becoming a sea
trout. The first year back she (for a sea trout is usually a
female) becomes a finnock. Alternatively, she can stay at
home in the burn of her birth for four years, never growing
beyond 15cm (5.9 inches), a wee 'brownie'; or she can sink
to the bottom of the loch and eat her brothers and sisters
and become an ugly distorted ferox; or she can sit in the
brackish water, never quite making it to sea but eating all
the goodness that comes up the estuary and become a fat
'slob trout'.

Sandpipers bob over the rocks and I begin to enjoy
myself. Fishing is meditation, they say, like yoga. But I don't
feel chilled out, I feel like I desperately want to catch a fish.
Perhaps I am a Paleolithic hunter after all? I am aiming for
the dimples where the fish are rising but again George beats
me to it. This time it really is magic; he's caught two. We
think the second is on the drop line but then realise it has
been caught by its tail and it's silver – a finnock. It is an

extraordinary coincidence and we laugh at the impossibility of it, the joy of fishing. You can see why four million people are addicted.

When I eventually catch my own trout, on Loch Damph a few days later, for my own fly I copy George and choose a little brown job (I have no idea of the name but it looks a little like the midges flying around my head). The light is fading and the bats are just coming out. It is only on the first few casts that I feel the tug of a trout. He is the colour of the loch, his belly creamy yellow like the sandy beach, his back golden and black like the surface of the water.

His tiny teeth shock me, like needles. He could kill if he wanted to, he could be anything. I lower him back into the water, the environment he has adapted to so well, and let him breathe for a moment before he darts off – who knows where? It's a lovely feeling. Most fishermen do let their catches go. But if I want to eat one, eventually I am going to have to kill one.

As with shellfish, the science on whether fish feel pain is mixed. In 2003, scientists from Edinburgh University claimed to have found the first conclusive evidence of pain perception in fish. They injected bee venom into the lips of rainbow trout and observed them rubbing their face in the gravel in response to some kind of stimulus. Other reports say fish do not have a suitable brain system or enough sensory nerve receptors to experience suffering.

There is no doubt that fish are sentient creatures. They build their own nests, they communicate in shoals, they can escape an inexperienced fisherman clumping around on the bankside. They bleed, just like us.

Fish, such as brown trout, are also an important part of the ecosystem and in the UK are often under threat. Overabstraction in South East England is drying out tributaries, sewage is being dumped in rivers during storms and the use of fertilisers is causing algae to bloom in waterways. Most of us barely notice; it's the fishermen who fight for the habitat of their prey. Fish Legal, an arm of the Angling Trust, is one of the least known and most effective environmental charities in the UK, often the first to sound the alarm when pollution is dumped and the only ones to pursue the perpetrators.

When they do take fish, anglers kill the animal immediately with a knock to the head, rather than letting them suffocate in the hold as they would do on commercial ships. And they take very little. These are the people protecting our rivers. If they take one or two for the pot occasionally I'll forgive them. I'll forgive myself.

Anglers are a friendly bunch and I am never short of invitations to practise my inept casting. Andy Richardson, a gamekeeper in Fife, says he can 'guarantee' me a fish. We set off from his house, Devil's Lodge, with the requisite labrador in the boot and some secret handmade lures that I could tell you about, but I'd have to kill you.

It is spring and the wood anemones are just coming out on the River Eden. As we tramp through the wild garlic I spy the first swallows of the season and what I think is an otter print, but am soon corrected by Andy – it is a badger.

'Oh, the river is dead, dead compared to what it used to be,' he says, nodding towards the fertilised fields around us. When he was a child the river was full of brown trout, as well as salmon and sea trout. The brown trout are now artificially stocked and salmon and sea trout are rare. Local volunteers prune the trees and fight with the sewage board and farmers to reduce pollution but nothing brings the sea trout back; perhaps the problem is the fish farms or the overfishing at sea?

I cast into the shallow water, watching a dipper dart back and forth, building her nest, or feeding her babies; I'm not sure. When we eventually catch a brown trout, Andy is ready with a priest (a heavy object used to kill fish, in this case a piece of weighted antler). I hit the fish sharply behind the eyes and though it flips its tail a couple of times it is soon still. It is a brutal act – Lord Byron complained of the cruelty of killing fish, though I believe he still ate them. I stroke the iridescent skin; it is more silvery than a loch fish. Perhaps it is because it is a cold-blooded creature, so different from us, that I feel okay. Or perhaps I am cold.

I gut the fish, running a knife from the vent, the hole just in front of the anal fin, to the chin. The guts scoop out easily. I run my fingernail along the spine to remove the 'bloodline'; it is surprisingly red. Andy has given me a bunch of wild garlic and instructions on how to cook it. I smear the fish in butter and stuff the belly with the pungent green leaves, then wrap the whole thing in foil. When it comes out of the oven 20 minutes later it smells like garlic bread. But somehow you can still taste the trout; it is strong and delicate.

Fresh fish pulled from a stream, killed and gutted ourselves, is a common dish. Many of us have, at some point, enjoyed the experience of catching a fish. It is often a happy memory from childhood, time to enjoy a little bit of advice from the family fishing enthusiast, and a lot of silence. It is hunting at its most gentle and contemplative.

But killing an animal with feathers or fur is different. It involves noise, violence, blowing the world apart. It involves a gun.

I don't have a gun licence so I can't purchase my own gun and lessons would be extremely expensive, so I have to rely on my dad. It's an odd moment. My brothers were taught to shoot as a matter of course. But I have never asked to even see inside the gun cabinet before. I realise I am lucky. It is an incredible privilege to be taught by my father, but I feel a little nervous. Not just because it's a gun, but also because it's a little 'loaded', if you'll pardon the pun. I am no good at this sort of thing; I tend to be naturally clumsy. Also, I feel under pressure to prove I can do it as well as the boys.

Dad opens the steel cabinet and selects an antique gun. It is a single barrel shotgun made around 1890 by Charles Boswell. Dad takes it out of its canvas case, carefully reinforced with gaffer tape around the handles, opening it as he does so to check the barrel is empty. It is a beautiful object. I have no desire to fetishise guns and I always approach them with caution, but you cannot deny the workmanship in the curlicued engraving of the shotgun's chamber or the elegance in the long barrel and walnut stock.

Shotguns are completely different to rifles in both their design and purpose. Firstly, they tend to be fancier. Shotgun shooting is considered more of a 'sport' – there is more fuss and decoration in the stockings, the bags, even the guns. Secondly, they work differently to kill a fast-moving animal that is often flying through the air. Cartridges full of lead pellets, 'the shot', are loaded directly into the barrel, instead of bullets in a magazine loaded from the bottom. When you pull the trigger the shot is thrown out of the barrel, spraying a lethal 'pattern' into the air, which has a better chance of hitting the target than a single bullet would have.

This gun is a 12 bore, referring again to the size of the barrel but confusingly, in the case of shotguns, a lower number means a bigger gun as it refers to how many round balls of that diameter would weigh 1 pound. So for example a 20 bore gun would be a smaller gun as the barrel fits a ball weighing 1/20th of a pound and a 12 bore would fit a ball weighing 1/12th of a pound. The gun was probably designed for a young boy to learn to shoot with. I wonder who he was and if he survived the First World War; what a generation to be brought up in. Or perhaps it was designed for a woman, one of those ladies who look so elegant in the Victorian pictures posing with their guns.

Shotgun shooting is all about etiquette, but that's just another word for automatic gun safety. To endanger anyone else is considered worse than rude. At every stage there are ways to do things correctly, and eyebrows will be raised if you get it wrong. My father shows me how to hold the gun broken with the stock over my arm and the barrel hanging down, like a long evening coat, so everyone can see the barrels are empty. The most important rules are listed in a child's poem hung on many the loo wall of a country house. 'Never, never let your gun pointed be at anyone ...' it begins. It ends rather sweetly, but ominously. 'All the pheasants ever bred, won't repay for one man dead.' I memorise it in the bath.

'The Bos', as it becomes known, is not an easy gun to shoot with, so I have to get used to it. For a couple of afternoons, I take the gun, unloaded, 'for a walk' around the farm. Only when you are sure there is no one else around do you lift it to your shoulder, rest your cheek on the stock, take the safety catch off and take aim. At regular intervals I stop, snap the gun closed ... shoulder ... cheek ... safety ... then under my breath whisper 'bang'.

Dad takes me to try shooting some clay pigeons. We realise that while I shoot off the right shoulder I am left eye dominant; therefore to line up my line of aim with where I am looking it is better to close my left eye. It takes a bit of practice but eventually I am shooting clays out of the sky, with satisfying consistency. Dad tells me to look at the target, not at the end of the barrel: 'see the doo, shoot the doo,' he says. That's how most novice shots learn to shoot, by taking pot shots at feral pigeons, or 'scutty doos' as they are known in Scotland. The birds are universally hated by farmers for eating young shoots just as they are poking through the earth and for destroying whole crops. Young boys and, increasingly, hobbyists will spend whole afternoons shooting hundreds of pigeons for free.

There are pigeons roosting in the barns at my father's farm where the grain is stored. Dad goes into the grain store and claps his hands. The birds come clattering out, rising into the air like leaves in a thermal, banking to right and left. I lift the gun, trying to remember everything I have been taught: shoulder ... cheek ... safety ... 'Oh.' They have gone.

Dad comes out. 'Well, did you get one?'

'No.' I try to keep my voice steady.

We try a few more times. Dad roars at me – quite rightly – for pointing the gun at him in a moment of distraction. I have completely lost my nerve. It's no use. I am useless at this. I am close to tears. This is not like clay pigeon shooting. There is no time to think. It is difficult and dangerous and I'm not capable of what a small boy would have done for pocket money.

I retreat and decide to do it my way, for food. The best pigeons for shooting and eating are woodpigeons or *Columba palumbus*. The scientific name sounds like their flight, it always reminds me of summer days, walking into a wood; shaking branches and that sound, flap, flap, flap. The birds have increased in number in recent years to 20 million as farmers grow crops through the winter and the climate warms. Like feral pigeons they are a huge problem for farmers, who allow hobbyists to come in and shoot the birds eating their crops. You can buy wild pigeon from butchers and game dealers but strangely most of the pigeon served in UK restaurants are caged squabs from France.

The wild birds are much better eating and, to many, a much more sporting quarry than reared birds like pheasant.

Pigeons are not easy to shoot; they are known as 'grouse on speed' for their ability to dive and to swoop. Like any wild animal, the only way to catch them is to watch them closely and understand their natural environment. In a way I am seeing pigeons for the first time. For once I am really looking. I watch how they fly: they remind me of children on scooters, flapping their wings for a final wheeeeee! Swooping downhill, the white bars on their wings like go-faster stripes.

Pigeons are predictable; they come in on 'flightlines', like the roads we use to navigate. Professionals will put out decoys to attract the birds. But I know where they come in to roost every night. I stand in the orchard just as it is getting dark. I have the Bos over my arm, but I seldom take aim. Usually, I would prefer to just stand here and watch the sunset, to listen to the 'hoo, hoo' of pigeons in the wood behind and have a wee think. But something has changed. I want to do this. Not like the boys, but in my own way, calmly and quietly.

I am about to give up when I see a pigeon come flapping in; for a moment it soars. I take my time, 'see the doo, shoot the doo'. An explosion of feathers, and the pigeon disappears into the canopy of trees. I make sure the gun is safe and crawl into the dark understory of the plantation to find the body. It is a different world under here, a pine-scented night-time. I pick the quarry up, admiring his dusky pink neck and the grey-blue feathers of his breast. They pluck out so easily as I walk home, disappearing into the wind as the sky also turns pink.

I'm not sure whether to feel proud, or ashamed. I go to see my Grandma, an elegant lady, even now. I expect she will be shocked at my nerve, nosing around as usual, looking where I shouldn't. But instead she surprises me.

'Oh, yes, I ate pigeon once,' she says. 'With a man who was in love with me…'

'What? Not Grandad?'

A Canadian officer stationed in Edinburgh took her to dinner at the Royal Northern, now the Balmoral. It was the war, so there was no chicken, only pigeon. Now of course it is on the menu again, alongside grouse, as a game dish.

I imagine the beautiful young Beatrice Flockhart picking at her pigeon. She never saw the Canadian officer again – and she never ate pigeon again. I ask whether Grandad brought game home but she says he never shot much, not after Arnheim. He was a prisoner of war and it put him off guns, seeing what they could do, the maimed young men.

I go home and slow-cook the pigeon in red wine with cinnamon and spices. You can see why the Balmoral is serving it as a main course once again. It may not be considered as exclusive as grouse, but it is just as tasty. The meat is ruby red, almost like beef. I eat the tender meat slowly, thinking about my experience of shooting so far. I will never take it lightly. I think of Grandad, a stickler for etiquette, for doing things the right way.

Chris Wheatley-Hubbard cares about etiquette, the knowledge and understanding implicit in any pursuit of a wild animal for food. He teaches men and women not only how to shoot properly, but also fieldcraft and marksmanship. Softly spoken and slight, with a ginger beard, Chris doesn't look like a typical field sports enthusiast. He insists I come down to his farm in Wiltshire one evening and stay the night camping in a wood to truly understand his theories.

Over tea by the campfire he explains his 'holistic' approach to stalking. He believes that humans are still linked to the skills we needed to track and kill just a few generations ago. All we need to do is to tune back into those atavistic instincts. It's not about some testosterone-driven caveman impulse, but rather knowing how to slow down and stop, and start to truly see, a skill any man or woman can remember. Perhaps shooting can be contemplative too?

Before we even start to think about handling a gun or stalking a beast, we have to get down to some 'dirt time'. We lie on our bellies staring at a quadrat of earth marked off with four sticks. 'What can you see?' asks Chris.

'Um, grass, leaves, dirt?'

'And what else?' Chris makes me look at the earth and look and look until I start to see patterns and shapes. He points out leaves that have recently blown onto the area, then investigates beneath. 'Is that a deer print? Can you just see an outline?' I don't believe it until we find a hair. Chris snaps it in two. It's hollow: a deer hair. 'Tracking,' says Chris, 'is all about stories. What stories can the earth, the leaves, the other animals, the smells, tell you about who has been here before? What was the character of that person or animal passing through? Are they bold? Timid? In a hurry? Gradually you can piece together a story and then you can understand so much more.'

Chris takes me on a practice stalk, crawling through the undergrowth after cut-outs of deer placed in the woods. I am to use the three S's – safe, suitable and sensible – to judge whether the targets are worth shooting. Is there a backdrop to absorb the bullet? Where are the other deer? Are there any obstacles in front of the shot? Chris teaches me to place my boots carefully, to not make a sound. Most importantly, he encourages me to sit in the wood and listen. Why are the birds sounding an alarm? Is there a bird of prey overhead? What is that smell? Through tracking and observation skills, I find I am reconnecting with nature at last.

'Fieldcraft' means understanding the ecosystem. We do it every day in the city, checking our phones and iPads, but we've forgotten how to do it in the countryside. We are so busy rushing about in all walks of life that we forget to slow down and just absorb. It was not a lesson I expected to get shooting, but it was one I needed.

Like pigeons, the roe deer or 'elf of the woods' is considered a pest by farmers, eating brassicas like oilseed rape and even strawberry crops. It's not difficult to find a farmer willing to let me stalk a roe buck.

The first time, I go on a morning stalk in the Cairngorms with Sam Thompson. He's like a character out of a John Buchan novel. In his own words: 'As big as a house.' Usually clad in estate tweeds, checked shirt and fleece gilet, he strides around the sporting world like someone from a different age. When we meet at the Royal Highland Show, he immediately invites me stalking. I tell him I have caught a trout and killed a pigeon already.

'Aha, a Novice Macnabber!'

'A what?'

He explains that a Macnab is killing a salmon, a grouse and a red deer all in one day. I am doing the poor man's version – a brown trout, a pigeon and a roe buck over a period of months. A Novice Macnab indeed.

Sam is a good teacher. He gives me a rifle shooting lesson and sneaks in a dud bullet. I fire and even though there is no bang, I flinch. 'Aha! Now you see The Flinch,' says Sam. 'Yes, now I see The Flinch.' Another name for it is buck fever, when the heart rate spikes and you fail to be still for the shot. It is probably what happened with the rabbit. The next time I fire I concentrate all my energy on not flinching. It sounds silly not to have noticed it before, but it was such a natural reaction. Now I know it is there, I can master it. I calm my breathing and in a moment of absolute concentration, I feel my mind lift and, almost in slow motion, move forward with the bullet. 'Good shot,' says Sam.

The next morning, we set out roe stalking in the summer dawn. The glens are washed clean, the leaves silvery with dew, making the colours softer. I can smell the birch and bracken, hear the birdsong more clearly. Anything could happen at this hour. A buck stands on the horizon, legs akimbo in the 'Bambi pose', before he springs away. We scan valleys, watching does graze among the silage bales and dotterels.

Up on Glenbeg we sneak over springy heather looking towards the Cairngorms; there is still a sliver of snow up there, even though it is July. We loll in the heather and watch does grazing up on the hill and all this is part of it: glassing the hill a bit more, gossiping, listening, waiting. As the sun comes up the colours change again. It is too bright for our clumsy forms, too clear; the roe have gone. We are in the harsh human world now.

We return empty-handed and sit in Sam's bachelor pad cottage eating rhubarb crumble and custard for a late breakfast. On the wall is a roe buck 'trophy' called John McClane after the *Die Hard* character. 'I pursued him for years,' says Sam. 'In a way I regret it but then … I'm glad it was me, not someone else.'

The ethereal roe continue to elude me. I try again, this time an evening stalk through the Angus countryside. I take a television crew, which is not particularly helpful. The producers of BBC *Landward*, the Scottish equivalent of *Countryfile*, approach me to make a programme about the woman who only eats animals she kills herself and suggest filming a stalk. 'I may bottle it,' I explain. 'I'm not going to do it just because you are there.' 'That's OK,' they say, like doctors about to remove a plaster. 'You don't need to do anything you don't want to do.'

We set off in high spirits to explore the brassica fields along the Auchmithie cliffs. The evening sun has turned the

sandstone cliffs red and gulls float over our heads. Walking
the field margins, just planted with wild bird seed, I chat to
Sarah Mack, the pretty presenter, about all the skills I am
picking up learning to shoot.

As the evening sets in and roe venture out of the woods
to feed, we crawl along drystone walls and down ditches,
always against the wind that carries our scent, the camera
creeping along behind, in pursuit of the deer. We see the
spiky antlers arching briefly above the oilseed rape and
silhouettes on the horizon, but the weather has turned
against us and the roe deer are skittish. Deer rely on their
senses of smell and hearing to detect predators, as well as
sight. If the wind is up they have to be even more alert and
nervy than usual. Taking a whole camera team is tricky. We
do our best but also can't help giggling, at one point coming
across an angry Hereford bull in his field – and deciding
quite sensibly to take another route.

Eventually, we find the perfect quarry, a 'black buck', his
fur darker than the others, showing he is older and suitable
for culling. But the farm manager comes around the
corner – no doubt to check on his prize bull – and another
opportunity is lost. Sarah asks me if I'm disappointed and
I confess I am not. Perhaps I am even glad? I'm always
nervous about making a kill and there is a part of me that is
glad the black buck lives on.

As dusk falls we feel the world change: the bats come out,
the pheasants go up to roost and the baby owls start
screeching. We leopard-crawl under dripping branches,
thorns and nettles stinging my palms. I feel closer to the
deer, like I have more senses too. I can smell the damp earth
and pine needles. We talk in whispers, and even though we
are uncomfortable we all agree we are enjoying crawling
about in the undergrowth at this magical hour.

A buck has been spotted in the wood but disappears
again, and the doe comes out. I have her in the sights of the
rifle, close enough to see her ears twitch. I can't kill her at

this time of year – not that I would want to – so I have the opportunity to watch her. In a way it is worth all the waiting. She is so alert, looking up every few seconds, her face and black muzzle much darker than I expected, even more beautiful close up than when you see them in elegant springbok-motion.

We stay there watching her so long that darkness falls, and I have to let the barrel fall and admit defeat. We have a flask of tea laced with whisky and watch the tattie fields turn from purple to black. I apologise to the team, a little embarrassed at my continued failure to complete even a Novice Macnab. 'Oh no!' exclaims Sarah. 'We've enjoyed the evening. And that's the whole point, isn't it? That's what this is all about? We take meat for granted. But it's not easy if you do it yourself, it's not like going to the supermarket. It means that when you do eat it, you appreciate it for what it is.'

She's right, in a way. I am enjoying beginning to learn how to stalk and shoot. I am meeting interesting people and learning a lot about the countryside. But it is also about meat in the supermarket. It's simply not realistic for everyone to source their own wild meat. To truly be an ethical carnivore I need to find out how meat is raised and slaughtered on our behalf.

CHAPTER THREE

Minions

Sapere aude.
Latin translation: *Dare to know.*

I wasn't prepared for my first slaughterhouse. I did not research the abattoir in question or tell my friends and family where I was going. I wore a new blouse from Topshop with startled fawns on it. But the worst thing I did was to meet the pigs beforehand.

Gorgie City Farm seemed like such a positive place to start the project. The pigs, a cute rare breed called Gloucester Old Spot, live a happy and productive life. Not only do they grow fat for sausages, but they also entertain children from deprived areas of Edinburgh. As I walk around the farm one morning in mid-November a family are admiring the latest litter. The children throw handfuls of grain into the pen and watch the piglets skitter across the straw, wagging their tails in such excitement they lose control of their back legs, like puppyish cartoon characters. 'Aw, Mum, look at them! They're like the Minions …'

Ross Mackenzie, the general manager, smiles. He is spotlessly clean for someone who spends most of his day ankle-deep in manure, perhaps as a result of being in the army for many years. He knows every volunteer by name – 'This is Steven who dropped out of school and is now studying agriculture …' And every animal – 'And this is Gandalf, an abandoned hamster …'

The farm is squeezed between tower blocks at the tail end of the M8 on the west side of Edinburgh. It was one of the first community farms in Britain, fighting to retain a scrubby wee patch of green space in the 1970s before anyone realised a farm in the city would become their last link to the countryside, or that a whole generation would grow up not knowing where milk or sausages come from. It was also one of the first farms to be brave enough to turn its main attraction into bacon sandwiches. Ross came up with the idea in 2013. The former project manager and captain in the Royal Logistics Corps has a clear and unsentimental eye and could see an opportunity staring him in the face over the top of the stalls. Gorgie City Farm gets a little bit of money from the council for providing a free facility for 100,000 visitors a year, as well as working with problem teenagers and disabled kids, but it's never enough. Keeping the farm afloat is a constant struggle and fundraising ideas are always welcome, no matter how controversial.

Fortunately, the timing could not have been better. The horsemeat scandal meant that people were more eager than ever to know where meat came from. At the same time chefs were keen to buy whole free-range animals, not only because of the new fashion for different cuts of meat, driven by celebrity chefs such as Hugh Fearnley-Whittingstall, but also because they taste better. Pigs are sociable animals and enjoy life on a petting farm. A happy life means less adrenaline, which taints the meat. Also the pigs here are kept on a varied diet, including fruit and vegetables from local supermarkets, so their fat is richer and full of omega oils.

Best of all it made sense financially. As every pig farmer knows, it is virtually impossible to make money selling whole live pigs straight into the market unless you can keep costs ridiculously low – and we all know how that is done. But like any fair trade transaction, selling a whole pig to a restaurant direct means more of the profit can be kept with the farmer. It costs around £100 (US$130) to raise a pig, yet they will barely sell for £50 (US$65) in the market. In contrast, selling the whole carcass to a chef will raise £300 (US$390), just about covering the transport and abattoir costs. Gorgie also sells its own sausages in the cafe to bring money back into the farm.

I hear about the enterprise via a French chef who suggests I use it as a genuine example of connecting food back to the farm. Like many of the visitors, I am keen to learn about where food comes from, although I want to go a little deeper into the process. Despite being told it will be impossible for me to get into an abattoir, the whole process is remarkably easy. I realise that a good chef can put you in touch with butchers, slaughtermen and farmers all the way back down the chain because this is how they ensure the best ingredients. Fred Berkmiller is more than a good chef, he is a great chef, engaged with his producers and passionate about making sure every aspect of his food comes from a positive place. He is keen to support my project, though upset that I refuse to sample his latest pig's head terrine – brawn, or potted heid, as they call it in Scotland. He suggests I follow the pigs from Gorgie all the way to his restaurant and puts me in touch with Ross himself.

Ross is similarly unembarrassed about the fate of his pigs. After all, there is no question they are happy pigs. The sows are not kept in farrowing stalls, which prevent them moving when feeding the litter, as they would be in most industrial units. Sure, a few piglets will be lost every year by the sows rolling on them, but that is just a fact of livestock management and another reality Ross is trying to educate the public about. The piglets don't have their tails docked or their teeth cut because they are not so crammed in that they attack each other. The big old boar, who is much admired, and the pregnant sow, about to burst with piglets, have their own comfortable stables. We walk past to see the young sows going to the abattoir in a couple of days. They are towards the back of the farm, away from the main 'petting area'. The teens, like many of the volunteers, are a wee bit forgotten. 'The fact is they do get uglier ...' says Ross.

The four sows seem content enough, snuffling at me through the bars of the stall, their eyes obscured by huge ears, like a floppy fringe. I am struck by their intelligence. They have a water tap they work themselves by pressing on a knob. Everyone knows you have to be careful with locks as pigs will let themselves out if they can work out how to. Everyone has read Dick King-Smith's famous children's story *The Sheep-Pig* or seen the film *Babe*.

'What are their names?' I ask.

'Oh we don't give them names,' says Ross. 'Well, sometimes the volunteers do, but I try not to encourage it.'

Ross invites me to try one of their sausage sandwiches and my mouth waters. Of course I cannot partake since I have not killed it myself, so I have to make do with a coffee. 'At first I was scared we would get a kickback on Facebook and of course there is *Peppa Pig* ...' Ross explains. 'But people love the idea.' The sausage baps at Gorgie Farm sell for £1.50 (US$2); there are no posh condiments or labels extolling the virtue of organic, just a quiet pride in wholesome food. They sell out quickly. It is refreshing to see someone outside the bubble of middle-class foodies become passionate about providing good-quality meat. 'Why the hell shouldn't poor people get to think about these things?' says Ross. 'Or buy them.'

The father of three admits he is a relative novice with animals; his job is giving the people a chance. When it comes to the question of managing the pigs, he turns to Denis the livestock manager trundling past in his overalls. Unlike Ross, with his neat hair and clipped fingernails, Denis Rankine is everything you would expect from a farm manager. He is big and ruddy and takes no nonsense from volunteers or animals. He is a traditional stockman and tells me with some pride that he once raised rare breeds for royalty. Each species is different, he says, you just have to understand them to keep them calm. A sheep will always follow on; a pig will back up. That is why the slaughterhouse they send them to is so good; the animals are kept calm for the few hours they spend waiting in a new place, outside home for the first time. The lairage, as it is called, is as far as most farmers will ever go. 'The funny thing is it's a quiet place, the slaughterhouse,' he says. 'Very calm.'

We move on to visiting an abattoir for the first time and, perhaps because I am being so open about my nerves, or perhaps just because of the subject matter, the conversation goes somewhere else entirely. Ross has seen men trained to kill, but not to kill animals – to kill men. 'Soldiers are desensitised to it,' he says. 'They have to be professional. It's not because they don't feel; it's because that is what they have to do.'

The ex-serviceman was in TELIC 8, one of the operations that lost the most men in the Iraq War. He was at the heart of coordinating supplies of bullets and bombs. He controlled the drivers and the ambulances. He saw soldiers go home dead. 'We did a lot of repatriations,' he says quietly. I realise we are not talking about pigs any more; we are talking about death. 'We had something called Traumatic Risk Management or TRiM,' says Ross. 'Medics were taught it. You talk about what happened and it becomes a story. As if it didn't happen to you.' I take notes and wonder if he is trying to tell me something about my impending visit. Is it advice for me or him?

As I am leaving I bump into Charlene, a pretty blonde I met earlier, who has left school and wants to be a veterinary nurse. She is mucking out the pigs. 'Do you eat the bacon?' I ask, trying to make a joke. She looks at me with open contempt. 'I buy bacon from Aldi, cos it's all I can afford.'

I set off for the abattoir from work. I have been doing shifts at *Scottish Field* and everyone knows about my project. Like most people they are being incredibly supportive, but at times like this they are also a little perplexed, frightened perhaps. 'So, I'm off to a slaughterhouse now.' They continue typing. What is there to say? We've chatted about it and a few agree that as meat-eaters they ought to know, but still, they don't want to, not in detail. 'Well, anyway. I'll see you later!'

I gather up my notebooks and march out the door. I realise I am trying to normalise the day as much as possible, otherwise I will bottle it. I jump in the car and set the sat nav. It's a straightforward journey down the M8, the road that connects Edinburgh and Glasgow. I know the route well from my days as a rookie reporter for the Press Association, driving around Scotland picking up speeding tickets and doorstepping the families of boys from the Black Watch killed in Iraq. I know the landscape too, the way the green deepens the further west you go, the accent changes, the rain comes. A fine spray rises over the Lanarkshire hills, refracting the light as I pass what is left of industrial Scotland: New Lanark, old mines, the empty offices they built to try and replace the proper jobs.

By the time I drive into Wishaw, the low winter sun and country music on Radio 2 has made me a little melancholy.

The town reflects my mood. The after-school club is boarded up, the pub has a metal grille on it and the community centre is closed. Carrier bags limp over acid green lawns in front of pebble-dashed homes. I drive down the high street thinking, surely an abattoir can't be this close to the centre of town? I remember the one we used to drive past on the way to school that was in the middle of nowhere. It always smelt of dog food.

Eventually I spot the slaughterhouse opposite Classic Touch Cakes: 'Cakes * Balloons * Candy cart * Tiara's [sic].' There is also a bridal shop, one of those discount grocery stores – 'ShopSmart' – and a pet grooming parlour and boutique: 'Braw Dogs'. I think people must marry here, fall in love, get a job, feed their families. It might be deprived, you might have to work in an abattoir, but you still groom your dog, marry your sweetheart, crown your daughter a princess.

The abattoir is green corrugated iron with smart red gutters and has 'Wishaw Abattoir' in big letters above the door. No one is hiding what they do here. I park in the car park; it smells strongly of manure, like a farmyard. I tap on the receptionist's window and an attractive blonde woman called Audrey comes to say hello. 'I'm here to see Philip,' I say. 'We spoke maybe a few days ago?'

'Oh', she looks embarrassed. In the background I can see the general manager huffing and puffing as he puts on his overalls. He is called Philip Goodwin. I check the name written down on my notepad.

'Does she have safety equipment?' He isn't even addressing me.

'Er, no, was I meant to?' I do not even know what abattoir safety equipment would be.

He mutters under his breath and leaves the office. Audrey lets me in. The office smells of pig shit too. But Audrey is smartly turned out. She has worked there for seven years and seems to like her job, despite not quite fitting in with the surroundings. She admits she has never been into the

abattoir itself. The nearest she got was watching a
documentary with that nice girl from *Countryfile*. She
couldn't watch it happen, she says, it would be too awful. So
what kind of men work here? I ask. The ones who can take
it, she says. Some men stay. Some decide after a day it's not
for them. They train people up. Are they mostly local
men? Mostly. A few from Eastern Europe; they tend to
work in the 'gut room'. I wonder what that is.

Phil comes back still huffing and puffing. My overalls are
a few sizes too big and hang over the equally enormous
boots like pantaloons. I rip the hairnet and struggle to get
the hard hat to stay on my head. I look ridiculous, like a
clown. Why do I need a hard hat anyway, I think. What the
hell is going to fall on me?

'Come on then.' Phil opens some huge metal doors like
we are entering a bank vault, letting out a waft of cold air
that smells like antiseptic and old fridge. We tramp down a
cold concrete corridor. I am concentrating so hard on trying
not to fall over my huge wellies, I almost go careering into
the back of Phil when he stops suddenly. 'You don't speak
to anyone, OK?'

'Oh, right, OK.'

We enter the slaughterhouse and now I see why I needed
a hard hat. Above me chains and metal clank and creak into
life. Gantries criss-cross the ceiling swinging hooks and
carcasses like the opening of a steampunk graphic novel.
The first thing I see are cattle hanging by their hind legs.
They look monstrous – like the prehistoric beasts of cave
paintings, blood red – the size of at least two men – and that
is cut in half. I'm looking up, holding on to my oversized
hard hat, and when I look ahead I see blood splashed up the
walls. Shocking red against the white bathroom tiles. It
looks like the post-massacre scene from a gangster movie.
Its seems a cliche but it's true; that is the only place I have
seen anything like this. I desperately try to concentrate, to
think of a sensible question.

Phil starts walking through this foreign land, speaking a language I can barely understand. 'Kill-out, live weight, dead weight, cold sale …' Men move around the room silently, with purpose. They wear wellies and plastic aprons over blue overalls, often cut off above the elbow to show off tattoos. Most are big blokes and the hairnets look oddly effeminate. They have belts filled with clanking knives. Some have chain mail aprons and gloves. I hear a chainsaw and a man goes past with half a sheep on his shoulder.

Phil is explaining the process. He talks about the mandatory on-duty vet checking the slaughter process, the Food Standards Agency (FSA) officers checking the meat. I notice the animal is never slaughtered, but dispatched. They are not gutted, but eviscerated. I take a moment to savour the word, eviscerated … I'm not sure I've ever heard it before, in its absolute sense. The 'pluck' – heart, lungs and liver – lie on trays for inspection. Stomach fat hangs from a rack like an old woman's pants. I think if I wasn't so shaken, I would find that funny. Pieces of animal I can't even identify roll past on trolleys on their way to the 'gut room'. I feel like I have gone back in time and landed in the centre of a medieval meat market.

'OK, let's go and see your pigs.' This time I don't give myself time to think. I follow Phil into the 'killing room' and force myself to look instead. The pigs come in two by two, because they are the most intelligent, 'the most pally', of animals, and because they do not like to be alone – least of all in an uncertain situation. Like us, it keeps them calm to see another. They blink, a little uncertain, confused about where they are. The two slaughtermen stand above the pigs in a small stall – strong men, able to keep the pigs back with their legs. The first animal is held in the electric tongs, around the size of large garden secateurs; it barely struggles and goes down immediately, although the current stays on for longer, to make sure. The second pig looks perplexed for a moment but not panicked, then its moment comes and it is down. They are winched up immediately. One, two, three, four, less than 15 seconds then its throat is cut and blood gushes out. That's it.

I write all sorts of things in my notebook to describe that moment, but not 'dispatched humanely'. They say it happens quickly and it does. But you know what? It is not the killing that is the most violent thing. It is what happens next: it is the skinning, the burning, the boiling ... the evisceration.

I am standing to the side in this churning room, trying not to get in the way; it feels dangerous with fire, knives, cloven hooves flying around. The sows hang upside down, their heads soaking in blood, dripping off their ears, their eyelashes. Phil is explaining it in his language. 'The "beater" removes the epidermis layer.' I see a pig I saw just a few days before bouncing violently along a metal conveyor belt. 'It is lowered into the water. We say scald – not boil – a pig'. The body comes out clean. The wrinkled haunch is like elephant hide. 'The mouth and anus are scraped off.' The hair is burned off with a naked flame and the flesh is branded, adding the smell of burning flesh to shit and blood. I keep my head down, trying to write, but my mind has gone blank. I'm concentrating on keeping calm, on stopping my legs from shaking. My notes make no sense. 'Legs spread up, pig goes round, then stuck, flame, skiing beaters, rust, blood, oceans of blood ...'

'The men can kill 20 pigs in an hour,' says Phil. 'They work eight-hour shifts from 7 am to 4.30 pm, with breaks.' It is real old-fashioned industrial work, a hard, physical job, not like in those offices off the motorway. Men sharpen the knives as they go along to cut off the trotters, the tail. They are as strong and unfeeling as the iron equipment, busy, alert, with ruddy pink cheeks and 'sleeves' of tattoos; one has diamante earrings like David Beckham.

Denis said it would be silent, but that's because he didn't go inside the killing rooms – farmers never do, only the lairage. The rusty equipment rattles and bangs, flames roar. I am warned about the pigs screaming, but never hear a squeak. Weeks later a Spanish friend told me about seeing a pig killed in her home village. 'I never forget the screaming.' There is no screaming 'like a stuck pig' here, but I wonder, would that make it better? To be part of something, a tradition, a family event, like the ones happening all over Europe every winter. I feel terribly alone, confused, out of my depth.

I am aware Phil is testing me but I don't care. I have to leave the room. My hands are shaking and I have to concentrate to move my legs; it's not just the huge boots slowing me down now, it's the effort to stop shaking. 'I never ever ever want to see this again,' I write. 'I am NOT eating something that has been through a slaughterhouse ever again.'

The men move around me. One is whistling. Some guts go flying past my head. I think they are taking the mick out of me now. A trolley of offal goes past and blood is poured from milk churns down a drainage channel. I look at the floor – it is painted red. Of course it is. It has to be, otherwise it would be constantly smeared in blood; only clots of blood can be seen. Like Lady Macbeth's hands, you would never get it clean. I wonder, do all slaughterhouses paint the floors red?

I think no one could ever film this, it is too strong – the maroon foaming blood pouring out from milk churns. People would not believe it; it is too much, like a rich dish. Like drinking the blood from the can. I didn't need to go undercover to be shocked. The very nature of it, even legal, even 'best practice', is upsetting. 'Bring on the CCTV', says Phil. 'We have nothing to hide.' No indeed, I think, only everything. People could not bear to see one part of this. There is a reason the only way you can see it on the internet is protest videos; there is no tasteful way to film or photograph – or write – about this.

Phil comes out to find me; he looks at the walls, at the men, anywhere but into my eyes. 'Do you not like what you see?' he says.

'No, no I don't.' I feel a surge of anger. What do you want me to say, Phil? I see him feel bad for me, standing here in my clownish outfit, with my scrawled notes and shaking hands.

'Now don't just be going down that tree-hugging route Louise. If you stop rearing animals where the hell are they all going to go? I am 100 per cent sure these animals met their end in a humane way.' I'm not, but then I'm not sure of anything any more. 'We as mankind have to decide if we are to eat meat or not,' he continues. 'See when the lions stop killing antelope on the Serengeti? That is when I will stop. Tell you what, I'd rather go like this – a pig with no idea – than with a lion holding on to my bum.' No, I think, I'd rather anything than this hell. I'd rather have a lion holding on to my bum, I would, in a million years. Phil sighs.

The clean-up has begun and steam and spray fills the room. I'm glad of my overalls now. I don't want this water on my clothes, with bits of God knows what – brain, offal, blood – in it. It smells of a launderette, like a new wash. More fragrant than Fairy liquid or washing powder, but also more cloying, knowing what it is covering up.

We walk back to the office. I stand in the corner, as if I've done something wrong. As if I was part of all this. 'I do believe I have traumatised you,' says Phil, not without some satisfaction. I believe he may be right. I peel off my hairnet and overalls and faintly regret wearing my new shirt. 'Ha! Bambi …' laughs Phil.

Audrey is still there but no one offers me a cup of tea or even a glass of water. Phil sits down at his desk and begins eating his lunch. He has white rolls – well fired, a Scots tradition – filled with ham, of course. 'Has a vegetarian ever worked here?' I ask, trying to engage them all in conversation. They laugh, 'no.' I ask about his family and he softens at last. It's a family business. Phil's dad was the manager. 'I wanted to be like my dad,' he says. 'Doesn't every son?' He has four grandchildren. His five-year-old grandson has been in the abattoir, but he hasn't seen the kill – not yet.

It is clear Phil is proud of his job. He hands me his card. 'Let us meat your requirements,' it reads. 'I get satisfaction from doing a job well', he says, 'from feeding people. Do you want to eat American beef – and not know where it is coming from?' he asks. 'I'm making sure farmers can get their meat to a local market.'

He's right. Who am I to judge someone doing a proper job? I feel spoilt, stupid, judgemental. This abattoir may not be the most slick, up-to-date operation but it has a good reputation. It employs local people and, most importantly, while other small abattoirs shut down, it ensures that smallholders can continue to keep animals for meat – the same smallholders we all want to see thriving and providing our sustainable meat.

Phil puts his feet up on the desk. 'Politicians and journalists are under more stress than me ...' I can attest to that, I think. 'I'm doing a good job, that I'm proud of.' I ask him about the effect on the workers. 'I don't think they can think or look at it mentally; they just see a shape and it disappears. It is just an object. Listen, no one works here who doesn't want to,' he says. 'Men who take to the slaughter room stay for life, men who don't leave in the first few days.' Abattoirs do tend to employ men over generations – like Phil – but also labourers who 'float', who go from town to town doing this sort of job, who can disappear. Phil tells me about a 19-year-old boy who has just moved here from a dead-end job on the car wash. 'He's doing really well, he could go all the way ...'

Pam Morrison, the line manager, comes in looking neat even in a white coat and wellies, her shiny hairdo unmoved by removal of the hairnet and hat. Pam used to be a Marks & Spencers store manager and looks like she could get up now and walk into a department store. She wears a little make-up and gold jewellery. I am surprised she decided to come here instead but she insists it is an interesting, well-paid job. Like most people in the business, I am finding, she is from a family of butchers.

'Aye, it's a very male environment,' she says. 'But what do you expect? They have to be strong.' She can be rational, careful, practical, all the skills needed to work here. 'We do not deliberately harm animals,' she says. 'I am an animal lover.' I am making to leave, shaking hands and trying to smile, but she insists on showing me pictures of her dogs, two Japanese spitzes. I should sigh and say how cute, but I am too numb; I just see white fluff. 'I would harm a human if I saw them harm an animal,' she says.

I get back in the car and wait for tears, but nothing comes. I need to speak to someone who knows me well and phone my sister. As usual she is looking after the children and a little distracted, so I rush through my description of what has just happened. I tell her I feel shocked, dirty, like I did something wrong. She tries to comfort me like a child. 'You did nothing wrong, it's fine, you'll recover. You must intellectualise it, distance yourself.'

I don't cry but I tell her I love her, which is unusual; we are not the kind of family that do that – not unless it is an emergency. Then she asks, 'Should I be vegetarian? Should I not be feeding the kids meat?' And without thinking I say 'no' and it is an interesting moment. I come back to myself. Surely this should be my first thought, to stop this happening? But it's not really. My first thought is I don't want anyone else to have to see this. No one should ever have to see this.

Everything has changed. I no longer feel we should all visit a slaughterhouse. We should be protected from it, retain our innocence, like children. Nowadays we no longer see the neighbour's pig being strung up and stuck. Not unless you live in the villages of France or Spain where the traditions are still followed. We are too weak, we have to disconnect — to protect ourselves, to survive. But a small voice says, isn't that what makes bad things happen? Wars? Torture? Shouldn't you be brave enough to look? If you want to make things better?

'Now, Louise,' says my sister. 'Don't get into one of your spirals …' Then a child cries and she is gone.

I pull myself together and start back home. I leave the radio off, thinking perhaps I can process all this as I drive. And I'm not thinking about the pigs, I'm thinking about me. I'm worried I've opened a Pandora's box I can never close. I can never explain this, never share it. I am alone. I pull off the M8 and let the tears come.

The smell lasts for days. At first I think there must be manure on my shoes — or blood — and then I realise it is me. I am sweating anxiety; I can smell it, like animals can smell fear. I get flashbacks. I hear it in dreams, see it in a nosebleed in the sink, red on white tiles, in the meat counter at a supermarket, in the news: another war in Palestine, more bombs in Iraq, Syria. Once you open the box …

Eventually I summon up the courage to go and see Fred and the pigs. The kitchen is all pepper and steam and gleaming copper pans. Fred floats from counter to oven to sink, shouting instructions. 'Look!' He lifts a lid and there are bay leaves and cloves — and trotters; he takes out a roasting pan and crackling snaps. He slaps his sides, his shoulders, his bum … 'Loin, shoulder, ham.' The pig has become something else, an object. 'Do you want to see the head?'

'No! OK, yes.' It does look different; it looks OK. Then I see the Gloucester Spot, the prickle of black hair, *Peppa Pig* … I wonder how something so positive, from Gorgie Farm, from Fred Berkmiller, could have turned into such a nightmare.

'Oh Louise,' says Fred. 'You can't get to know the animals — especially not pigs. The farmer doesn't do that, no one

does that ...' Fred has asked farmers not to send him photos
of the cows he is using for beef, because it is too upsetting.
'Everybody hates it, nobody likes it,' he says. 'But as a chef,
I have a responsibility: the customer is trusting me to feed
them, to feed their children. You have to know, but you have
to give yourself distance.' Fred insists on visiting the farm at
least once to see animals are well looked after, finding out
about how they are killed and using the whole carcass.
'I want a link between the men who raised and killed that
animal and me. I want to make sure they all come from guys
who have a passion for food.'

He accepts death as part of the process, and one that
everyone should know about. 'We are weaker than we used
to be,' he says. 'Because we are completely disconnected
from our food.' Fred blames the supermarkets. 'We have
been conned into thinking Tesco will be responsible for
where our food comes from – but they're not. Look at the
horsemeat scandal. In the end it did good because it made
people think.' Fred points to his temples. 'We have to know
where an animal comes from, for the flavour, the quality.'
He puts his hand on his chest. 'For your own heart.'

Since the horsemeat scandal, Fred has done a roaring
trade in horse burgers and also found new customers are
coming in to eat meat, from tail to snout. 'Food is freedom,'
he says. 'Understand it and you can make a choice. Ignore it
and the supermarket does it for you. I know where the
animal comes from and I know how to respect it. I use
everything, except the teeth and the bones.' He opens up a
pan to show me the pork belly sitting in sauerkraut, points
to marinating loin chops, pulls out a tray of crisp ears.

I think back to what Ross said about telling stories to get
over a traumatic incident, TRiM. Fred is telling stories
through food. It is what I am doing, talking to Fred now. We
are all telling stories, all the time, making sense of our lives,
our choices, our food.

CHAPTER FOUR

Henry

Treasure the farmer.

Alice Waters

I need to go back to the beginning: birth, new life, the lambing shed. I think perhaps it is my favourite part of farming – isn't it everyone's? The lambs standing up for the first time on tottery legs, a small miracle we can admire every spring, beyond Sunday school and childhood. Television programmes like *Lambing Live* allow the nation to rejoice in the drama of twin births and triplets. We even manage to handle a stillbirth, then the grisly spectacle of the farmer skinning the dead lamb and 'grafting' it onto an orphan who needs a new mother. We watch as the ewe who has lost her own lamb sniffs the stranger as if it is her own, then lets it suckle. It's like the perfect soap opera or Sunday night viewing (to watch after the roast), a bit gory but always with a happy ending.

When the fashion for live television shows from the lambing shed was at its height, I was sent by the *Daily Telegraph* to be 'a shepherd for the day' on an Oxfordshire farm. I will never forget it: waking in the dark to stumble downstairs in a stranger's cottage, climbing into oversized overalls and wandering bleary-eyed into the dark April morning.

The lambing shed is a deeply intimate place, thick with the sweet breath of ruminants, the sound of shuffling hooves and the soft cudding of haylage. The sheep were not lambing yet, so I got chatting to my tutor Roly Puzey, a young tenant farmer taking on his own flock of sheep for the first time. Roly and his wife Camilla used to work at the charity Linking Environment and Farming, or LEAF, and are passionate about sharing their experiences as farmers with the rest of the world, even as they cheerfully admit they are still learning themselves.

As the sun rose over Didcot Power Station, Roly wandered around the stalls showing me what to look for. One ewe ready to lamb pawed the ground and gazed at the sky. 'Star gazing, we call it,' he whispered. Gradually, lambs began to be born and I found myself caught up in the drama of real lambing live.

Roly found a ewe lying on her side, panting heavily. He knelt down and gently inserted his hand to inspect the birthing canal, his other arm looped over her belly, like an embrace. 'OK, we're going to have to give her a little bit of help,' he said.

'We?' The ewe rolled her eyes.

'You have smaller hands.'

Actually, they are quite big for a girl. Still, I took on the challenge, closing my fingers as Roly had shown me and gently inserting my hand, aware he was trying to teach me something important. Almost immediately I found the tiny, soft hooves. All I could think about was keeping my grip. 'OK, I think I have the legs.'

'Both? OK, now very gently, pull.'

The lamb slipped out covered in blood but mercifully alive. I placed it by the anxious mother so she could lick the newborn's nose, quickly clearing the birthing sack so the tiny animal could take its first shuddering breath and even let out a rather pathetic bleat. The wet fleece of the lamb was covered in blood and the slimy yellow film of afterbirth, but blood can be beautiful, as well as frightening.

I stood up, to give the ewe some space, but Roly held me back. 'Just watch.' Within moments a second head was emerging. This time the lamb came easily, diving out head first. He even managed to flap his ears in surprise as he slithered onto the straw. Just one more to go, and a few minutes later we had triplets before the sun was up.

'Pretty good going for your first day as a shepherd,' said Roly.

Of course, I had done nothing. I later wrote a rather naff piece about the miracle of new birth in the early dawn and all that … But looking back it wasn't that which impressed me; it was the intimacy between man and beast, the absolute trust. As we went around, Roly pointed out Henry, a ewe that was hand-raised as an orphan when they first started the farm two years ago. 'She slightly sticks her nose up,' he said. 'Thinks she is better than the rest.' He gave her a scratch, a rare moment of connection between a shepherd and a named ewe. She shook her head and went to tend to her newborn twins.

After we finished, just as everyone else was getting up, I remember smiling to myself as Roly spooned brown sugar into his porridge and said: 'I don't really know anything about farming, you know …' Roly Puzey might be one of the most humble and exhausted people I know. I think I decided then he was also one of the best.

Roly and Camilla are now the first stop in my road trip down to South West England, famous as the livestock heart

of England. Since I last met them, they have moved to West
Sussex to take on the tenancy of a National Trust farm, have
two children of their own, even more sheep, and are as
busy as ever.

You could not get a better example of livestock shaping
the land than Saddlescombe Farm. For more than 3,000
years humans have been here, cutting back the forests
initially, then running cattle and sheep to nibble down the
grass like so many lawn mowers, creating the rolling
landscape we know and love.

I avoid a tempting cream tea at the National Trust cafe and
read the information board on the biodiversity of England's
chalk downland, apparently 'more rare than tropical rainforest'.
While the rest of the country was ploughed up after the
Second World War, leading to the loss of 80 per cent of
England's chalk grassland, this ancient farm survived because
of its steep hills that a tractor could not get up. There are up to
50 plants in one square metre (11 square feet) of this land and
14 types of orchid thrive here, a quarter of the species found in
the UK. As the National Trust information board says: 'If the
animals disappeared so would your enjoyment – these wide
open spaces would soon be replaced by impenetrable bramble
and scrub.' And how could one serve cream teas on that?

I eventually find Roly, moving sheep with his loyal collie
Belle and his son Freddie riding either side on the quad bike. I
squeeze on and we set off up the steep hills to admire the view.
It's not just the ground that is chalky; the air is soft too, the
colours dusting into one another like a picture on a blackboard,
Brighton a hard white coastline before the sea. Roly points
out hedges that have been laid by volunteers to create another
habitat that is dying out in England, the hedgerow. Since the
Second World War, some parts of England have lost half their
hedgerows. But farmers are bringing them back. Since 1995,
50,000km (31,000 miles) of hedgerows have been re-established.
The hawthorn is just in bloom, creamy buds opening up as
the sparrows and chaffinches flit in and out.

Saddlescombe Farm itself has been here at least since 1086, when it was registered in the Domesday Book. But Roly and Camilla are the first family to settle here since the 1940s. With their two young children they are bringing an energy and a life to the farm that is wonderful to see.

Back down on the farm Freddie is keen to show me the young lambs. Volunteers still help out and people come up from Brighton to be a shepherd for the day. In many ways it is an old-fashioned way to farm: relying on local labour, keeping mixed livestock and selling the meat direct, through farmers' markets, a box scheme or mail order. But on the other hand it is a very modern approach. By keeping a blog on their website, Roly and Camilla share the experience of farming, including the difficulty of taking animals to the abattoir. Camilla admits to crying when they took the first pigs, adding 'you can't farm without feeling'. In a world that in many ways doesn't want to understand where food comes from, they are helping people to see. 'It feels right and whole to grow and eat our own food,' says Roly. 'But also to share it. There is a bond between the consumer and the producer.'

As I leave, I have a look again at the information boards. There is one showing a scene from 1890 of a shepherd with his sheepdog. Except for the fact he has no quad bike and Roly has no beard, not that much has changed.

Livestock farming may look pretty, but there is no doubt about it – in terms of land use it is inherently inefficient. It doesn't take a genius to work out that eating grain ourselves, rather than feeding it to an animal so it can eventually be made into meat, would require fewer acres.

Back in 1813 Percy Shelley, the poet – and genius – who was a passionate vegetarian, pronounced that eating 'plants from the bosom of the earth' was ten times as efficient as eating the meat from an ox. He probably wasn't far wrong. (Interestingly, his wife Mary Shelley and her vision of the future, Frankenstein's monster, were also vegetarians.) Although the figures vary wildly, it is generally accepted that beef takes up to ten times as much energy to produce as the equivalent calories in a vegetarian meal. The way it is worked out is called the feed conversion ratio, which shows how many plant-based nutrients are needed to grow the equivalent weight in meat. So for pigs, the feed conversion ratio is four, for chickens it is 2.2, for salmon 1.1, and so on. It can change depending on the measure – whether you are considering calories or just protein, for example – but it is always less efficient to eat meat.

Environmentalists also point out that raising animals takes more water than simply growing plants. Again the figures vary widely, but we can take it as read that growing soya, then feeding it to a pig, takes more water than eating the same soya in an edamame salad. The fact livestock eat food, burn energy and drink water means that they require a much greater footprint than a vegetarian diet. Nearly 30 per cent of the available ice-free surface area of the planet is now used by livestock, or for growing food for those animals. In Britain around 70 per cent of land is used for agriculture, and of that around half is used to raise livestock.

For many it is the strongest argument for vegetarianism. *Planet Carnivore* by Alex Renton is one of the many books published recently about our insatiable demand for cheap meat. How can we justify using 40 per cent of the grain the world produces to feed animals, when 870 million people are hungry? Eating meat is an 'extravagance' we don't need. It is something that uses up land, water and energy that could be used to feed malnourished humans. All the true mavericks are vegetarian: Gandhi, Tolstoy, da Vinci, Einstein. But then the true mavericks never accepted the obvious easy answer. What about all the by-products we use from animals? The manure as fertiliser? Medical products? And what about the contribution to the landscape and community, places like Saddlescombe?

In 2010 a true maverick wrote a book: *Meat: A Benign Extravagance* by Simon Fairlie set out the 'pro-meat' arguments and for a time was an oft-quoted text that converted many a vegan environmentalist to occasional meat. Unexpectedly, it was not written by a butcher or businessman; it was written by a self-confessed 'hippie' fed up of watching the hypocrisy of vegans and vegetarians replacing meat in favour of exotic foods imported from abroad. The book came out of genuine frustration at living in a commune for more than a decade and watching the butter, meat and milk produced by livestock raised on the farm rejected in favour of soya spreads, tofu and almond milk.

Today Simon truly lives his message. He stays in a commune in Monkton Wyld Court, Dorset, where he looks after the livestock. For a man who crunches the figures, he does not look like a geek, with his beard and tweed coat; he looks like a man of the land, which is exactly what he is. Yes, he agrees that raising livestock is inefficient, but there are plenty of places in the British Isles where you cannot grow vegetables, but you can grow grass. And there are plenty of waste products such as food scraps or spent grain from brewing that could be fed to animals. Simon calls it 'default livestock': the animals raised on waste or land that cannot be used for anything else, or are themselves used for other products. Surely it makes sense to eat them? You see, we can eat grass; we just need to convert it first.

There are many benefits to growing grass. Ancient unploughed grassland like Saddlescombe is thought to hold a huge amount of carbon, but unlike in forests the carbon is found mainly in the soil and the roots. This 'carbon sequestration' is often used as another 'excuse' for raising meat in places like Britain. There is even a word for it: 'carbon farming', or in the USA, where it is taking off, 'carbon cowboys'. The biggest proponent of it in the UK is Graham Harvey, the author and agricultural editor of BBC radio soap *The Archers*. In his book *The Carbon Fields* he argues that instead of ploughing up fields for grains, we should be growing pasture. This not only locks in carbon but also can provide more nutritious milk and meat than from grain-fed animals.

An oft-quoted statistic is that emissions from livestock make up 18 per cent of global greenhouse gases – more than the transport industry. Actually this is a much contested figure. It stems from a 2006 UN report, *Livestock's Long Shadow*, and in 2009 UN scientists pushed it up still further to 50 per cent. The calculations are based not only on the carbon dioxide exhaled by cattle breathing but also the methane they burp out (despite the belief more gases come out the other end, it's not actually farts that are responsible). Methane is a much more powerful greenhouse gas than carbon dioxide as you need far less to cause more warming. It also includes the amount of carbon dioxide created in producing the fertiliser and growing the grain for the cattle, and greenhouse gases produced chopping down forests to provide grazing.

As Simon points out, you don't need to deforest to grow cows, or feed them grain. He says the figure is more likely to be around 10 per cent. A recent report by Chatham House put it at a conservative 15 per cent. So yes, cow burps are something to worry about, and you should eat less meat if you want to reduce climate change, but you should also drive less, fly less and turn the heating down. Simon criticises the UN report for suggesting white meats like pork and chicken, which can be farmed industrially with a much lower carbon footprint, are a better option for meat-eaters. What about the animal welfare? He argues that instead people should eat less meat – 'default livestock' only – and more pulses and grains instead. 'If the human race can only be saved from

global warming by a diet of turkey twizzlers, one wonders if
it is really worth saving.'

I drive from Sussex, through half the chalk grassland in the
world, into the red soil of Devon and true farming country.
The Devon County Show is all colour and noise, candy floss
and dried mud. I remember getting lost as a child at the
Suffolk Show and grabbing on to the nearest tweed-clad
leg; it wasn't my dad. I wouldn't have that problem here. The
Devon farmers are in shorts or jeans or red trousers – or
skirts. Perhaps it is the weather or perhaps farmers are just
more fashionable these days.

   Country shows are shopping sprees for farmers; there is
an area for whatever you are into: machinery, food, animals,
mood rings. I wander towards the livestock section, past a
stand for public schools, the RSPB, puppy therapy, pulled
pork, handmade soap, bee pottery, fudge, more fudge and a
nail bar. Only a small number of people here will be
farmers, but it feels like the rest of the country is coming
together and seeing what they do. Why are we so interested?
The UK has had a predominantly urban population since
1815, yet we long to be connected to farming. Perhaps we
miss the animals, the way of life it affords us. When I
was born in 1978, 1.2 per cent of the British population
were employed in farming; by 2007 this had fallen to
0.78 per cent.

   I move on to the sheep tent; it is like stepping back in
time. Thousands of years of history, hundreds of years of
farming and decades of family businesses are gathered here.
It almost has the air of a prehistoric cave, with the humans
living with the animals. The owners sit on camping chairs
by their sheep with just a flask of tea at their side. I doubt
they have been outside all day – unless to get a quick burger.
In the shearing sheds, young men show off their muscle and

their might. And in here old men sit by their prize-winning tups to get the latest gossip on the competition.

I think again of the lambing shed. Humans have a bond with livestock. It's a two-way relationship. 'We look after them and they look after us.' Sheep were the first meat animal to be domesticated around 10,000 years ago, providing humans with clothing as well as nutrition, and indeed later a sacrifice to the gods. The Greeks were even said to name individual animals.

Not much has changed today. We have created more than 1,000 breeds, of which 60 are in the UK. The Bluefaced Leicesters looking down their long noses at the rest of the flock, the dreadlocked Wensleydale, the Devon and Cornwall Longwool like puppies, my favourite the Herdwick with its slaty blue-grey coat, and my least favourite the ugly Texel – which looks like a truck yet is often bred into British flocks to increase the meat. We have even bred an 'easy care' that sheds its own wool.

You can see why people get addicted to sheep breeding. It's like a fun game, mixing up all these characteristics and seeing what you get. Like playing God. Each breed reflects a different part of the country, different soil, different geography, different climate, different characters. It makes up the diversity of Britain; it would be a shame if a monoculture took over. Yet, that is exactly what has happened. We have lost tens of different breeds already. Between 1900 and 1973, 26 breeds went extinct in the UK, including the Sheeted Somerset cow, the Lincolnshire Buff chicken, the Dorset Gold Tip pig and the Limestone sheep. Personally I'd keep them all just for the charming names. I mean, perhaps it's not as sad as losing the giant panda, but still, why throw something away? All of these breeds had a purpose. Take the Lincolnshire Curly Coat, a robust, outdoor pig with a coat of long white hair, the last of which was sent for slaughter in 1972. It would have been invaluable in the extensive outdoor farming systems we now use for pigs – but it's too late.

In the Rare Breeds Survival Trust (RBST) tent I meet the real enthusiasts. A Manx Loaghtan sleeps in the corner – 'they make lovely smoked leg,' says an admirer. The RBST was set up in 1973, with the support of the Royal Family – perhaps they know the feeling of extinction just over the horizon. Since then no more breeds have gone extinct. The charity is now setting up a gene bank so that no more special characteristics are lost. Chefs in particular are interested in the different kinds of meat rare breeds can produce. In a fancy London restaurant it is now common to get salt marsh lamb from North Ronaldsay or home-cured bacon from a Tamworth pig. It's like those plants in the rainforest – we don't know what we might want to use them for, so we better keep them just in case.

I pause at the main arena, where Girl Guides are showing their rare breed sheep: Dorset Down, Greyface Dartmoor, Jacob, Scotch Blackface. The young handlers stand erect by their charges like they are being judged in a look-like-the-owner competition.

'What the hell is that?' says a man leaning on the fence, next to me.

'It's a sheep.'

'That doesn't look like a sheep, it looks like the Devil.'

Soay sheep are little devils. They can run circles around any sheepdog and are almost impossible to farm. The dark-fleeced sheep come from an island off St Kilda, a tough place for anything to survive, and will happily live outside in all weathers. They have the most primitive appearance of any UK breed, almost like goats, with curling horns.

The difficulty of farming the sheep meant that, as with many rare breeds, by the 1970s they had almost gone extinct. But now their very wildness could ensure their survival.

The sheep are recovering as farmers use them to graze marginal land in remote areas. On the north-east cliffs of Scotland, near Inverkeilor, a flock has been a great success in terms of conservation. The sheep graze down the sward so that rare species, such as small blue butterflies, can thrive. There is only one problem: controlling the population. Of course they are impossible to round up, never mind take to an abattoir, so the only way to stop the population from getting out of control is to shoot them in the wild. Local enthusiasts or soldiers from a nearby army base will come to help with the culling in return for a leg of lamb for the Sunday roast. I get permission from the farmer and ask George Burgess, a retired vet, to take me with him to cull one of this year's lambs.

George takes me out for target practice with a .222 calibre rifle. For some months I have been practising with a .177 air rifle and my aim is now fairly good. I have also, thanks to practice, gotten over The Flinch and learnt to remain calm when shooting a gun.

It is a soft autumn afternoon when we set out, the sea in the distance overhung by a pink haze. The sheep are grazing on the top of the cliffs. They are suspicious of humans, though it is easier to get close than with truly wild animals, so we leopard-crawl in. George is just behind me. In whispers we identify the best cull lamb – a ewe with a lighter fleece, almost golden – and ensure I have a safe backdrop. We load a bullet and I try to get comfortable. It feels like I am taking forever, trying to steady myself and slow my heartbeat. Keeping still when you are looking at a target is easy; when it is a live animal, it is far more difficult to remain calm. I am aware of the birds singing around me, the feeling of my face against the stock of the gun, my elbows on the ground. To his credit, George waits, letting me get comfortable. I can feel my heart hammering. I wait and wait, breathe, breathe until my hand is steady, my shot sure, the cross hairs moving up and down as I breathe, in and out. And squeeze.

One shot and she is down, her body twitching like a dog in its sleep. I make the gun safe and run to her; she is still, a clean kill, the eyes gone, dead. George cuts the throat for the bleed-out; a surprising amount of blood gushes onto the grass. He cuts the stomach open and eviscerates the lamb. The warm rumen is stuffed full of macerated grass; we leave it for the crows and foxes. The body leaves a trail of blood as we drag her from the field to the larder.

We hang the lamb on a steel contraption that looks like a coat hanger, one leg through either side of the steel. It is small, this year's lamb. I can smell the lanolin from the wool, the lambing shed. George plucks at the skin and describes the anatomy in veterinary terms: 'cut the fascia', that's it. Slowly we peel off the skin and the wool. The fat on the surface is so warm it's still soft, like butter, and underneath the firm pink muscle looks like a diagram from one of George's old textbooks.

We take out the liver and cook it for lunch. It tastes delicious, with a taint of iron in the back of the throat, like rust, and the texture melt-in-the-mouth. The shoulder and neck I take back to Edinburgh and feed to my friends. Soay lamb is not like other lamb; it is tastier, leaner, perhaps from feeding on the seaweed. Just now it is fashionable in restaurants as a 'prehistoric' lamb. Jade, a yoga teacher, slow-cooks a roast and our friend Zoe says she can taste the love with which it was harvested. Even my vegan friends have some at a barbecue. They are not disgusted with me; they are pleased to be able to eat meat that has not been intensively farmed. It's the first time they have had the opportunity.

After the Second World War, Britain moved to a much more intensive way of farming. Livestock, like everything on the farm, had to be more efficient. This meant bringing chickens and pigs and cows indoors – more of which later. Beef and sheep also had to compete on an open market and we started cutting corners with feed. Cattle, herbivores of course, were fed bonemeal to provide protein and make them grow faster. It led to bovine spongiform encephalopathy (BSE), more commonly known as mad cow disease, and the end of the reputation of British beef as the best in the world.

I remember watching the news reports as a child in the nineties, the cattle so weak their legs collapsed under them. I was frightened to eat a burger from the Suffolk Show again after hearing about the deaths of young people from the horrific disease. Of course in our household – like on most farms – we carried on eating beef, probably the animals that had to be slaughtered for being over 30 months old, the new cut-off point for commercial sale.

I also remember foot and mouth disease, the next scandal to hit the livestock industry in 2001, this time blamed on the consolidation of abattoirs and cattle markets and the movement of animals around the country. I remember slopping through hygiene washes if you wanted to visit a farm, and livestock burned on pyres 40m (130ft) high. Six million animals were slaughtered and the price of cattle went through the floor, forcing many farmers out of business.

The trauma of that time had only just receded when along came the horsemeat scandal in 2013. Once again, cutting corners had led to a food scandal. Horsemeat was found in cheap processed 'beef' meals including Tesco burgers and Findus ready meals. But this time, the farmers were ready.

Nicola Bulgin slams down a lamb shoulder glistening with blood and fat. As a butcher's daughter and farmer's wife she knows the value of good meat. So when she was offered a price lower than it had cost to raise her beef and sheep she said no. 'I knew the meat was worth more than that,'

she said. 'And I knew it was safe, so I thought, alright then, I'll sell it myself.'

Like many farmers in the wake of the foot and mouth crisis, the Bulgins decided to go it alone, rather than accept the ridiculously low prices offered by the market and go out of business. It has been hard work sending their animals for slaughter and butchering, and then picking up the cuts to sell in farmers' markets or through direct sales. But it has paid off. Their farm in Norfolk has expanded and been awarded for its environmental principles, grazing cattle and sheep on flood land used by rare wading birds. Beat Bush Farm now supplies Harvey Nichols and regular customers buy every cut of beef and lamb. The market is expanding, with the internet providing another place to sell the meat. Box schemes, when customers order half or all of the animal, with no choice about cuts but full knowledge of provenance, are becoming increasingly popular. When the horsemeat scandal came along Nicola's orders went up even more.

It is a story I hear more than once, often led by the women working on the farm, who are unwilling to accept the prices of the supermarkets any longer. Instead they make the brave decision to sell the meat direct. It has not made many of them rich, but as the consumer looks for brands they can trust, they are coming out on top.

I go along to a fete on a trendy estate in south London organised by Farmdrop, a new online service that provides people in the city with produce direct from farms. It was set up by Ben Pugh, an ex-banker and entrepreneur who could see that many people wanted to know exactly where their food came from, especially meat. Hipsters with beards and girls in summer dresses try samples of meat produced by Nicola and other farmers. Despite living in the city, these people still want a connection to the countryside and the food they eat.

Open Farm Sunday is also growing in popularity. In 2015, 291,000 people visited farms on the first Sunday in June. I went along to Deersbrook Farm in Essex, one of the few beef farms in the county. The pastures are a relief to see in the largely arable landscape and the car park is jammed. Children are feeding the chickens, scratching the pig and marvelling at the cows, including the huge Angus bull. Anna Blomfield, the farmer, is rushed off her feet making burgers and trying to prevent small children climbing on the pig. She has done this all free of charge, except for selling the burgers for charity, but it is worth it. 'People should be able to ask questions – it's their food,' she says, before she is collared by another curious visitor. It's not just animals people want to reconnect with – it is the farmer.

Almost half a million people in Britain work in the farming industry. But the number is going down, along with earnings. The average age of a British farmer is 59. Traditional livestock farming in particular is struggling. The population of sheep has halved in the last 20 years to just 20 million. It reflects the move to a more industrial way of farming. But have we lost something in the switch that connected us to our food and our landscape?

When James Rebanks sent his first tweets in 2012, he didn't think it would make him famous. At the time of writing @herdyshepherd1 had 78.2k followers all over the world and growing. It is very simple – in his tweets and a bestselling book, *The Shepherd's Life*, he shows what is happening on a hill farm: the passage of the seasons, the herding, shearing, feeding, castrating, deworming, doctoring, mending and mucking. The living and dying. Why are people so interested? I think it is because they long to be connected to the land and a way of life that brings them into contact with birth and death.

Of course, there has been a backlash from the people who believe the uplands would be better left for the trees and 'rewilding'. But what would happen to the Rebanks and 300 other farmers who sustain another kind of landscape that we love – and a food we also enjoy? 'No one who works in this landscape romanticizes wilderness,' he writes. James Rebanks does not hide what he does; he celebrates it. He is producing meat and keeping the land alive and we love him for it. A living conservation.

I manage to interview him between lambing, tweeting and being profiled in *The New York Times*. I ask him if he worries about raising animals for meat. 'No offence to vegetarians, but I genuinely think it is a muddled concept; their hands are covered in blood, as are mine. There is a growing and strange view that you can somehow opt out of having an impact in the landscape – but if you eat then you can't. You live, and other things die. It is really that simple – whether you are a vegan or a vegetarian. The only choice is whether you are aware of your impact and expressing rational choices or not. Or flying blind,' he says. 'I don't feel sad about sending sheep for meat. I am entirely comfortable with the idea that animals die so we can eat. I'm not sure that there is any real alternative to shedding blood to eat, so it seems sensible to me to accept it and live with it.'

For James and other famers keeping our landscape alive it is about more than producing meat; it is passing on a way of life to a next generation. 'I see traditional farming systems as a kind of cultural diversity – a depository of the knowledge humans acquired over millennia about how to live and eat in different places,' he writes. 'I think losing those systems and the knowledge and skills that they require is a very dangerous thing for our species. These are insurance policies for the future if it goes wrong, and places to go to for ideas, DNA and inspiration even if it goes right.'

Jade Barlett and Oli Parsons are taking up the baton, running a small livestock farm in Halwell, South Devon. The young couple rent land to graze Galloway cattle and Lleyn ewes and sell the meat via a box scheme, linking customers to the meat.

Jade, a former outdoor education instructor, is unusual in the countryside for her skinny jeans and her questioning attitude to meat. Brought up in the Home Counties and well travelled, she thought she wanted nothing to do with the raising and slaughter of animals. But as an adult she felt a need to connect with the land in a real and meaningful way. 'I was vegetarian for 15 years because I did not know about meat and I did not understand it. But I always wanted a connection to the land, I was always looking for a way in …'.

When her father bought a smallholding she came down to Devon to help. Being vegetarian on a small livestock farm, where all the ducks one year happened to be drakes, meant changing her views. 'We had to kill them because no one wanted to buy them,' she says. 'We were responsible for bringing them into the world, so we were responsible for killing them too and not wasting the meat.' Eating meat for the first time, she said she felt a 'wholeness'. It is a word I hear often when talking to people about meat; it is the link to the land and former generations. 'I felt thankful for the sunshine and water and the grass – those animals,' she says. As we scratch the backs of cattle grazing by Dartington College, Jade tells me about meeting Oli years before, rounding up sheep. She laughs as she recalls meeting his cattle as well. Just when they started going out he was given a Belted Galloway calf in lieu of payment for a job he was doing. He kept it in a cardboard box in the kitchen and called it Humbug. Jade fell in love. Humbug will never leave the farm.

Jade is not sentimental and she's not stupid – she's a farmer and businesswoman. Just because she's thought about welfare doesn't mean she's not trying to run a successful business. 'We have not just inherited a farm. We chose to do it. We worked for it. We are questioning everything we do all the time to ensure it is a good thing to be doing for the world, a good thing to be doing for society and a good thing to be doing economically for us,' she says. 'We are responsible for breeding the animals so we are responsible for them for the rest of their lives and they can't all be pets; that's not a viable business. It's not how farming works. So if we are going to do it, we have to be 100 per cent responsible for it. We've been to our local abattoir to work out exactly what happens. It wasn't nice but we take responsibility for it. The hardest thing is that every time, every time we take them I think should we be doing this? Should we be using these animals? I am still questioning it. I always will.'

I phone up Roly to see how this year's lambing is looking. The sheep have just been scanned. 'Henry's having triplets!' The first she's had since she started lambing six years ago.

We chat for a while about the book. I am still struggling to find a way to explain, to make sense of the journey of meat. 'It's always difficult, it's difficult.' I imagine Roly in his overalls by the phone, his hands grimy with work, thinking about his sheep. 'I don't know how you're going to do it,' he says. There is a pause. 'When I go to the abattoir, which is just down the road, when I'm waiting with the livestock trailer to let the lambs out, I'm always struck by the amount of birds and wildlife in the hedgerows right next to …'

He can't quite say the words: where there is life, there is death, especially in farming.

CHAPTER FIVE

Gobby Teens

If to be feelingly alive to the sufferings of my fellow-creatures is to be a fanatic, I am one of the most incurable fanatics ever permitted to be at large.
William Wilberforce, co-founder of the RSPCA

'Would you like to see a poleaxe?' It was the last thing I expected to see at the headquarters of the Royal Society for the Prevention of Cruelty to Animals (RSPCA): an instrument of death and torture. I was stunned, knocked for six, poleaxed. But there it was, in pride of place in a glass cabinet, like a family heirloom or the crown jewels, at the heart of the country's softest, fluffiest, cuddliest charity: a poleaxe.

I'm not sure I had ever thought about what one really looked like or what the phrase poleaxed means. It had a

wooden haft around 90cm (3ft) long and a heavy steel head
with a vicious spike on one side. Traditionally the poleaxe
was used by medieval soldiers as a 'tin opener' to cut through
the breastplate on a suit of armour. Oddly it is still the
weapon of choice for those long-haired men who enjoy
re-enacting famous battle scenes at the weekend. But towards
the 19th century it was mainly the instrument for killing
cattle. A poleaxe was used to stun the animal by hitting the
forehead with the spike in one huge concussive blow.
The trouble was that it wasn't always accurate.

I track down accounts of the time. Some tell me that the
men were exhausted and more often than not full of beer.
There were tales of animals taking 12 agonising minutes to
die. This is where the RSPCA steps in. Despite its reputation
today for rescuing neglected cats and dogs, the charity was
in fact set up to prevent cruelty to farm animals. Back in the
1800s, abused animals were not something you saw on
YouTube; they were on every street corner. Animals were
born, worked and died in the city. The 'shambles' or butchers'
quarters were in the heart of the commercial district – as
you can see from street names in cities like York. It was quite
normal to hear the death cries of slaughter and see rivulets
of blood creeping out of certain alleyways.

Aside from the hygiene concerns, it was becoming
increasingly clear that such gruesome images were a
'demoralising influence' on the small children who would
dare one another to peek in through the doors. A radical new
idea was also creeping into fashion – that perhaps animals
could suffer just like we do. A growing branch of philosophy
was questioning the strict rationale of the Enlightenment
that dismissed any animal that could not reason and suggesting
sentience was also important. As philosopher Jeremy
Bentham wrote in 1789: 'The question is not, Can they
reason? nor, Can they talk? but, Can they suffer?'

Richard Martin or 'Humanity Dick', as he was known,
was the first Member of Parliament brave enough to speak

up for these 'dumb brutes'. At first he was sneered at and depicted in cartoons with the ears of a donkey, even though he was no ass, having survived hundreds of duels. Gradually his argument gained support; it was the Romantic Era after all. In fashionable coffee shops around London the intelligentsia was beginning to question whether those of a different class or sex or colour were really so very different from them. For a few, the next logical step was to discuss the rights of animals too. In 1822 the UK was the first country in the world to implement a law protecting animals. 'An Act to prevent the cruel and improper Treatment of Cattle' or 'Martin's Act' was at first seen as a pet project of the sentimental upper classes so they wouldn't have to see starving beasts beaten to death as they rumbled past in their carriages. Down in the shambles, it was a joke and the police considered it almost impossible to enforce.

It was only when other prominent figures joined the cause that animal rights started to be taken seriously. In 1824 a group of men including Richard Martin, William Wilberforce, a leader of the movement to abolish slavery, and the campaigner Reverend Arthur Broome met in the appropriately named Old Slaughter's Coffee House. The Society for the Prevention of Cruelty to Animals vowed to send inspectors into the shambles to make sure Martin's Act was being followed and cattle were not being mistreated. The charity went on to lobby Parliament to abolish bear baiting, cock fighting and other blood sports. The cause of 'dumb brutes' was suddenly glamorous. So glamorous, they soon won the support of the young Princess Victoria, who later added the word Royal and a cat to the charity's masthead design. During her reign the trend for humanitarianism and indeed sanitation would see slaughterhouses moved from the centre of towns to the outskirts and methods of slaughter transformed. They even gave the slaughterhouse a fancy new French name, 'abattoir', from abbatre, to fell.

In the 1920s a new invention, the bolt gun, began to
replace the poleaxe as the best means to stun a cow. The
cartridge-propelled captive bolt was a steel cylinder up to
10cm (4in) long by 1cm (0.4in) in diameter. Unlike the
poleaxe, which relied on brute force, it relied on a blank
cartridge to drive a bolt into the cranium, destroying brain
matter and causing immediate unconsciousness. The gun
seemed like the obvious method in an age when firearms
were being mass produced, and even though it was fiercely
resisted by butchers at first, who claimed it was dangerous to
operatives, it soon spread.

Again, the RSPCA, the new 'animal rights' charity, was
one of the first to promote this new idea of 'humane
slaughter'. Next to the poleaxe in the glass cabinet I am
inspecting is one of the country's first bolt guns, alongside a
certificate from the local police force assuring the public
that 'this firearm has been disabled'. It is definitely not what
I thought I would find when I visited the oldest and largest
animal welfare organisation in the world.

When I was little I was a member of the Junior RSPCA. One
of my favourite pastimes was marching around car parks
slapping stickers on the windscreens pronouncing: 'DOGS
DIE IN HOT CARS!' It didn't matter that there were no dogs
in the cars, or that it was raining; it was the idea of rescuing
someone, something, anything. We all want to be the hero.

But already in this visit to a very modern charity most of
my preconceptions of the RSPCA have been broken down.
Except for the traditional collection box in the shape of a
dog and a few pictures of 'star fundraisers' holding cute
kittens on the wall, the glass and steel building could be the
headquarters of any large corporation in Britain. The men
and women before me are pragmatic, clear-eyed and
unsentimental. In a way, they remind me of farmers.

'It is going to take an awfully long time to stop human beings from eating meat so while they are eating meat it is up to us to ensure those animals do not suffer unnecessarily – or at all – and have the best quality of life possible,' says John Avizienius, Deputy Head of the charity's farm animals department. 'There is no point in sticking your fingers in your ears, shutting your eyes and going la, la, la …'

Since its inception, the RSPCA has become a pillar of British society, famous around the world for rescuing abandoned pets and a key part of our reputation as soppy animal lovers. But behind the scenes it has never forgotten its commitment to ensure farm animals have a good life and a humane death – and it is still a radical charity. 'Some 200 years ago William Wilberforce and the other founders of the RSPCA faced an audience of people who thought those with a different skin colour or who didn't speak English didn't think or feel or suffer like we do. Now we have to prove that fluffy creatures or animals with scales who don't speak or think, feel and suffer like we do,' says John. 'I think the safest default position is to assume they do and then go backwards from that …'

One hundred and seventy years after Humanity Dick suggested those Regency ladies should lower their fans and take a look at what was going on in the shambles, another 'animal hero' suggested the modern shopper should look at how their food arrived on the supermarket shelf. In 1994 the then Deputy Chief Vet of the UK and Head of Farm Animals at the RSPCA, Alistair Mews, suggested setting up a labelling scheme that would tell shoppers whether animals were being raised and slaughtered in a humane way. For him it was a 'no-brainer', a way to force farmers and processors to behave correctly by offering them a 'stamp of approval' and potentially improving the lives of millions of farm animals. But it was also controversial.

Imagine you run a charity that relies on people perhaps being a little sentimental about animals and suddenly you are suggesting working with the industry that kills them. Many in the charity and the wider animal rights movement thought Mews was mad and some left the organisation in protest. But as Margaret Boyde, an RSPCA assessor who spends her days looking at cattle and sheep in abattoirs rather than at pet rabbits, says, the clue is in the name. 'It is the Society for the Prevention of Cruelty to Animals – all animals. It is not a fluffy charity, it is a head-on organisation that deals with welfare rather than just what the public want to see,' she says. 'We could have sat on the sidelines and had a vegetarian/ vegan agenda but that is not what we are about; we are about improving the lives of animals, including farm animals. This was such a huge opportunity to change that. We would improve the lives of millions of farm animals.'

Plus, the time was right. It was the 1990s, and people were increasingly concerned about the food they were eating. Mad cow disease had knocked people's confidence and made them question the claims on the packets. Suddenly there was a real hunger to know exactly how meat is produced.

In the background, veterinarians had already developed an animal rights agenda. Animals should have the right to the 'Five Freedoms': freedom from hunger or thirst, discomfort or pain, injury or disease, fear or distress, and the freedom to express most normal behaviours. Mews thought the public deserved to know that at least those five freedoms were being observed and thus the 'Freedom Food' label was born. He accepted the harsh truth, that there are a lot of farm animals – now more than a billion reared in the UK every year – but that means there is a lot we can do to improve their lives.

The idea was to work with farmers and abattoirs for the first time to encourage them to treat animals better, rather than just waiting for them to go wrong and sending in the inspectors. Those in the scheme would be inspected regularly, including random spot checks on issues like stocking density, access to feed, transport and humane slaughter. In return they would be able to use the Freedom Food label to add a premium to the food.

It was not an easy road: farmers were mistrustful of the 'animal police' and the supermarkets were set on pushing down prices rather than adding any extra costs. But Mews, a charismatic vet with steely determination, had worked with farmers all his life; he knew most of them wanted to do the best thing for their animals. He was also wily enough to know how supermarkets work, and despite one pushing for exclusivity he insisted this scheme would be across all retailers, or none; it was for all animals – or none – after all.

In 1994 the Freedom Food assurance label was launched as a separate organisation to the RSPCA. The first farm to join was Day Lay Eggs in Tring, Hertfordshire, now Noble Foods, and soon afterwards Bowes of Norfolk, a pig enterprise. Sadly Mews died shortly after the launch of the scheme, but he is remembered as a hero to this day – he certainly did more than slap stickers on car windows.

Freedom Food was the first label in the world to concentrate solely on animal welfare and remains the most well known and respected. Today more than 90 per cent of eggs and 40 per cent of pork meet RSPCA standards. On the day I visit, the RSPCA reveals plans to extend the scheme even further. In another brave move, they are changing the name from 'Freedom Food' to 'RSPCA Assured'. Even though it is a risk to associate the RSPCA with meat – that is, the farming industry and slaughter – it is judged that using the brand name in such a way will help more animals.

'It's the right time,' says Jez Cooper, the new Chief Executive of Freedom Food, brought in to increase 'brand awareness'. 'A busy mum needs meat to be high welfare, but she hasn't got time to scan labels or do research. She needs to recognise a brand that she can trust, that will not add too much extra cost.' It's a little depressing to think we need to be told – or that mums have to do all the shopping – but I can't help admiring the pragmatism of the RSPCA. Here for the first time are people who care about animals but accept we eat meat and want to make a difference.

Margaret, whom I personally would not mess with, slams down a pile of thick booklets on each of the 11 species covered by the RSPCA, with up to 400 standards for each. I start to flick through each of the pamphlets noting directions on depth of bedding, hours in transport, stunning voltage … 'People don't want to look at slaughter but we literally have everything there – to the length of the knife,' says Margaret. 'We are not shirking from anything. It is the truth. That's why we started in the first place, because people say they don't want to know, but they do.'

The standards are developed by a committee of farmers, vets and researchers and they are always being updated. The idea is to 'stretch farmers' so animal welfare is constantly being improved, 'step by step'. 'But don't farmers mind?' I ask. 'More red tape …'

'You have to remember it is good for them too,' replies Margaret. 'Many of our farmers prefer working under the RSPCA conditions; it is better for them.' It is also in the interest of abattoirs to be RSPCA Assured. Workers are given more training in animal welfare; moreover, if animals are not stressed no adrenaline taints the meat and therefore it tastes better. One of the key RSPCA requirements is that CCTV films the workers at all times and the tape is kept for three months so that inspectors can check back anytime. This now happens in most abattoirs and there is hope it will be enshrined in legislation.

I ask Margaret, who has been a farmer herself for 25 years, about the workers in abattoirs. Aren't they 'brutalised'; can they really be expected to care? Sure there is the odd 'bad apple', she tells me, but CCTV and inspections should ensure they are weeded out. 'As a farmer you have an incredibly high standard of care and caring. If you spoke to any of our abattoir assessors, the vast majority are extremely caring people because, remember, they are looking those animals in the eye; they are not shooting them at 300 metres.'

As we sit in the RSPCA canteen with office workers sipping coffee and munching sandwiches, we discuss the best way to stun an animal, the shackling of hens, the caging of pigs. For the first time in this journey, it doesn't feel odd. I wonder why this is, and then I realise: this is their bread and butter, looking at what no one else wants to see. I feel less alone; I am not the only one mad enough to want to uncover my eyes and take my fingers out of my ears.

The RSPCA is even brave enough to suggest that eating veal is a 'good story to tell'. For years it had a bad reputation as the worst kind of farming. The male calves of dairy cows were kept in crates and fed only milk so that their meat would remain pale and tender. It was horribly cruel and has been outlawed in the UK. I remember the images of the veal crates from the 1990s from my Junior RSPCA *Animal Action Magazine*, the eyes of the baby cows green in the camera flash, the light showing up the chain at their neck and the shit on the floor.

But what happens to male calves of dairy cows now? Mothers still need to be in calf every year to keep producing milk and while the heifers are put back into the dairy system, the males are often destroyed at birth. Although less common in the UK than in France or Italy, up to 99,000 dairy calves are still shot every year, and as many as 10,000 calves are exported to the Continent each year, possibly to low-welfare veal farms. The RSPCA believe that the males can be given a good life and be eaten as 'rosé veal', which is a little more pink because the calf has been given solid food and lived in a barn on straw rather than in a crate. 'They can live a happy life for up to eight months,' said Margaret. That's a lot older than the lamb and chicken people eat quite happily. 'You could almost call it baby beef.'

Julie Bunt has to speak up to make herself heard over the lowing of veal calves. 'They're like gobby teens,' she says. 'Hollering and bellowing. The best thing to do is to ignore them.' We are in the lairage, where the cattle are kept before slaughter. Julie, the motherly Technical Manager at St Merryn Foods, has decided to take me under her wing. Veal day is the noisiest day at the RSPCA Assured abattoir I have come to visit, because the younger cattle tend to be more vocal. 'They're just telling each other what is going on,' she continues. 'But you can see they are quite relaxed.'

The animals swish their tails and blink at me through the gates. They look more like fully grown cows than calves. At eight months old, they are already at least 200kg (440lb) and just getting to the point where you couldn't bucket feed them without a friendly nudge sending you flying. Julie points out what to look out for: alert ears, glossy coats, no lameness. If anything is not right the farmer is reported. Also the haulier, who is RSPCA Approved, cannot transport animals for over eight hours and must make sure they have adequate bedding and water.

The lairage itself is spotlessly clean; it is hosed down each time before a new consignment comes in and the cattle stand on washed concrete. Julie shows me the etching to stop animals slipping, and padding on the gates so they don't bang. Each pen leads on to a circular cattle chute that leads in turn to the slaughterhouse, so that animals can be moved easily without too much disturbance of the rest. Anything that can alarm an animal, even an old pair of overalls blowing in the wind, has been removed. CCTV cameras are everywhere, watching everything. 'No one shouts in the lairage,' she says. 'It should be a calm place.'

Julie, a mother of five, has been working in the industry for 19 years. She is bullish in her defence of her work. 'The moral dilemma is not "to kill or not to kill". You are born to eat meat and we always will. This is something that is going to happen anyway so if it is going to happen, my job is to make sure it is done in the best possible way.'

The official vet or 'OV', who will check all animals before slaughter in any abattoir, is there making notes on the clipboard. He nods. They are ready to go through.

You always go backwards in an abattoir, from the packing plant, to the boning hall, to the killing hall, to the lairage. It is to avoid contamination. So, backwards – from the beginning. I arrive at St Merryn Foods on 1st June, the first day of summer. After a week interviewing livestock farmers in the pillowy fields of Devon, I feel vulnerable again. Despite the evidence of farming maintaining the landscape and caring for the animals, it has also made me sensitive to the softness of the animals and the land, of me.

The abattoir is hidden behind Asda in the corner of an industrial site on the edge of Bodmin, the bleak moor just a few miles beyond. Like most slaughterhouses, it seems an ordinary industrial estate as you drive in, except for the telltale smell of manure. As I wait by the security gate some Eastern Europeans sign in for the first time. Their friend, who has better English, has to come and do it for them. It is a sign of the changing social make-up of the people who work in abattoirs. Although the skilled and highly paid jobs in the killing hall are usually taken by local men, the unskilled jobs in the packing halls, especially near urban centres, are increasingly being done by migrant labour.

In the 1970s there used to be 1,000 abattoirs in Britain, many just a room behind a butcher's shop and practically all owned by family firms. But as more and more regulations have come in as part of the European Common Market, it has been impossible for the smaller units to exist, and there are now around 200 red meat abbatoirs. There are 12 or so large units like St Merryn, which process up to 100,000 animals a year, usually owned by holding companies that are part of a larger food processing business. Half are medium-sized units, owned by supermarkets or farmers' cooperatives. Most of the remaining small abattoirs are family-owned units and it is these that are struggling to survive.

St Merryn is owned by 2 Sisters – at one point the largest food processing company in the UK. Everywhere I go I hear about its CEO, Ranjit Boparan, but struggle to get an interview or indeed even a response from the press office. The company, based in Birmingham, came from nowhere on the back of 'added-value' food – ready meals – processed in big units near urban areas, where cheap, often migrant, labour can be sourced. Since then they have gone on to buy up smaller companies and are one of the main suppliers to the supermarkets.

St Merryn has been at its current location since 1987 and has the capacity to slaughter and debone 1,875 cattle and pack 200 tonnes (220 US tons) of meat per week. As I wait lorries come and go through the security gates. Finally, they let me through to the car park, where I find Sarah Cutler, a Freedom Food Assessor, and Roger Briddock, an RSPCA Farm Livestock Officer. They are dressed in smart blue overalls and immediately put me at my ease. Sarah is about my age and pretty, with kind brown eyes and a ready smile. Roger is a little more gruff, but open to any questions. 'Shall we?' They lead me across the car park. Like at any big industrial site with large machinery, you must stay within the yellow lines. You must not stray.

It is a completely different experience to Wishaw. Before we go into the slaughterhouse, we sit down for a coffee to discuss the process, so I understand everything that is going to happen. So I don't panic. Kevin Blemings, the most experienced slaughterman in the plant, has come up to the boardroom to answer my questions. He sits opposite me tapping his fingers, looking no different from the farmers and fishermen I met in Devon. I read his knuckles upside down: 'I LOVE CORNWALL.'

'So, how did you end up being a, erm, um, a slaughterman?' I feel like an idiot.

But Kevin looks unperturbed. 'Never known any different,' he says. He's been at St Merryn for 28 years. His kids are here, his brother, his nephews and nieces, his ex-wife, probably one day his grandchildren. 'Slaughterman is a word of mouth job, you do it from a young age,' he says. 'We are just normal people, it is just the job you end up doing.' He does not look unhappy about it. He is clearly well respected, making training videos on animal welfare. 'When I started slaughtering there was no such thing as animal welfare,' he says. 'The job has changed so much; it is much better. We look after the animals better and we look after ourselves better.' He looks proud. 'It is quite complex getting to know all the health and safety stuff.'

'And, er, well, what does it feel like?' Now I feel like a complete idiot.

But again, Kevin doesn't flinch. 'Look love, you are not going to move the best part of 1.5 tonnes if they know they are going to die; you have to treat them with care and respect.' He pauses. 'I'm getting softer as I get older. I do not want to see the poor things die but it is a job that we have to do and as long as it is done properly that is all we can do. I know that it is an animal but if you were so soft, thinking "poor little calf" all the time … You have to disconnect. To a certain extent you have to switch yourself off to do what you are doing. Not totally, but …'

We've reached a point where it has become more of a philosophical discussion. Can he even explain that moment? There is an uncomfortable pause. 'C'mon love,' says Kevin. 'I'll show you around.'

Before we go in, Sarah takes a moment to explain the system here: a Jarvis stun box. The cow walks into the stun box, she explains gently, and is clamped by the neck so the nose is resting on an electric plate. Sarah puts her palm to her nose. Immediately a three-second current is passed from the neck yoke to the nose electrodes, knocking out the brain. Then another electrode is rested on the brisket – she touches her chest – stopping the heart. Finally, an electrode at the rear end disables the spine. The animal falls into the steel cradle below. The final shock stops everything. It has stopped twitching. No 'paddle' action. No 'clonic, tonic' reflexes. No swimming in the air, as if they are trying to get away.

They lead me into a dressing room where overalls, a hat and boots in my size have all been laid out ready. It is spotlessly clean in here. The walls are a white container metal. It is a cold sort of environment. I wonder how no one gets lost; everything looks the same. We go through the usual routine: hairnet, sanitiser, wellies, footbath. I try not to look too hard at the bits of gristle in the rotating brushes at my feet. It must be fat, right? Like when you wash a pan that has cooked sausages and been left on the side. Or is it something else? Brain, bones, skin? I try to calm my imagination, to be objective. We pass through the store room hung with carcasses: a forest of red trunks, the labels like leaves showing the farmer, age, slaughterhouse, time in stun box.

In the killing room it is strangely silent except for the sound of the radio. It smells of the latest deodorisation, masking the hot fug of beef dripping. The men are waiting by the lines for the next consignment to come in. They work a long day: 7 am till 4.30 pm with just short breaks to go to the loo, have a smoke, catch up on the gossip. Someone is phoning in on the radio. I wonder, do they ever get a call from here? 'Hi! It's Terry. From the slaughterhouse …' The floor is grey, not red. So they can see the blood, they say, keep things clean. I look up at the gantries as they start clanking; the men adjust their hairnets, cover their noses, but I can see their eyes. Work has begun again.

I feel my heart hammering as the machinery comes to life. We are following the lines along the floor. For some reason it goes behind a queue of freshly slaughtered cattle, their tongues lolling out their mouths, dripping blood. I start to feel claustrophobic. I want to take a different route. Men stand on platforms above me ready to skin the animal, known as 'peeling the jacket off'; the carcass moves down the line … decapitation … evisceration … sawn in half and whish! Along the rails, into the forest.

We are at the foot of the ladder up to the 'knocking box'. There is a bang. They just used the bolt on a young cow. That's the trouble with veal calves – often they are too small for the Jarvis and it is quicker to use a bolt gun rather than stress the animal manoeuvring it into the right position. It unnerves me but I put my first foot on the ladder. I climb up, followed by Sarah. It feels crowded in here, with three of us including the slaughterman. I don't just feel claustrophobic now, I feel sick, and my thighs are shaking.

No, I can't afford to do this again, to spend months getting over this. 'Sorry.' I turn away and climb down before the next calf comes in. Back on the scrubbed concrete, they all crowd around, protective now. We walk on to the lairage; we don't leave the yellow lines.

Sarah did this nine months pregnant on a hot day. 'I do find it difficult,' she says. 'I always have, but I do it because

I want to make sure it is being done properly.' Sarah is on farms and in slaughterhouses every day, talking to farmers and butchers. She has a PhD in animal science; she knows the challenges and the solutions. 'I put my wellies on every day and look at livestock and hen houses and I am using my brain too. I absolutely love my job. I do not always find it easy but in terms of making a difference, I really, really feel that I can,' she says. 'And when I drive away, I think people should appreciate where their food comes from, people should understand what goes into it. It is so undervalued. They should value the meat that they eat.'

It is all that Humanity Dick would have wanted. For the animals to be treated with respect.

A lot has changed since Humanity Dick transformed the slaughterhouse. But then again, a lot has stayed the same. Slaughtermen are still considered the lowest of the low. I am told more than once by animal rights campaigners that people who work in abattoirs are sadists. Strangely, none of them have any UK statistics to back this up. In the trade, they don't know any statistics either. Off the record I am told, sure, there are a few guys with criminal records. Where else would they get a job? What about giving people second chances? But sadists? No, they'd get sacked.

Personally, I wouldn't be surprised if the criminal rate is higher. There is a significant proportion of men, of low-skilled workers, of drug use and alcoholism. A 2012 Australian study found that slaughterhouse workers are more inclined to commit acts of violence. The lead researcher found that their levels of aggression were 'so high they're similar to the scores ... for incarcerated populations'. The findings corroborate a 2010 Canadian study that found that violent crimes, including sexual assault and rape, increase in towns once an abattoir moves in.

The only UK study I find is 'Sacrifice and Distinction in Dirty Work' led by Brunel University. It's about butchers and it's about the loss of their status. It's rather sad. It makes me think of Kevin. I think he deserves our respect. If you are going to eat meat, even a small amount, you have to support the people who provide it for you, not look down your nose.

Looking through old copies of the *Meat Trades Journal*, I find a letter from 1894 in response to the new 'vegetarians' trying to close down slaughterhouses where they could be seen by passers-by. I imagine him, the 19th century slaughterman, standing proud in his blood-spattered apron, the fountain pen tiny in his huge calloused hand. 'People don't treat me as an unclean creature that I know of; and as to talking about the "deep degradation of the nature of the whole class of men," I can tell him that he does misrepresent me and others and that I do my duty as well and am quite as honest as this vegetarian agitator. We are not even now dregs and never were.'

CHAPTER SIX

Grown-ups

I think using animals for food is an ethical thing to do, but we've
got to do it right. We've got to give those animals a decent life,
and we've got to give them a painless death.
We owe the animal respect.

Temple Grandin

I have had many arguments with editors over the years, but
one of my favourites was trying to convince the *Daily
Telegraph* news desk that the slaughter of cows was more
interesting than the birth of Prince George.

It was a hot summer's day during the silly season and
every other journalist was outside the Lindo Wing of
St Mary's Hospital waiting for poor Kate Middleton to do
her duty and produce an heir. I was thoroughly bored by
the whole affair, as were most of my colleagues stuck on

a sweltering pavement in central London, so I thought I would take up an invitation to tour a Waitrose abattoir with Prince Charles. It seemed like a good idea at the time. I had never been to a slaughterhouse back then and I presumed most people would be interested to know where their meat came from. Of course my news desk was more interested in whether I could get the inside scoop on the Royal Baby.

Now, reporting on royalty in the UK is not like reporting on normal people. There are rules, and strangely, given it is now the the 21st century, we stick to them. You cannot approach Their Royal Highnesses and you certainly cannot ask them direct questions. Instead you follow them around all day, never getting too close, rather like a game of grandmother's footsteps. To find out information you talk to the people they have just spoken to.

So it was I found myself walking around a meat packing plant near Pontefract asking perplexed individuals whether Prince Charles had let anything slip about *The Baby*? Every few minutes the news desk would ring: 'Anything? Have you got anything yet?' 'No!' I would hiss and return to playing grandmother's footsteps as His Royal Highness walked down the sausage-making line. Eventually, I started ignoring the calls and looked around at what was happening, and it fascinated me.

We skipped the actual killing hall but visited the lairage, where the animals were kept on thick beds of straw, and toured the boning hall, where huge carcasses were broken down into steaks. I decided I had a much better story right here and phoned the news desk to pitch an article about the future of the modern abattoir. They didn't even let me finish my sentence.

'But there are women on the boning line!' I insisted.

'Don't care.'

'But they're wearing chain mail and they have HUGE KNIVES!'

'Don't care.'

'But they're playing classical music to the cows!'

'It's the birth of the future King or Queen of England, Louise, no one fucking cares!'

Of course, I maintain that they do, so a couple of years later when I came to write this book I phoned up Waitrose and asked if I could come back for a return visit. Being Royal Warrant Holders and knowing their manners, they said yes. The supermarket chain is not the only business to use Dovecote Park, the largest independent abattoir in Britain, but they are the main customers.

Nothing about Dovecote Park is like a normal abattoir – though they insist from the beginning I call it a 'food processing plant'. Usually they are hidden in industrial estates out of town, out of sight, out of mind. But this is different. The landscape around the complex is planted with trees, like stately home parkland. Prince Charles must have felt very at home. The walls are painted a tasteful pale green, like a Farrow and Ball shade, 'abattoir mint' perhaps. There is a gym and a huge staff canteen. The offices are converted stone-walled barns, like the hotels and wedding venues in the surrounding Yorkshire countryside, though it used to be where the cattle were kept before being driven across the yard to be slaughtered.

Now the office is scattered with cow skin rugs and trendy furniture. A smartly dressed receptionist gives me a coffee and I leaf through copies of the Waitrose magazine while I wait. David Gunner and Richard Canvin, the joint chief executives of Dovecote Park, pop their heads in. They are unembarrassed and urbane, chatting easily about the business, interested in my book, offering reading advice from José Ortega y Gasset to Wendell Berry and a name that keeps on cropping up, Temple Grandin.

Richard shows me a picture of a butcher's shop in 1899; like most people in the meat trade he is from a long line of butchers. I look at the huge cows strung up in front of the sepia shop, just like the carcasses that gave me such a fright in Wishaw. But this was out in the streets; passers-by could see the cows and even inspect them, admiring the fat around the kidneys, the suet, which they would later use in mince pies. Nowadays we cringe from the sight of our meat. I tell Richard about JBS butchers in Sudbury, a town near where I grew up. The family butcher received complaints after putting up a display of seasonal meat in the window including pigs' heads, rabbits and pheasants. I wanted to go and see them but of course, like a lot of high street butchers, they've closed down. 'How sad,' says Richard. 'We don't hide anything here, there's nothing to hide.'

Again, we go backwards, first through the packing hall. The lady butchers are still there, slicing sirloin in their 'gauntlets' or chain mail gloves. The factory is working full pelt because it is the first 'barbecue' weekend of the year. There is a carnival atmosphere in the air; the smell of spices in the sausage-stuffing department and the excited chatter about what they'll all do after work reminds me of Christmas. My tour guide Simon Peters, the abattoir manager, knows everyone by name. It is almost like following royalty again; he shakes men by the hand, makes a joke, asks after the family. 'Alright lads!' he shouts as we pass a plastic greenhouse. Even the smoking area is light and airy and clean in this abattoir.

We move on through the cold store. Even though it is the hottest day of the summer so far they have given me a puffa jacket to wear over my white coat and the usual wellies, hairnet and hard hat. It is another huge refrigerated forest of red meat and I shiver, despite my layers. 'Hanging allows bacteria to start breaking down the meat, making it more tender and easier to digest,' explains Simon. Dovecote hang all quality beef for at least seven days on the bone. It also dries the meat out, meaning it loses weight, which explains why most supermarkets choose not to hang their meat for as long.

We are getting hotter, moving toward the real butchery, the killing hall. It has to be warm in here so the skin comes off easily. A man stands on a platform and attaches the machine to the top of the cow so the hide peels off in one. Carcasses move around the ceiling on a bright metal carousel, clean and shiny now. It is less steampunk, more a demonstration video of exactly what a factory should look like. So clean and efficient. But the men are real.

'We process 18 cattle an hour,' says Simon. 'That's about 110 in a day. We could kill 400 but the idea is to be efficient, not fast.' Dovecote has made a conscious decision to stay small, so that the workers can be involved in the whole process, rather than concentrating on just one area, which is what happens in a bigger unit. 'Job enrichment', they call it. 'You could be taking out the back end one day, the front end the next.'

The men nod as we walk past. They wear green aprons over their overalls, the obligatory tattoos peeping out. Some are whistling, despite the sound of machinery, wearing yellow ear defenders and hard hats over hairnets. Again there is that odd combination of the hardy and the feminine. 'It is a gentle process,' emphasises Simon. 'You have to make sure the dressing is spot on.' In front of me a man is using what looks like a fan to shear the fat and membrane off a carcass. 'It's the latest technology,' explains Simon. Compressed air powers a circular knife to delicately cut off the fat. It's VL,' he says. 'Visual lean. The housewife' – it's always the housewife – 'wants lean meat.'

We move further down the line to the evisceration. The insides of the cow are hung up like Widow Twankey's washing line – lungs, liver, brain, kidney. The FSA meat inspector is poking about, checking each one. The cow is always inspected by a vet before slaughter and afterwards by the FSA for disease showing in the internal organs. 'Ah, look at this.' He prods a liver and I see a tiny grey slug. Liver fluke. The farmer will be informed so he can treat the problem in his cattle, but it is extremely common. The liver will be condemned but the rest of the carcass will be fine.

Simon slaps the inspector on the back as if congratulating him on his great find. In the background trolleys wheel past filled with offal. Everything is being removed that can be used. The pizzles go to China, the snouts to Nigeria, the hides to India, the toenails for dog chews, the oils for industrial use. Only the brain and spine – Specific Risk Material – will be incinerated because of the danger of BSE. We have reached the back of the killing hall and my chance to see the gut room at last.

A short man, known as Little David, ushers me in. He has rubber gloves up to the elbow and a huge grin. 'Come in, come in.' The smell inside is a combination of silage, the beef dripping my granny always had in her kitchen and washing up liquid, from when they regularly 'deodorise the place'.

Apparently David is the happiest man in the plant – despite having a job most people would struggle to do. They recently sent him to Brazil to learn about the latest technology in creating 'casings', the stomach skin used for sausages. In other abbatoirs the guts are sent abroad to be sorted, where I doubt there is any CCTV.

We walk in past vats of guts, cauldrons of stomach fat. 'Don't fall in!' The floor is slippery with fat. David scoops out a handful of small intestine – 'It's 28m long!' – and runs it through his hands. 'Feel it, so soft; I think it might be the softest, silkiest, most beautiful substance nature invented, no?' He puts his mouth to one end and blows it up like a balloon. 'Look!' He dips his hand into another vat and brings out the manifold, the cow's third stomach. 'They call it Bible tripe.' With its layers of soft white leaves, it does look like a Gideon Bible, each page softened by years of thumbing. I balance it on my hand – it feels like a child's rubber toy – and realise I am giggling, in the gut room.

Perhaps I am being naive, but there is a sense of industry and pride here – even in the gut room. Ever since the mines closed, Dovecote has been one of the main employers in the area and, unusually for modern factories, people stay on for their whole working lives.

My car is so hot from sitting in the sunshine that I take a moment to change into sandals before driving home. Lads from the plant lounge about in the sunshine on their lunch break, teasing one another about sunbathing like a girl. 'Alright love!' One flexes his muscles. 'Sun's out, guns out!' I laugh. It's the first really hot weekend of the year; they all just want to do a good job and go home with a fat wallet. It all seems very British: sunburn, barbecues, sport on the telly. Beer and beef and Prince George.

Beef has traditionally been associated with our sense of national identity. The navy sang songs about 'the roast beef of old England', the army refused to march without barrels of salt beef and on feast days or Christmas we traditionally ate roast beef. We are even nicknamed 'Les Rosbifs' by the French, for our national dish and perhaps, at times, rather oafish and uncivilised ways, especially around food.

We still love beef but increasingly we can't be bothered to cook it. If we eat beef, we eat it American style – in burgers. While the amount of red meat sold over the butcher's counter and made into a Sunday roast is falling, the number of processed burgers sold to Brits continues to go up and up.

Following the provenance of a Waitrose burger is all very well, I think, but the burger I really want to get my teeth into is McDonald's.

The biggest fast food chain in the world now serves 68 million people each day – that is one per cent of the global population. In the UK, there are around 1,250 McDonald's restaurants, and the number is growing, with up to 30 new outlets opening every year. Every day three million of us chow down on a Maccy D's – surely we should know where our burgers come from?

Apparently not. I approach McDonald's on a number of occasions requesting an interview, but am politely refused despite a pledge of greater transparency. Perhaps it is because I am too honest, emailing the press team repeatedly about my book, trying to explain it is a balanced look at the meat trade. I could have taken a softer line but I know too much about McDonald's. They'll do a pretty thorough background check on me anyway – and they do, dragging out an article I wrote in 2012 about the fact the McDonald's restaurant in the Olympic Park was not serving exclusively UK beef. 'But I'm an environmental journalist,' I want to scream. 'Of course I've written rude stories about McDonald's!! If I didn't question powerful corporations I wouldn't be doing my job …' I am told my readers probably won't be the kind of people who eat McDonald's. Really? Since 90 per cent of the population has eaten a McDonald's at some point, I rather hope they will. In any case, what's to say McDonald's customers don't read books? Or care about where their meat comes from?

Eventually after six months, I wear them down. They agree to an interview in their London offices, but I have a strictly limited time and I'm not allowed to record the interview. I have no idea why. McDonald's has a good story to tell and anyway Jo Roberts, Head of UK Media Relations, and Dionne Parker, Communications Director, are far too slick to let anything slip. I tell them about my experiences so far – about visiting abattoirs, trying to process the shock – trying to bring out their sensitive, open side. They are unmoved. Sitting there in their smart business suits they nod calmly. Oh yes, they've been through abattoirs. 'All the way through.' All the team have. They're in the business of selling meat. It's no big deal.

The truth is McDonald's in the UK sorted itself out long ago. In 2009 after the McLibel legal case and the documentary *Super Size Me*, the company was losing customers fast and profits were falling. In a smart move, it decided to 'revitalise the brand' by improving animal welfare, bringing in Fairtrade tea and coffee and full traceability of meat – then showing off about it. All the beef in burgers sold in the UK comes from British or Irish cows, sourced from 17,500 farmers. The patties are made in a processing plant in Scunthorpe.

It has paid off. When the horsemeat scandal came around, McDonald's not only came out whiter than white, but was also held up in the government's report on what went wrong as the best example of a traceable supply chain. Compassion in World Farming (CIWF), the RSPCA and even the World Wildlife Fund (WWF) have queued up to praise McDonald's for its environmental policies.

I still can't quite believe how McDonald's can provide pure beefburgers at that price. 'It's scale,' insists Dionne. 'We are making three million burgers every day.' McDonald's are even showing off about the fact burgers come from cows, an unusual move in an industry that has traditionally done everything it can to hide where meat comes from for fear of putting off its customers. Posters appear showing the cuts, forequarter and flank, that McDonald's uses for its burgers, though it doesn't state that more than 100 cows can be used in each burger and dairy cows can be included in the mix.

The meeting goes well and I wait for the offer of a farm-to-fork tour. But like a date that will never call, I eventually conclude it's no good. For some reason, they just don't

like me. There is nothing for it – I am just going to have to
go and find out for myself.

Adrian Ivory is the kind of man my dad would have liked
me to marry: a farmer, rugby player and all-round nice guy.
He's also a bit of a beefcake, featuring on an Asda advert for
Scottish beef in 2011 and instantly becoming 'the Brad Pitt
of British agriculture' in the tabloids and a 'hot farmer' on
gay websites.

The married father of four laughs off the compliments
on the day I go to visit him and insists it's not about him –
it's about his beloved cows. Adrian keeps 250 breeding
Charolais and Simmental cattle on his farm, Strathisla, in
Perthshire, supplying not only Asda and other supermarkets
in the past, but also McDonald's. The brown and white
cattle look beautiful dotted over the rolling green hills of
Strathmore Valley. Like most British herds they are entirely
free-range in the summer, only coming in during the winter
months to be fed on silage, local grain and a small amount of
husks from local whisky distilleries.

It is a fairly typical story. Adrian insists that most burgers
will come from cattle like this, grazed outside at least some of
the year. Although so-called 'barley beef' does happen in
Britain, where young male cattle are kept indoors for their
whole lives and only fed grains, it is rare. Most are from small
herds kept as part of a mixed farm and only fattened on grains
for the last few weeks. The average herd size in Britain is
between 28 and 50. Pasture-fed cattle can have more omega-3
fatty acids in them and we all like to see cattle in the fields.

Adrian certainly seems to take pleasure from seeing the
cattle contentedly munching the grass, scratching their backs
and giving Attaboy, the huge Simmental bull, a scratch
between the ears. 'We give them as enjoyable and stress-free
a life as possible,' he says. 'But we also realise they are here

for a purpose.' Adrian is the only person to win Young Farmer of the Year and Farmer of the Year – in the same year. He clearly has an eye for detail. When he visited the McDonald's processing site in the north of England where he sends his cattle he was impressed with the processing of thousands of burgers but felt the handling of the cattle could be improved.

He takes an innovative approach to farming himself. His cattle races are all lined with plastic board to stop the metal clanging and are curved towards the light. It is all inspired by Temple Grandin, the American and autistic animal behaviourist I keep on hearing so much about. 'Cattle like to move back to where they came from,' says Adrian. 'We don't need to shout at the animals.' I was impressed. It was time I met this Temple Grandin.

I am picking blackberries with some friends when I get a phone call from Temple Grandin. 'Hello! This is Temple Grandin!'

'Wow! Well, er, great, thank you, wow. The thing is I haven't …'

She is already chatting ten to the dozen. 'Yes, you see the point you make about slaughterhouses. That's right people should be respected. It's all about good stockmen. People think they just have to buy the right equipment but it is about the right people too. The thing is …'

'Sorry Dr Grandin, I just don't have a pen.' I am scrambling around in my pockets trying to find something to write on. 'Could I possibly call you back later?'

'Oh, sure!'

'Who was that?' asks my friend Sarah.

'Temple Grandin.'

'Oh my God! You are joking?' Sarah just happens to be a speech therapist who works with autistic children and is familiar with the work of Dr Grandin. 'Oh wow.' In our excitement we hug and dance around. Sarah's wife Hilary looks perplexed. 'Temple who? Is she a rock star or something? A famous actress?'

'Duh! No! Only like the most famous animal behavioural scientist in the world!'

'And autistic!'

'And just really, really cool.'

Temple Grandin does this to people. In every single interview I have conducted with rather sober upright people in the meat industry her name comes up and immediately we all start chatting enthusiastically like superfans. She would find it all extremely odd, especially the hugging.

Temple Grandin does not like to be hugged. She hates it, in fact. She likes to be squeezed, in a machine, just like a cow. This extraordinary discovery was made as a child when she was staying at her aunt's ranch in Arizona. Like a lot of highly sensitive autistic people, the young Temple grew up accosted by noise and stimulation: her clothes itched, the air conditioning clanged, everything jarred and whirred and set her nerves on edge. Just like an animal she noticed every little change in her environment. So she watched what the animals did to calm down: they gathered together in a herd. In the ranch, the cattle coming through the chute to be vaccinated were put in a squeeze box. In the same way, deep pressure seemed to calm them. So Temple thought she'd try it too. She crawled into the squeeze box and she had a go.

Bizarrely it worked, and so she made her own squeeze box, or hug machine as it is sometimes called. The invention not only got Temple through college and enabled her to calm herself through her twenties, but is also now used as a treatment for other autistic children around the world.

As well as being a rock star animal behaviourist, Temple Grandin has become one of the most famous autistic people in the world. She's kind of the opposite to me: instead of thinking in words and emotions, she thinks logically, in pictures. It is an incredible journey: from a five-year-old who couldn't speak, to a woman who is the focus of an award-winning Hollywood film and a bestselling author. In a way it is an all-American *Rocky* story about someone who simply never gave up.

Despite advice to put the young Temple into an institution, her mother guided her child into art and science. At her aunt's ranch in Arizona she also discovered her affinity with animals. She went on to study animal behaviour at university and to apply her own understanding of the world – or 'thinking in pictures' – to designing slaughterhouses. By her twenties she was working in some of the toughest abattoirs in the US Midwest. The men she encountered there were threatened by this brilliant young woman. Bull's testicles were thrown at her car, but her ideas were right.

Temple could turn an abattoir around overnight simply by noticing the shaft of light or flapping flagpole that was spooking the cattle. Soon she was designing whole systems based on leading the cattle forward using their own natural curiosity and tendency to go back to where they had come from rather than frightening them from behind. Because of her systems, electric cattle prods are used far less and the lead-up to slaughter itself is a calmer experience. Half of the abattoirs in the USA and Canada are designed by Temple and many in the UK, if not all, are at least influenced by her. Dovecote Park was designed around Temple Grandin's ideas and has been praised by CIWF for its high welfare standards.

Later, in a two-hour conversation, Temple tells me how she revolutionised the slaughterhouse. She talks about the 'sloppy years' in the 1980s when the industry grew too fast and welfare suffered, and how she helped developed audits, initially for McDonald's. With her brilliant brain, Grandin devised an audit system to check the animals were being treated well enough, from the lowing in the lairage to the movement through the chutes and the post-mortem. She argues that large slaughterhouses can treat animals well as long as the right procedures are followed. She is passionate about encouraging more young people to study animal behaviour and to use it to improve the lives of animals.

At the same time, she wants to help young autistic people, not only by proving what can be achieved through her own story but also by encouraging parents and educational institutions to let minds that might just be a little different thrive. Just a brief look at the internet reveals all the parents, animal lovers and autistic people she has helped through her work. She doesn't use the squeeze machine any more, she tells me, but other people do, and their lives are the better for it. She even lets some people, a select few, hug her.

There is a scene in the film *Temple Grandin* when the young autistic woman sees cattle slaughtered for the first time. She stands there for a moment in her white hard hat, stunned, and then she starts yelling. 'Where'd he go? Where'd he go?' It's the one question 'the woman who thinks like a cow' cannot answer. She knows how a prey animal sees the world. The main 'emotions' of cattle, she says, are curiosity and fear. They are always on the lookout for food and changes in the environment that might signal danger: a loud bang, a shirt hung on the gate blowing in the wind. 'Curiously afraid,' she calls it. But she doesn't know where they go in the end; none of us do.

When I eventually see a kill at a UK abattoir that supplies McDonald's it is a Temple Grandin design: the 'stairway to heaven', she calls it. It is in one of the country's best abattoirs. I agree not to write about the kill, so as not to upset its current customers, but I don't agree not to mention

McDonald's. If this is the only way to see how burgers are made then so be it. It is not a bad abattoir, it's just careful with its customers. The stockmen stand around in overalls, checking over the cattle, chatting to the vet; there is an air of calm. Remember, this is where farmers drop off their animals. If they don't see anything else in the abattoir, they will see the lairage, and if it is not calm, if their animals are not looked after, they won't come back.

An Angus bullock is coming up the race. For a moment he looks at me through the metal bars. He is not scared, his eyes are not rolling, but he is not sure either; his ears twitch. Where are the others? Is there food? What is around the corner? Curiously afraid. I am trying to remain calm. I don't want to make a fool of myself again, but nor do I want to force myself to see what I can't handle. And nor do I want to frighten the animals, which may pick up on my nerves. I try to still my beating heart; I don't want to make this any worse for him.

The slaughterman is tall with a neat ginger beard. He whistles and pats the bullock's flank. The bullock moves forward. 'Would you like to?' He is so polite, so calm. I move forward, stepping up onto the platform. He has already shown me the instrument. It's a contact-fired instrument called a 'Cow-Puncher'. It is about the size of a bottle of hairspray. The slaughterman taps the animal on the forehead between the ears and eyes, and a blank cartridge fires the bolt into the brain, causing immediate incapacity. The animal should die without hearing the bang of a gun. He can't have heard a shot before it is all over and the body, meat now, is rolled into the killing hall below.

My mind is racing. I step off the platform, I can't wait to get away, but then I feel bad for the slaughterman. What has he done to deserve my abhorrence? I wonder if I am using manners to cover up a more complex emotion. Why am I worrying about the slaughterman? What about the cow?

What do I really think? I don't know. Where'd he go? I step back from the platform. 'Thank you,' I say.

I ask Temple what is was like the first time she killed a cow. 'It was an initiation', she says. 'There was no training back then, they just decide you are ready. I was ready.'

'But how did you feel?' I push.

'I remember driving out of the plant and it was a nice sunny day, the clouds were in the sky.' I know Temple will have an exact picture in her head of the Midwest skies she loves so much. I imagine it too. Flat-bottomed cumulus clouds heaping towards the horizon. That sense of space that Temple clearly loves, where no one can bother you. No irritations or noise. No people, just cattle. 'I guess …' She pauses. 'It makes you think about the meaning of life. Looking at death makes you want to do something a little more productive with your life rather than, I dunno, just make a lot of money and spend it on a lot of stupid things. You have to do something of value. Yes, I think the meaning of life is the things you have done to make the world a better place.'

CHAPTER SEVEN

Swine

… if slaughterhouses had glass walls,
we'd all be vegetarian.
Linda McCartney, *Linda's Kitchen*

I must have been more nervous than I thought about visiting my first proper factory farm, as when it looked like the whole thing might fall through I burst into tears.

I had spent 24 hours wandering around the cobbled streets and spires of a Danish city, Aarhus, and now I was waiting to be picked up by my contact Jens – except he seemed to have stood me up. When I phone his number, he doesn't answer. All I can hear is the holding music for Danish Crown, Europe's largest meat processing company, cleverly interspersed with the sound of knives being sharpened and the sizzle of bacon. Eventually a woman's voice comes back to me. 'I'm sorry to say Jens has completely forgotten you. He is in the south of Jutland with a television crew …'

'Oh, I see …' My voice wobbles as I explain to the girl. 'But I've come all the way from Scotland to see your slaughterhouse with glass walls.'

The hotel receptionist looks sympathetic. 'You could go to Legoland instead?'

I have come to Denmark to discover where our bacon comes from. Bacon sandwiches seem to preoccupy a large part of the carnivore's brain – at least in Britain. Yet more than half of our pork is imported, mostly from Denmark. Danish Crown, a cooperative owned by Danish farmers, is the main producer. I found the contact details on the website and within five minutes of sending an email I was invited to come over and see for myself. It is quite transparent compared to the UK; there are no background checks, like at McDonald's – or not that they are telling me.

My chaperone for the day, Agnete Poulsen, eventually arrives resplendent in zebra-skin, heeled sandals and a fluffy white jumper. 'I am not dressed for a farm,' she laughs, revealing a pretty, gap-toothed smile. 'But oh well …'

A blanket of fog is slowing lifting over Jutland to reveal red-roofed houses, low-slung barns and the bottom of wind turbines, the blades hidden in the clouds. Despite it being one of the world's foremost producers of pork and dairy, I don't see any animals. Come to think of it, I don't see any fields.

Agnete is taking me to one of their biggest and oldest farms. The drive is lined with beech trees, just dropping their yellow leaves. The farmhouse, built in 1788, looks like an illustration out of a storybook with its dark timbers and white walls. I can't smell the pigs and there is no mud in the yard, only rows of smart new barns. We enter the entrance hall, like the reception of a sports hall, with the same chlorinated smell and changing rooms for men and women. I put on overalls made out of a bright green material, like a giant J-cloth. Next to me an attractive young woman changes from her fashionable clothes into dungarees, before disappearing into the piggery.

Niels Aage Arve may be turning out tens of thousands of pigs a year, but he looks like an ordinary farmer with florid cheeks and a hearty handshake. He is keen to show me his whole system, from birth to death. 'We will let people see, we will let people challenge us,' he says. He is as good as his word, and we walk straight into artificial insemination. I feel painfully embarrassed, like watching a David Attenborough documentary with your parents. But then I guess this is the beginning of most of our industrially farmed meat – and a deep concern of animal welfare.

I imagine the whispered commentary: 'The mating ritual of the industrial pig is over quickly …' Sows in season stand in pens; in front of them a boar is wheeled along, his balls squashing out between the rungs of the cage. He snorts at the females and they snort back as a pigman clambers on their back and gives them a scratch, to imitate the feeling of being mounted. 'When she is ready she will stand extremely still,' explains Niels as another worker inserts a fake plastic penis and injects the sperm. I know they are Eastern European as they are not speaking Danish. I think it is Polish. I expect they are making jokes. Lord knows, they must have to.

I nod seriously – wishing fervently it was over – and feel mightily relieved when we move on to the next stage of the journey: the stalls of pregnant sows. Until recently pregnant sows were kept in gestation crates, where they cannot turn or lie down for the whole of their pregnancy. Nowadays these are officially banned in Europe, but still used in some countries, including the USA.

The sows have a few days between when the piglets are weaned and their next pregnancy, when they are kept in herds. We walk through these barren concrete stalls. The pigs are mostly sleeping; they are covered in scratches from the fights when they are establishing the dominant female. They look like the kind you get from a thorn bush or from scratching yourself in a bad dream. In the 'maternity ward', the mothers are in farrowing crates, still used widely for the first four weeks because of the risk of the sow crushing her piglets when she lies down. The cages are just wide enough for the sow to lie across the heated floor. As many as 17 piglets tear at her teats, struggling for a hold in this first key test of survival. Niels hands me a piglet; it is silky soft and feverishly hot. I resist the temptation to cuddle it like a puppy, against my neck. Within a few weeks it will be weaned and the whole cycle will begin again.

We wave at the girl from the changing room. She is busy injecting piglets. It turns out she is a trained accountant from the Ukraine, like many workers in agriculture an overqualified migrant making a new start in a rich country. 'Yes', admits Niels. 'We rely on foreign people to do the labour, especially during the economic good times.' About half of the workforce in agriculture in Denmark is from Eastern Europe or countries like the Ukraine. I wonder what they would do without these hard-working people?

It is surprisingly quiet as we go into the piggery to see the weaners, 'the slaughter pigs'. Many of them have been castrated and they don't squeal when they see humans because they no longer associate humans with a feed bucket, since feed comes automatically, all the time. For three months the pigs eat almost constantly to get up to slaughter weight, putting on 1.1kg (2.4lb) a day. Some 20 per cent of the feed is soya, much of it genetically modified (GM), with all the concerns that brings about clearing the rainforest in South America to grow the crop.

The silence is not the only strange thing. It is the smell. It's not like the slurry you smell when it is spread on the fields; it is pure ammonia, it has a chemical tang. It burns the back of my throat. The pigs are on a bare concrete floor, with a slatted area they will naturally keep separate for defecating. The phrase happy as a pig in shit makes no sense. Pigs are clean creatures; they will not roll in their own faeces unless they are overheating. The lighting is dim, to keep activity low and growth rate at a maximum. The stocking density is around 30kg (66lb) per 3 square metres (32 square feet). It looks crowded to me, with more than 20 young pigs crowded into a space it takes me a few small steps to cross.

'You can make more pig with less feed nowadays,' says Niels. 'We know how to keep them: right feed, right ventilation, the right genetics …' Everything is controlled: the light, the heat, the temperature, the feed, the medication. I notice a spider's web in the corner. It is the most normal thing to see in a piggery, yet it seems incongruous somehow when most of the dusty corners seem to have been swept away. I think of *Charlotte's Web*.

Yet the young pigs are still curious. The weaners crowd around me, their pink skin clashing with my bright green overalls. They are like puppies or small children, snuffling at my notepad. They have a buoy on a piece of chain but not much else to play with. I can't see if their tails are wagging, because they have none, just stumps. Under European law pigs are not supposed to have their tails routinely docked and they are supposed to have malleable material like straw to root around in. But in intensive units both rules are widely ignored. Tail biting is almost impossible to stop in such a crowded environment, while straw bungs up the efficient slurry system. Toys are minimal and not regularly changed, despite the fact pigs will quickly become bored.

There's not much back scratching either. Any small farmer who loves their pigs will almost always scratch their backs as they talk to me and talk to the pigs. Niels does not touch his pigs. 'Pigs are just like dogs …' he says. And just like us, I think: social, greedy, vicious, intelligent, curious, easily bored. Niels insists welfare is improving, largely because of mistakes in the past. Back in the 1990s all the piglets got antibiotics as a growth promoter and to keep infections down. 'Then we realised it was wrong,' he says. Antibiotic-resistant bugs took off across the globe and the finger was pointed at agriculture. Now the pigs are only given antibiotics to save the herd from serious infections, insists Niels.

Denmark may have cut antibiotic use, but in the USA it is still used as a growth promoter and in the UK the levels of use are still above the recommended amount. It is all very well to say the farming industry has cleaned up its act, but it may be too late. In China they have discovered a strain of *E. coli* resistant to antibiotics linked to intensive rearing of pigs. The genie is out of the bottle. Have we created a monster? An antibiotic-resistant bacterium that could wipe us out – just so we could have our bacon a bit cheaper? It seems too high a price to pay.

The slaughterhouse with glass walls looks like an ordinary factory. Pigs are delivered into one side, and packaged meat comes out the other end. We enter past lines of lorries ready to take the product to countries like the UK. Horsens was set up in 1887 to supply the British market. It was updated more recently to supply the world. It was the farmers of Danish Crown who decided to give it a viewing gallery. Like most farmers, they do not like spending money and, after spending £200m (US$288m) on a brand new building, they wanted to show off their 'jewel in the crown'. No one expected the reaction they got, with people from around the world queuing up to visit.

Danish Crown gets 22,000 visitors a year to the abattoir, where they kill around 20,000 pigs a day. The demand is so great they have set up a visitors' department with nine people. The waiting list is three to four months long. There are so many elderly people here coming for a free day out, they had to start restricting numbers. At least a third of visitors are from other countries, and school kids come from five years old upwards. 'The little ones love it, they are fascinated,' says Agnete. 'You should see their huge eyes …'

There is lots to show off about. The factory uses less water and less electricity – even though it cannot use windmills because of local protests – than other similar plants. The low carbon footprint is one of the arguments used to justify such industrial farming methods.

Horsens has always had a slaughterhouse, explains Agnete, partly because of the prison nearby. 'Because the rules are quite strict and as long as you follow the rules, you can make it. It is very good for people who have been in an unfortunate situation in one way or the other,' she says. 'It is a good chance to get into normal society'. The men are even given help coming off drugs, methadone or alcohol addiction. Just like in the UK, it is not high status to be a slaughterman in Denmark, but there is an opportunity to earn good wages without a higher education. It is good money for industrial work. Yet, unlike small abattoirs, where there is more variety in the job, Horsens struggles to find workers for often monotonous factory work. Danish Crown offers job opportunities and English lessons to refugees coming into the country. In the gut room are a number of Vietnamese women, and Bosnians work on the packing floor. Jens could not come and pick me up because he was interviewing Syrian refugees, a butcher and a mechanic, hoping to start at the factory soon.

There are 1,800 employees at Danish Crown in Horsens. At least 600 of them come from abroad, all organised by the union and receiving the same salaries and opportunities. 'You will find men pleased with their work,' says Agnete.

'There is a lot of identity and pride in being a slaughterman.'
Apparently the viewing gallery has helped. It gives workers
an opportunity to show what they do, to be seen and
appreciated.

We begin the tour, walking through an airy lobby full of
trees and light. It is like any other office, except the workers
who walk past on the way to the canteen are splattered in
blood. 'I think you will be so impressed by how professional
it is. By how well it is run. It is the best you can find,' says
Agnete, briskly nodding to the men in their whites. 'You
will ask, how can they do this in such a well-controlled,
well-ordered way? You will be amazed!'

Everyone who goes on a tour has a guide, explains Agnete.
It's necessary to be able to absorb quite shocking scenes.
'Instead of imagining what it is like, people are experiencing
what it is like,' she says. 'You need courage and knowledge
and broad shoulders to take it.'

We pass a school trip from South Korea obediently
listening to their guide. They seem completely relaxed. Either
teenagers have changed since my day, or slaughterhouses are
totally normal to them. We are standing at the end of the
corridor looking through the glass down into the lairage. The
sheer size shocks me. Some 3,000 pigs could be waiting at
any one time, though it is usually more like 1,000. Only three
men are needed to herd all those animals; the rest is done by
machines. It looks like a futuristic city in a computer game.
Perhaps that is why the teenagers are so comfortable with it.

The pigs are moved through in their social groups. It is the
middle of the day, so many lie down and sleep; they do
appear relaxed. I put my ear to the glass. There is the occasional
squeal as the automatic doors push pigs onwards toward the
last door, the final stage in the game. It is the moment I have
been dreading but we don't see it. We see the pigs herded

into the chamber and then the door closes and the elevator sinks down into somewhere dark. The slaughterhouse may have glass walls but you can't see everything. My heart sinks, my stomach lurches. We move on to the next stage.

Agnete is careful to explain what is happening, to warn me of what is coming next. 'The pigs are in the chamber for three minutes, and the animals die within 30 seconds from a combination of carbon dioxide and acid. They go to sleep,' she says. 'I don't think the pigs know anything about their death; I don't think they suffer.'

The pigs arrive on the moving black ribbon, all 'floppy'. I am disjointed. I see the bodies go in: pigs. I see the bodies come out: meat.

'Do you find it disgusting?' asks Agnete. I feel trapped. Why do they always ask me that? What can I say?

'No, but I do feel disturbed.' How can I explain? It may be the most 'efficient, gentle' method, but this way of killing does not feel honest somehow. This is the moment of disconnect, yet there is nothing to disconnect from.

The pigs are moving along a row of men. We watch through the glass walls above. The men wear headphones so they can choose the music or radio they like. They switch knives for each carcass, so they can be sterilised, and take out heart, trachea, lungs. 'The men do 160 sets of intestines per hour,' says Agnete. Guts and statistics fly past. It looks like monotonous work. 'It is a production line; everyone has their job.' I watch the man at the end of the line delicately take out the brain with two fingers so as not to break the membrane.

Next the gut room. It is barely visible from behind the glass because of the fug, the steam rising from the insides. I can see the dark shapes of men and women at the tables cleaning the intestines – the most similar to those of humans. The casings are sent to China to be sorted, then sent back to Denmark for filling with sausage meat.

We come to the end, where the carcasses are lined up in rows, the red forest. This is where you are allowed to take a selfie, where everything is clean, packaged, explainable. See? Pig carcasses. What do ordinary people know of what happens in between?

The packing area looks like another computer game. Carcasses come through and are broken down into little bitesize chunks to be sent all over the world. Parts of pig are being broken down into how each country would like them. Because they have such high safety standards, Danish Crown export to 130 countries. Flying along conveyor belts are US baby ribs, Japanese corned beef, spam for God knows where. Specificity and uniformity means they can always get the high-end market.

Then there are all the medical uses. Agnete takes me through all the properties of a pig's carcass. Collagen from the stomach lining to plump the lips of vain pop stars. Heparin to stop blood clotting – though it can be synthetic. The heart for transplants. Agnete shows me two vials of the different potions we can make from the blood: the white cells make protein powders, the red cells can turn anything almost blue/black, like pet food. As well as being a leader in meat, Denmark is a leader in pharma – because of all the medicines you can get from animal-derived products. Could this factory be the future? Where people see exactly where their meat – and their pharmaceuticals – have come from?

On the wall of the lobby is a huge picture inspired by the Hans Christian Andersen fairy tale *The Swineherd*. It shows a scene from the end of the story, when the spoilt princess who rejected the prince disguised as a swineherd is rejected herself. It is a well-known allegory against snobby girls. She watches from her ivory tower as the prince sits in the mud with the pigs, laughing. It is typical of Andersen – and Danish Crown – to be quite so clear about what they think makes a happy ending.

'When you are living by killing you have to tell the truth; you have to show it to people and let them make up their own minds,' Agnete says. 'It can't be just the story – unless it is the whole story.' But is it the whole story? Linda McCartney said if slaughterhouses had glass walls we'd all be vegetarian. Having seen the biggest slaughterhouse with glass walls in the world, I'm not so sure. I think you have to do more than look through a glass pane to understand what is happening in a slaughterhouse: you have to hear it and smell it and think about it. You have to know the alternatives.

In the UK it is a fairly common sight to see pigs rooting around outside. Compared to Denmark, where just 3 per cent of pigs are free-range, in Britain it is 40 per cent. I go to visit some pigs in the now familiar domes we see scattered around the countryside. The Saddlebacks come rushing up the field to greet us, ears flapping, their curly tails all in one piece. Watching them root in the earth, you can see why 'malleable' material is such an important aspect of porcine welfare; it seems like such a normal behaviour.

Tracy Worcester scratches their backs. The Marchioness of Worcester looks a little like the *Swineherd* princess in her long flowing skirt, a chignon piled on top of her head. The former model once played Miss Scarlett in a television adaptation of Cluedo and retains some of that glamour, despite wearing wellies and an ethnic cardigan. But it would be unfair to dismiss Tracy as another posh greenie. She has worked long and hard to expose the truth about industrial pig farming and to promote outdoor reared systems like this. In her 2009 film *Pig Business* she jumped fences to film gestation crates inside industrial units in Poland and interviewed communities in Chile who blame outbreaks of skin disease on the effluent from pig mega-farms polluting the water.

Tracy focused her ire on Smithfield, a US-based company now owned by the Chinese company WH Group, which is expanding pork production all over the world, including

Europe. She argues that these massive companies are making it impossible for smaller farmers to survive. Indeed, the British industry continues to decline as pork raised with higher welfare standards struggles to compete with cheap imports from abroad. Even in Britain we fail to buy our own pork. Tracy has set up a new charity called Farms Not Factories and is asking members of the public never to buy pork without an animal-welfare label. Her most recent campaign shows photos of celebrity friends, like Vivienne Westwood and Jeremy Irons, turning up their perfect noses at industrially farmed pork. As a marchioness, Tracy is quite aware she will be accused of elitism for suggesting everyone should buy pork with a label showing high welfare, RSPCA, outdoor, free range or, best of all, organic. She points out that one-and-a-half high-welfare sausages cost the same as two sausages with no welfare label. She also urges people to buy direct from the farmer online or at farmers' markets, or to find a butcher who sources animals from high-welfare farms, if any of us still have a local butcher…

There used to be some 22,000 butchers in Britain in the mid-nineties. Now there are fewer than 7,000. They certainly no longer display pig's heads or carcasses outside their shop, like old-fashioned butchers.

During the writing of this book I make a habit of sticking my head into butchers' shops to see what is on offer. I find quite a lot of Danish pork, as well as butchers who can give me chapter and verse about the animals and farms where they source their meat. Again, it can be expensive, but butchers also offer unusual cuts, which are just as good meat and much cheaper. There is also the joy of establishing a relationship with your local farmers via the traditional means of a butcher.

Thanks in part to celebrity buzz such as Tracy's #TurnYourNoseUp at pig factories campaign, butchers are coming back into fashion. Some shops are now opening late so people can buy their meat after work, like they do on the Continent, so they can compete directly with the supermarket. Others offer butchery courses and display photos of the animals taken when they were skipping through fields. Perhaps it is more than a middle-class trend and butchers will experience a revival as consumers take more interest in meat?

I never consider home butchery myself. I am aware that home slaughter and butchering the animal yourself is fashionable in the USA, where there is more of a frontiersman attitude. I believe that Mark Zuckerberg, the founder of Facebook, who only ate animals he killed himself for a year in 2011, did it by butchering animals on a farm. But I don't think I would be able to do it, unless it is with someone I absolutely trust.

My friend Angus Buchanan-Smith first makes the suggestion in the summer. He is passionate about producing meat locally, having spent his childhood watching his family farm give up both dairy cows and then pigs because of competition from factory farming. The idea would be to slaughter the pigs on the farm, so they do not have to suffer the stress of the abattoir, and then teach butchery to a group of the public with the carcasses.

We go through the details, back and forth over tea in a vegetarian restaurant, loudly discussing how we will bleed the pigs, collect the guts, use the trotters, etc., until we are politely asked to keep our voices down. 'Please, this is a vegetarian establishment.'

It is winter by the time we are ready, the traditional time to kill a pig, to see the family through the cold months ahead. In Spain they call it matanza – the big killing time. It is a festival. A family or even the whole village will take part in the slaughter and the processing of the pig. It still happens today, linking people to the village they come from, their people and their food.

I find Angus, his brother Charlie and his father Jamie preparing a wooden frame on which to hang the pigs. There is a little ice and snow over the ground and over everything a blanket of freezing fog, making the bare branches of the trees stand out. Jamie, a farmer and former soldier, is quite calm. He has done this sort of thing before when he had to take injured or sick pigs out of the herd. He will kill the pigs and, if we all feel we can do it just as well, Angus and I will also take our part. Angus and Charlie, both in their twenties, look to their father to guide them through the experience. I feel honoured to take part in what is, like the matanza, a special family event.

The pigs are young too, bumping about the barn wagging their tails. There are two Berkshires and two Saddlebacks, used to humans, curious and always, always hungry. Their hair shines black and glossy even though it feels brittle. They honk at the food but don't squeal too much. We are all calm.

One by one we take them into a pen, urged forward by a feed bucket. Jamie stands in the pen and takes aim with the gun. It is a .22 rifle and only loaded when he is sure of the shot – aimed diagonally between the eyes. The pig does not notice anything: a small crack and it is down immediately, just like the stunning at Wishaw. The gun is made safe and the boys go in to tie a rope around the pig's hind foot and haul it up onto the pole. This is the most difficult bit; it twitches violently before it is stuck. The blood runs straight into the soil, back to the earth.

Once a second pig is hung up, we start gutting them. It is a huge, messy job. We stand on upturned milk crates to reach inside the pigs and haul out the grey guts, or 'casings' as I know them. The livers and hearts or pluck, are put to one side. Our breath hangs in the air, mingling with the steam billowing from the pigs. Already we are learning how hard this is, how you must think of everything in order not to waste a drop; an art that has developed over millennia, that I failed to appreciate before in Wishaw.

Imagine in the past, in medieval times – everyone knew the anatomy of a pig, the anatomy of death; they saw it every winter, they smelt it and felt it. We are puzzling it out. The testicles are removed and the cavity that holds the intestines is cut open, being careful not to puncture anything. The guts squelch and oink as they fall to the ground. 'Woah, intense ...' says Angus. And I think it really is intense; for once the word is being used as it should be. We are not experienced butchers, no one has taught us. We have been protected from all this, we had no teaching from our forefathers, we have to work it out for ourselves.

The visceral nature of the experience heightens my senses. In the mist, the colours stand out: Angus's yellow fleece, Jamie's orange boots, the blood on the ground, my purple hat, the glowing beech hedge. At lunchtime the water tastes different, of earth and salt.

When it is my turn Jamie quietly tells me when I have the gun at the right angle. The pig's eyes are covered by its ears but I have to look; I have to see I am in the correct position. I squeeze the trigger. It falls, straight down. I have to concentrate now, remain focused. I make the gun safe and follow the pig down the hill. 'Show me where to cut, Angus. Show me.' I slice through the layers of fat and flesh. The blood pours out, leaving a puddle.

The boys haul up the carcass. It is almost like an out-of-body experience. I am standing here in front of this warm pig with a knife but I do not feel afraid. The light is fading fast, the temperature dropping. I feel perfectly calm, ready. 'OK, well, I'll make a start shall I? While you guys do the last one?' I do not feel panicked, like I did in Horsens or Wishaw – I feel privileged. I make a first cut and start skinning out the guts.

Who is this person, able to do this thing? An adult, I guess. I feel more mature, as if before I was a child, sheltered from these difficult truths, but now I have had to face up to them and take them on. In his book James Rebanks says, on a farm 'everything and everyone is at times covered in shit or snot or slaver or afterbirth'. Or blood. 'I would rather my children saw the blood and knew it was real than had a childish relationship with farming and food,' he writes. 'Everything in plastic packaging and everyone pretending it had never lived.'

Doing it all yourself is a much more immersive experience. You literally immerse yourself in the pig. We talk about Leonardo DiCaprio's recent role in *The Revenant*, his character crawling inside a horse carcass to keep warm, as we wrench, elbow deep, the steaming guts from the carcass. The whole process gets into your pores, your bones.

I feel a stab of sadness when we lay the carcasses on the back of the quad bike and Charlie says that's how they sleep. It's true. All day we talk about how intelligent and how affectionate pigs are. We talk openly about how horrible the killing was, how difficult it was for us all to focus and be calm, to see it through.

To do it properly, to care so much, to be so deeply involved, covered in the smell and the blood of the animal, and tired from the work, feels like a true privilege. In comparison, Denmark felt sterile and unreal. It was all so unfeeling – everything just torn into neat little strips, done the same as all the others; no one cares, no one feels. Yes, no suffering, but what do we sacrifice to have that taken away from our control? One of the first things I said to the boys was that no one appreciates this. No one appreciates how hard it is to kill an animal, to do it properly and care about it. To respect the animals. The hours it took were full of activity and laughter and blood and sweat and intense questioning, conversation, life, death.

Angus refers to it many times as ritualistic, even beautiful. I guess I think ritual has more structure to it. This is more chaotic, but yes, the repeated monotony of skinning, the almost out-of-body state to kill, the worship of the animal and the celebration in the butchery and the eating does feel like some sort of ceremony.

The next day when we arrive the pigs are sawn in half and laid on tables in the old stable. Perhaps it is because it is one of the few places I have seen a carcass before, but it looks like a painting. Somehow the colours have deepened as the animals cooled. The throbbing, moving body is still: an object, more solid somehow, less transparent. Fat mixes with the blood and it deepens into a more orange poppy colour, like oil paint. I think of Rembrandt's *Ox* stretched out in a slaughterhouse, splayed like a crucifix, a sacrifice to human greed.

We all put on our aprons. We are awed by the sight of the meat, excited by the task ahead. What a bunch of hipsters. Young people desperate to know where their food comes from, how to cut up meat. I imagine the horror of my grand-mother to learn I was paying to be a butcher for the day.

The hair has been scorched off the skin and the smell of burning hair has added to the deep piggy smell of fat. We will all smell of it for days. The carcass has acquired a new set of names to further distance it from the animal it was before − chump, loin, chaps, rump. You don't carve or cut up a pig; you break it down. First the ham between the aitchbone and the tail bone: York ham. I cut out the bone, finding the joint sitting in its own liquid, an exquisite piece of engineering. I count down the ribs: one, two, three, four, five − and cut. I slice the loin from the belly, the knife in my fist; the meat gives itself to you. My favourite is cutting the pork chops from the spine. I slice through the flesh then cut through the bone using the cleaver − tap, tap, tap.

Of all the things to butcher, a pig is the most flexible, adaptable; it can be so many different things, because of our imagination, our greed. In France every region has a recipe for pig offal, as a way to celebrate the pig. I guess we all did once.

We have an old borrowed sausage machine that hardly works; we crank the wheel and laugh as I struggle to control the sausages, like girls at a hen party. In the cold we all take on the complexion of a butcher – ruddy-cheeked, veins appearing in our noses, blood under our fingernails, sleeves rolled up, specks of blood on our glasses. At the end of the day we all go home stinking of pig, with bags full of meat, proud and rosy. I have one small nick on my thumb.

The pork is nothing like any pork I have eaten before. It tastes of pig, it smells of pig, it is a pig. I wonder, what do they do in supermarkets to stop pork smelling or tasting of pig?

I find it difficult to tell anyone about Denmark. It is efficient alright, but I struggle to find the words to explain what was going on – it was so distant and sterile; behind glass. In comparison, the experience with Angus and his family felt real, a worthy story for the pork we are eating.

It tastes good but I don't want to eat too much. I feel like we have been tricked into eating more pork than we need to in modern life by making it taste like nothing. I take my homemade sausages to a party and am surprised at how readily my friends accept the latest offering from my year only eating what I kill myself. Many want to do a butchery course too – despite the fact there are way too many breadcrumbs in the sausages and some are a very weird shape. Perhaps it is our generation – we are hungry for something. Not necessarily pig. But something like matanza, a ritual, a way to honour the animal we are eating; almost something spiritual.

CHAPTER EIGHT

Ishmael

Whoever is kind to the creatures of God is kind to himself.
The Prophet Muhammad

I am supposed to be sleeping in the upstairs bedroom but the sacrificial lamb is in there, so it is decided I will sleep in the living room instead. This has the advantage of regular Arabic lessons. The disadvantage is the lessons start at 6 am, just after the muezzin's call to prayer.

The children troop in, whispering at first and then, gathering confidence, begin to prod me awake. 'Louiseeee, Louiseeeeee! Wahed, jouj, tlata …' I am waking in a labyrinth of streets beneath a vivid blue sky, the air full of spices. I am not sure whether I am still dreaming or not.

'Erm, wahed? Jouj? Thlata?'

'No! Tlata, tlata!' More prodding.

'Erm …' I want to go back to sleep. The children can't believe that this new addition to the household, all the way from the UK, could be quite so stupid as to not be able to count. They are determined to teach me.

At the turn of 2006 into 2007 I am staying in their tiny living room in the old town of Fez, Morocco, because my stepsister has fallen in love with Said, a dreadlocked tour guide. I have come along to visit, feeling a little like the spinster chaperone in an E. M. Forster novel: swept up in the romance of it all but unable to quite let go of my fear, or my disapproval. Over a few days I follow Said in his Rasta hat and Georgina in her H&M top we bought in the airport to keep her swelling belly warm, feeling like a bit of a gooseberry. I can't help noticing the curious stares of the locals as I allow myself to be pulled along in the slipstream as they float along the streets of a medieval city, entirely indifferent to the rest of the world.

The family welcome me with open arms. 'A thousand welcomes,' they say. Soon I am eating dates and watching the Arabic version of *Pop Idol*. It's better than ours. I remember Georgina's mother Claire telling me about visiting Fez, after her daughter secretly married Said. She sat in this same room, sweets and mint tea laid out, all the little kindnesses, while the women hennaed her hands to celebrate the wedding. She had no language to say thank you and was overwhelmed by it all: the shock, the sudden joy of a grandchild, the uncertainty. She began to cry letting the tears run down her cheeks, unable to wipe them away for fear of smudging the henna.

Except for the television talent shows, Fez is like going back in time. Donkeys carry Coca-Cola bottles through ornately decorated gates, palm trees sway behind the fort walls, men gather in white to pray in the square. In the medina, shadows from the loose palm thatch covering the street market dapple the light, making it feel like we are walking underwater, a current of people trickling through the streets. I wonder where we are all going? There is a feeling of expectation in the air. A festival is coming, a feast is being prepared.

It is the day of Eid al-Adha, the Festival of the Sacrifice. It celebrates the passage in the Qur'an when God tests the obedience of Abraham by asking him to sacrifice his son Ishmael. When Abraham is about to kill his son, thus proving his faith, God sends the angel Gabriel to tell his loyal servant to sacrifice a lamb instead. Now every year, two months and ten days after the end of Ramadan, families that can afford it are to sacrifice a sheep to remember the faith of Abraham. The men have already been to the square to pray; now the slaughter has begun. I can smell sheep, like in the lambing shed, bleating from behind closed doors; there are skins over the balconies, guts on the washing lines and blood coming out of the alleyways, just like the shambles.

Men in djellabas walk ahead of me, their knives in sheathes. Women pass in groups, their faces covered. Shopkeepers beckon me into tourist shops stacked with jewelled slippers, Aladdin's lamps and stacks and stacks of spices; the smell is glorious − cinnamon and cloves, cumin, ginger and nutmeg − and as you walk out into the street, that smell again: lamb, alive and dead.

Everything happens in the street: sleeping, eating, drinking, talking, buying, selling, cheating, cleaning, pissing, living, dying. People live communally, as a huge family. Even the roof of the house is a communal space, like an exotic scene from *Mary Poppins*. Up here the children jump over to their friends' houses, dipping in and out of different families, conversations, arguments, ceremonies.

On our roof the extended family is gathered. The 'spare room', as it turns out, is a shed on the roof. The sheep is taken by the horns and led solemnly to the centre of the crowd. The ram has a black nose and black socks, black marks around his eyes and downward-curving horns, as if they are drooping. An uncle − called Ishmael, funnily enough – has come to carry out the slaughter. There are neighbours and cousins; I lose track of the faces and names. I just remember blocks of colour, the bright blue sky and the white walls, and then, with one swipe of the knife, the blood. 'He said a prayer, you know,' Said whispers to me. Everybody nods. The blood flows so violently it nudges a stray flip-flop, like a twig in a gutter, as it rushes towards the drain to join the blood from all the other sacrificial lambs.

Within seconds the sheep is hoisted up on onto the washing line and immediately everyone has a job. The men peel off the skin and scoop out the guts. The children come carrying buckets of water and the women sort the intestines like wool. The hair on the head and trotters is singed off over a fire. The meat is butchered and distributed to each family, and the tripe hung out on the line to be made into cured meats. This is one of the few times in the year the family will eat meat and every part of the animal is used. The stomach casts a shadow like a lace curtain. We troop downstairs where warm pitta is ready for lamb's liver kebabs.

Later I come upstairs. The guts have already been replaced by washing but my room still smells of sheep. I opt to stay in the living room instead and continue my Arabic lessons, until I can count to ten, 'inshallah'.

Years later I realised I had witnessed halal slaughter. At the time it just seemed like part of a surreal world I was experiencing. I had gone back in time to a world where men carried knives and recited prayers to the animals, like whispering a secret.

When I came to write about halal slaughter in the UK, the first thing I thought was how can it possibly happen here? The Muslim community cannot slaughter lambs on the roof. They cannot hang the stomachs on the washing

line or burn the hair off the cloven hooves over an open fire.
So where does it happen? It feels like going back to the
beginning, before I had any knowledge of how animals are
raised and killed. The internet is full of information on halal.
I listen to sermons by imams and ask my Muslim friends for
an explanation, but it is all very confusing. None of them
seem to agree on the exact details. It doesn't feel much
different from trying to work out the standards for any
other label on meat: organic, free range, RSPCA Assured.
Perhaps they are all religions of a sort?

In the end I go for lunch in Leicester with a scholarly and
serious Muslim, Nadeem Adam, from the Halal Monitoring
Committee (HMC). We have a shaky start when I confess
I am a vegetarian most of the time. 'Oh, in that case!' Nadeem,
a stocky man in his thirties, stands up and bustles us out of
the Turkish restaurant. 'Sorry brother, she's a vegetarian.' 'It's
OK,' I insist. But Nadeem is insistent. This is the joy of
multicultural Britain; if you are going to eat vegetarian food,
you want to be in a completely different area of town, where
there are plenty of South Indian restaurants.

Finally we sit down in front of steaming dosas and biryani.
Nadeem has a kind face, a full beard and bristly hairs on the
end of his nose. 'Halal means permissible, ethical if you like,
exactly what you are looking at!' We tuck in.

But as I know only too well, ethics are complex. How do
Muslims decide if a certain animal is halal or not? Unlike the
other labels I have investigated, I am aware this area requires
more sensitivity, as it is not just standards imposed by an
earthly authority, but by Muhammad ibn Abdullah, whom
Muslims consider God's last prophet on Earth. The rules
were laid down in medieval times and as such make perfect
sense in terms of hygiene. The most important rule is that
the animal is 'alive'. Of course all animals are alive before
they are killed – the reason it is specified is to ensure the
animal is healthy and can be bled out properly, rather than a
carcass that could be contaminated.

There is also a deep spiritual element. Nadeem emphasises that halal considers the whole life of the animal. 'The Prophet Muhammad, Blessings Be Upon Him, said the animal must be healthy and have had a good life,' he says. To paraphrase, God gives an animal life, so if you are going to take it, it must be with good reason, as painless as possible and in the name of God. The slaughterman must be Muslim and use a surgically sharp knife, 'that can cut paper', so death is quick. With one cut the throat, windpipe and blood vessels in the neck are severed, causing the animal's death without cutting the spinal cord. Lastly, the blood from the veins must be drained. As the animal dies a prayer is said to invoke the name of God. Most commonly 'Bismillah' (In the name of God) and then three times 'Allahu Akbar' (God is the greatest).

There is some debate within the Muslim community as to the interpretation of 'alive' at the point of slaughter. For some this can include animals that are stunned but still technically 'alive', but for others, like Nadeem, they must be fully conscious. 'You can cover his eyes, but not his ears, as the animal must hear the blessing,' says Nadeem. 'The animal must be alive when it dies. Otherwise, if it is not conscious, it does not know it has been blessed ...'

For the cold, hard, secular statistics on halal in Britain, I find the answers in the most unexpected place: the Agriculture and Horticulture Development Board (AHDB). Based in the Midlands, this is where farming policy for the whole country is developed.

The Beef and Lamb section is quite understanding of halal slaughter in the UK; after all, it is a huge market, especially for export. Already the halal market is worth £2.6bn (US$3.6bn) in Britain alone. Muslims may make up 5 per cent of the population, but in England they eat

20 per cent of red meat sold. By 2030, the UK Muslim population is expected to rise to 8.2 per cent. The export market is also growing, especially in the Middle East, where organic and free-range halal lamb is a prime market for British farmers. Where do you think Harrods or the seven-star hotels in Dubai source their halal meat? Places like Lord Newborough's Rhug Estate in Wales or organic hill farms owned by Arab sheikhs in Scotland.

Phil Hadley, Head of Supply Chain Business Development at AHDB, is keen to emphasise that most halal killed in the UK is no different to any other meat. This is because most halal labelling authorities consider meat halal if it is 'alive at the point of slaughter', even if it has been stunned. Around 114 million animals are killed in the UK using the halal method, of which the majority is stunned first before the prayer. Around two million are killed shechita, for the Jewish market, which are all non-stun. I have chosen to concentrate on halal because it is a much bigger and growing market.

Halal slaughter includes lamb, poultry and beef but not pigs, which are 'haram' (forbidden). The main species for halal is sheep. We have already seen how important it is in the Festival of the Sacrifice, proving man's faith in God. Sheep and shepherds run through all the Abrahamic religions – Judaism, Christianity, Islam – indeed, sheep are mentioned 247 times in the Bible. In the Prophet's home town of Mecca, there was a long pastoral tradition. In ancient times a lamb was considered a possession of high value; therefore it seems a fitting sacrifice to placate a fearsome God.

Around half of the sheep slaughtered in the UK are killed halal. Of these, around 80 per cent are stunned first. This translates to more than 2 million sheep killed non-stun, and the rest stunned. AHDB Beef and Lamb and the Muslim community themselves are open about what halal means. A video shows non-stun slaughter: the sheep come up from the lairage on a conveyor belt. They are alert, a little confused to be separated from the flock. As the sheep move slowly past the slaughterman one by one, he bends to cut their throats. The knife is so sharp it slices through the wool and thick flesh. The animal collapses, out of sight of the camera, but I know there is blood, just like in Fez and in Scotland. 'Bismillah Allahu Akbar,' says the slaughterman. The sheep has 20 seconds to bleed out; it seems like a long time in a slaughterhouse, where killing is usually done as fast as possible. The slaughterman turns to sharpen his knife, away from the view of the sheep, then stands waiting, staring straight into the camera, into my eyes.

I watch the stun video next, which shows how the majority of halal animals are killed. This time the sheep come up a V conveyor belt, nose to bum as they would be in a flock. One by one their heads appear through a plastic curtain where they are stunned by tongs for less than a second. The rigid body of the sheep falls to the side and the slaughterman cuts the throat, just as he would in secular slaughter except for those words: 'Bismillah Allahu Akbar.' That's it. That's the difference – three words. In English: In the Name of God. So why all the fuss?

Perhaps headlines like this have something to do with it: 'Millions Are Eating Halal Food Without Knowing It.' The *Daily Mail* article in 2014 revealed that big brand names including Tesco, M&S, KFC and Pizza Express all sell halal meat, without labelling it as such. It is only four paragraphs in when it is mentioned that most of this halal we are eating is stunned – so not that different from ordinary meat, then? In fact many commentators question why newspapers insist on bringing up this issue again and again. If it is only a question of a prayer said at the moment of slaughter, then what is the problem? Is it Islamophobia? And if newspapers are so concerned about animal welfare, why are there not more articles on how animals are treated outside the halal system?

Yet this news story appears again and again. It is an issue that has been bothering us since 1875, when the first parliamentary debate was held on religious slaughter. In the latest parliamentary debates, it seems we are not any closer to solving our confusion. As in most debates in the House of Commons, the MPs agreed that 'something must be done'. But what?

The UK carries out more halal slaughter than the rest of Europe. Slaughter without prior stunning has been banned in Iceland, Norway, Sweden, Switzerland and Denmark. In Germany, groups must prove demand from a religious group before non-stun slaughter is allowed. In Austria, Estonia, Finland and Slovakia, stunning immediately after the incision is required if the animal has not been stunned before.

The UK is also the most confused about halal slaughter. The FSA does not collect figures on religious slaughter, so most of the statistics are from daily snapshots. Even the halal 'authorities' themselves do not agree on what constitutes halal or not. For instance, the Halal Food Authority (HFA) will label pre-stunned animals as 'halal', but the Halal Monitoring Committee will not accept any pre-stunned animals.

The idea of banning religious slaughter goes against a strong British tradition of allowing minorities the freedom to practise religious beliefs. The other option is to label food, so at least consumers know whether an animal has been stunned or non-stunned. However, it is unlikely this will happen any time soon. Jewish and Muslim groups, teaming up in a rare display of cooperation, argue it is unfair to expect religiously slaughtered meat to be labelled without asking secular organisations to do the same. Can you really see Tesco agreeing to label its chicken 'gas-stunned'? I don't think so, and the retailers have considerable power.

In the meantime it is possible to use other labels to ensure animals are pre-stunned. All organic, Red Tractor label and RSPCA Assured meat is pre-stunned. Alternatively, find a good butcher and ask them about where the meat comes from. Just like with most of the meat trade in this country, in the end the emphasis falls on the consumer to do the hard work. MPs will bray on, as they always have, but in the meantime it is up to us to know the facts.

In the case of non-stun, the facts are hard to stomach. The British Veterinary Association (BVA) is quite clear: animals can suffer.

I met Sean Wensley, just a few months before he became the President of the BVA, in St Pancras International. The young charity vet from Liverpool is passionate and principled. He emphasises that the BVA has no problem with religious slaughter, it is just against non-stun slaughter. I can't help thinking of the vets that the BVA represents who have to watch non-stun slaughter as the government 'Official Vets' in slaughterhouses. They have clearly made up their minds.

Over the din of commuter traffic Sean explains the three main welfare risks: the pain of the cut itself, the delay to losing consciousness that means the animal can suffer for longer as it bleeds out, and the risk of inhaled blood becoming an irritant to the lungs and airways. Studies estimate that without stunning, the time between cutting through the major blood vessels and insensibility, as deduced from behavioural and brain responses, is up to 20 seconds in sheep. 'You'll appreciate that even 20 seconds is a long time to experience significant pain and distress,' says Sean. In contrast, he describes using a stun as 'blowing a candle out'.

It is a brave move by the BVA to come out so strongly against non-stun. But the evidence has been building up for years. In 2003 a Farm Animal Welfare Committee (FAWC) report concluded 'slaughter without pre-stunning is unacceptable and the government should repeal the current exemption'. In 2004 the European Food Safety Authority issued an opinion maintaining that 'there was more pain and suffering if there was no stun'. And in 2010 the EU DIALREL Project, which looked at 200 scientific references across 11 European countries, stated: 'It can be stated with high probability that animals feel pain during and after the throat cut without prior stunning.'

The BVA, along with the Humane Slaughter Association and the RSPCA, want non-stun slaughter to be banned in Britain. If it is not banned, they at least want non-stun meat to be labelled so that consumers can have a choice. The BVA are backed in their campaign by the public – a 2015 petition backing the change in the law got more than 118,000 signatures.

'Ah, but we got 137,000 signatures in five days supporting the right to religious slaughter,' says Nadeem, pointing a samosa at me. 'Who reported on that?'

The fact is how we eat food, especially meat, is about more than scientific studies; it's about community, belonging and faith. As Nadeem says, eating food he does not consider halal would be like a vegetarian eating meat. It upsets your sense of self, of who you are. 'As a faith-driven person, it is important to me where my meat comes from,' he says. 'I will only eat something that is ordained for me.'

Unlike the HFA, which has been around for almost 20 years and certifies stun halal for clients including Subway and KFC, the HMC is fairly new and a little more strict. Nadeem says scholars at the mosques originally looked to set up an independent halal monitoring board following a *Panorama* documentary on chicken in 2003. It revealed that pork, which is forbidden under Islam, was used in processed chicken, including 'halal' meals. The contamination issue was again brought up during the horsemeat scandal. Starting small, the HMC began to send inspectors into slaughterhouses to make sure animals were killed in accordance with their interpretation of halal. The HMC also inspect the packing plants, butchers and restaurants along the way to ensure complete traceability.

Nadeem tells me about chicken that is still labelled 'halal' where the birds are stunned and mechanically cut while a CD plays the prayer in the background. For some Muslims this is good enough, but for others it is not. The role of the HMC label – a yellow sticker with red Arabic script – is to give confidence to those who demand certain values. Nadeem insists the cost of HMC is not higher, even though the slaughter line must necessarily move a little slower. 'If I do something as an individual that is not in line with the faith that I follow that is my own choice,' says Nadeem. 'But when you are taking responsibility for other people's food you have to make sure you are doing things correctly. We are allowing individuals to fulfil their faith with their dietary requirements. If we were not doing that, we would be failing the masses.'

The strategy has worked. The HMC has quickly grown to be one of the most intensive halal monitoring systems in the world, and is extending beyond the Midlands to London, Tesco branches, and even other countries. All the certified producers, retailers and restaurants pay a fee, which they should earn back through an upsurge in Muslim consumers. If it isn't, of course, the cost is passed on to all the other consumers, Muslim and non-Muslim. As a charity, the money raised by HMC is not taxed, but must go back into developing the monitoring system or aid work.

Nadeem loves science; he tells me about taking his wife to visit NASA every year. 'But the science tells us that sheep do not lose consciousness immediately,' I insist. 'That they suffer …'

'As Muslims we do not believe the animal suffers at the point of slaughter because when you sever the neck with a sharp knife, you sever the connection to the brain, which

essentially is the stunning – that is what we believe,' says
Nadeem. 'It is spiritual, a way of life, something that has
been passed down to us ...'

I stare across the table. We have reached an impasse. He is
talking about faith, I am talking about science. I give way.
Nadeem must see my disbelief because he gives it one last
try. 'Remember halal is about the whole life of the animal,
not just the death. Why don't you go and see some Muslim
farmers and find out more about that?'

I find Ruby Radwan in the polytunnel weeding salad leaves.
'Here, try this.' She hands me a flowering mustard plant.
'Delicious, isn't it?' 'Yes!' The peppery cabbagey flowers
explode in my mouth. 'Good for you, too. All the nutrients
are in the flowers. I don't know why we don't eat them
more.' Ruby, in her red corduroys and wild hair, looks like
any other organic farmer. She speaks like one too: passionate,
earthy, idealistic, a little bit of a hippy.

We leave the polytunnel, taking handfuls of mustard
flowers to munch on as we tour the farm. Lutfi Radwan is
eventually located charging the electric tractor. In his
waistcoat and checked shirt he looks like a cross between an
organic farmer and an Oxford don, which is exactly what
he is. Dr Radwan used to work in international development
before becoming disillusioned with our efforts to 'develop'
other countries. Instead, Ruby and Lutfi decided to practise
what they preach. They bought 18 hectares (45 acres) of
agricultural land outside Oxford, Willowbrook Farm, and
began the UK's first halal and organic farm.

'It was a decision to take responsibility,' says Lutfi. 'We
wanted to leave a legacy.' It was also a decision to live a more
gentle and sustainable life in accordance with their religion.
It has not been easy. They lived in Portakabins with their
five children and struggled to make a living. But it has been

worth it: the farm is now thriving, a cobb house has been built and visitors come from all over the country to buy the meat or just visit the farm.

Most of all, it seems Lutfi and Ruby have created a peaceful place for both humans and animals. I feel it as we pass through fields of grazing sheep and llamas, past chickens scratching around the polytunnels and geese ranging around the pond. We have to stop for a thistle in my shoe. Lutfi sighs. Even after 13 years, there are still thistles, which is why he is charging the tractor – it is thistle topping time. The farm does not use chemicals as Lutfi and Ruby believe that halal is not just about the moment of death; it is about the whole life of the animal.

On Willowbrook the chickens are slaughtered with minimum stun halal at a small abattoir that only does 200 birds a day. Ideally Lutfi would slaughter the animals at home himself, as he believes the best way to kill the animals is calmly and in their own environment. 'My argument and the argument of most sensible people is that if you have a calm, quiet environment on a farm or in a small abattoir the animal really wouldn't actually be aware of what is happening until the moment of slaughter, which can be done peacefully without the use of a stun,' he says.

None of the meat is certified HMC or HFA as Willowbrook rejects both schemes on the grounds that they do not take into account the life of the animal, only the moment of slaughter, and certify meat from factory farms. Factory farming, Ruby insists, is not halal, not just because of the mass killing but also the treatment of animals throughout their lives. 'There are a lot of people making lots of money on awful factory farmed food, including lots of halal producers. But eventually education will push people towards something better ...'

The problem is, it is actually quite difficult for Muslims who care about animal welfare to find organic meat that has been slaughtered halal, or for the increasingly urban population to find ways to connect to the countryside and the food they eat. 'All these kids,' says Lutfi, 'getting worked up about Syria, something they cannot possibly understand – yet they have no idea about the meat they are eating.'

'The world is broken: Muslims and non-Muslims,' adds Ruby. 'We have to fix it and it is not just the Earth we are fixing … we are fixing each other.'

I can't help thinking of an expression I have picked up, 'tayyib', meaning pure, natural. That is how Ruby and Lutfi seem to me. We are sitting in the buttercups by the new house laughing as I take photographs and make the couple pose with chickens. The conversation has moved on to the meaning of life – that's what talking about food and death does to people. Lutfi and Ruby strike me as intensely spiritual people, determined to not only improve this small piece of land but also help a younger generation of Muslims connect to the food they eat – just as many non-Muslims have chosen to question where their meat comes from.

'If we see anything that gives us a reason to be in this world, anything that distinguishes us from brute animals, it is a verse in the Qur'an – we were made in the best of all forms and then we were allowed to descend to the lowest of all forms,' says Lutfi. 'The general understanding is that free will gives us the opportunity to take responsibility and choose which of these we want to be. If we don't exercise that responsibility and we destroy the Earth, then we are the worst of animals, but if we take responsibility as a religious or spiritual person, we can be the best.'

I can't help thinking that most of us are a little bit of both.

Sometimes, very rarely, our celebrations get muddled up – the lunar and solar calendars, secular and religious, collide. So it was in Fez: Eid al-Adha was also Hogmanay.

On New Year's Day, after we slaughtered the lamb, I wake as usual in the living room. The family begin to wander in, in their thermal pyjamas. The TV is switched on to watch the results of *Pop Idol*, and there is the sound of banging pots and pans from next door where they cook over a single gas ring.

With no warning or fanfare, set in front of me is a steaming lamb's head, the eyeballs still in it, like the scene from *Indiana Jones and the Temple of Doom*. I blink, still a little bleary-eyed from the celebrations of the night before, my head full of Gnawa music and blurred by illegal whisky passed under the table. All eyes are on me – except, of course, the lamb's. I cautiously take a little meat from the forehead. It flakes off and melts in my mouth. 'Shukrun,' I say in my faltering Arabic. The rest dig in. We turn down the sound on the television. A silence descends as we eat.

Maryam, the eldest of the children, holds up one greasy finger, then two: 'Wahed, jouj, tlata…'

'Wahed, jouj, thlata?'

'No! Tlata, tlata …'

CHAPTER NINE

Colin

A danger of accepting any form of life as cheap is that each
successive generation might accept lower standards.

Ruth Harrison, 1964

Chickens, as my young nephews are fond of telling me, are the closest living relatives to dinosaurs. Watch them closely next time you get a chance: their alert eyes, strutting gait, ferocious curiosity. They are like tiny *Tyrannosaurus rex* – chickens that is, not children.

Reptilian cunning is not the only amazing thing about chickens: they have a sophisticated social hierarchy based around the dominant male or female – ever wondered where the expression 'moving up the pecking order' comes from? They defend their young from predators – see 'mother hen'. They have different alarm calls for different kinds of predators, full colour vision, and next time someone calls me 'chicken'

I am going to laugh in their face. Chickens also have better numeracy skills than toddlers, making them – at the time of writing – more intelligent than the aforementioned nephews' younger sister, though I'm sure she will overtake both chickens and her older brothers one day. Who are you calling bird brain?

Chickens are also the most popular meat in Britain and, after pork, the second most popular meat in the world. Every day in Britain we eat 2.2 million chickens; globally it is 49 billion. There are already more chickens on the planet than humans. By 2020 it is expected to be the world's most consumed meat. How are we going to repay our debt to this species we have manipulated in so many ways and who we owe so much?

My nephews know all about chickens because for a while one used to live in their house. Lydia was one of four former laying hens rehomed by my sister, Anna, after she saw an item on the news about the conditions on factory farms. Half of the laying hens in this country are kept in cages as battery chickens. Even the 'free-range' birds will be killed after 18 months, when their 'useful life' is over. Charities and ladies of a certain 'mother hen' disposition themselves gather these birds into their bosom, even knitting them little jumpers when they have lost their feathers. Rather than going to a pet food factory, they are found new homes.

Anna picked up her 'ex-bats' in a cardboard box and took them home. They were a bit straggly but quickly grew back their rich brown feathers. Like true Essex girls, they fluffed up their tails, shook themselves down and got on with the job of showing the neighbourhood who's boss. In honour of their sass they were named after the girls on the TV show *The Only Way is Essex* ('TOWIE') – Lydia, Lauren, Sam and Amy. For a couple of years they scratched around the garden quite happily, laying eggs anywhere other than the hen house and chasing the children, until one by one they started falling off their perches or had a 'Jemima Puddle-Duck moment' with the local fox.

But Lydia hung on, until she was the only one left. As it became colder, she started coming inside, first nesting in the shoes by the door, then the laundry basket and eventually the sofa. There was a certain amount of damage to the upholstery, but no one minded too much if she wandered about the house occasionally. She had worked hard for 18 months in a factory producing the eggs we enjoy for breakfast. Surely she deserved a good retirement? The occasional rest on a clean pile of school uniforms?

Defying those who say chickens are happier indoors, Lydia would roam freely during the day and eventually took herself off to a neighbour where there were other chickens, to live happily once more among her own flock. Lydia had character, pluck and a certain amount of dignity. Even the children could see she was an animal – not a machine.

The phrase 'animal machines' was first coined by the 17th-century philosopher René Descartes to differentiate humans animated with a soul from mere 'automata', without the ability to think or reason. He argued that by comparing humans to animals he could prove the higher purpose of man within the universe. He could not have foreseen the abuse of his theory in the industrial age to justify using animals quite literally as machines, but yet that is what people have begun to do. Cows, sheep, rabbits – but particularly chickens and pigs – have become so many units in a drive to produce protein as quickly and cheaply as possible. Some would argue that this is the 'Cartesian' theory of 'animal machines' in action. I would argue it is the opposite. As thinking, feeling humans – as opposed to animal machines – isn't it our responsibility to treat animals with care and respect?

The slow industrialisation of our farming system would have carried on behind closed doors without anyone noticing had it not been for one woman. Ruth Harrison was a Quaker, a former actress and a friend of George Bernard Shaw. She was also the inspiration of the farm animal welfare movement in Britain.

The images of veal calves on a leaflet pushed through her door inspired this sixties mum to explore conditions in other units. She visited broiler chickens crammed into barns, battery hens laying eggs in cages, 'their eyes gleaming like those of maniacs', 'sweat-box' piggeries 'wet with urine and dung', and veal calves in crates. Many of these methods were brought in after the war to provide cheap food after the austerity of rationing. Ruth Harrison was the first person in post-war Britain to put on the brakes and say hang on, is this right? Are we really this hungry? Are these animals, or machines? And if they are animals, don't we owe them a duty of care?

Perhaps her most famous quote is: 'If one person is unkind to an animal it is considered cruelty, but where a lot of people are unkind to a lot of animals, especially in the name of commerce, the cruelty is condoned and, once large sums of money are at stake, will be defended to the last by otherwise intelligent people.' Her book *Animal Machines*, published in 1964, inspired a change in legislation and a generation of animal welfare activists. By the time I get around to reading it, it is out of date, almost quaint in places, but no less inspiring. I'm ashamed to say some paragraphs make me laugh, they are so innocent of the scale we would reach in farming animals. For example, Harrison worries about 200 million chickens going through the packing stations in Britain; today it is more like 800 million. She is concerned about them handling 3,000 to 4,000 birds an hour; today it is 14,000 – at least.

Most hilariously – sort of – she wonders how a chicken can be 'fully grown' at nine-and-a-half weeks. Ha! Today, an organic chicken might be eight weeks old, and the average broiler is grown for 43 days. The industry 'leaders' are growing 'fully grown' chickens in 35 days. I was told by one poultry farmer he fully expects breeding to develop so he could turn around a 'crop' of chickens in 28 days. We are eating teenagers.

I laughed also, in a slightly tired way, at the reaction of the industry, which also has not changed. Ruth talks about 'evasion after evasion' when she tries to get into the processing plants and that old, tired excuse: 'We are only producing what the public wants.' She warns of the consolidation of the business into a few powerful hands. The poultry processing business today is in the hands of just five companies: Moy Park, 2 Sisters, Faccenda, Cargill Meats Europe and Banham Poultry. She makes points that Hugh Fearnley-Whittingstall and others are still making today – that birds raised so fast they barely have time to move around, let alone develop fat, are tasteless.

Back in 1964, Ruth already had a sense of where chicken farming might be going. Egg-laying chickens were in battery cages. Chickens in barns, known as broilers – a cross between the cooking methods boil and roast – were becoming the first intensive form of meat. Already we were losing respect for chickens. 'Chickens can be turned out in their millions and are therefore considered a more expendable commodity than large and more expensive forms of livestock,' she wrote. 'But the principle is the same, the cheapness of life itself, the lowering of standards. A danger of accepting any form of life as cheap is that each successive generation might accept lower standards.'

Rachel Carson, the US author of *Silent Spring* and heroine of the environmental movement, who exposed the danger of using certain chemicals in farming, was sure the passion and insight of Harrison would change the system. In a foreword to the first edition of *Animal Machines*, she wrote: 'I hope it will spark a consumers' revolt of such proportions that this vast new agricultural industry will be forced to mend its ways.'

In a way, Carson was right. Following the publication of *Animal Machines* there was a public outcry and the government was forced to act. It seems even in the sixties, when people had so much exciting music, fashion and art to think about, they still cared about animals. In 1965 the UK government commissioned an investigation, led by Professor Sir Roger Brambell, into the welfare of intensively farmed animals.

The resulting Brambell Report stated that animals should have the freedom to 'stand up, lie down, turn around, groom themselves and stretch their limbs'. It stated: 'Animals show unmistakeable signs of suffering from pain, exhaustion, fright, frustration ... and can experience emotions such as rage, fear, apprehension, frustration and pleasure.' This was groundbreaking stuff at a time when animal rights were still a fringe concern.

Brambell summarised the main priorities for animal welfare as 'Five Freedoms' (see page 98), which later went on to inspire the RSPCA's Freedom Food. It is certainly a succinct and powerful list that helped campaigners all over the world introduce legislation. Typically, in Britain it took until 2006 to bring a basic version of the Five Freedoms into law, the Animal Welfare Act. In 2009, the Lisbon Treaty, agreed by all the EU countries, recognized animals as 'sentient beings'.

But did all the fine words inspired by *Animal Machines* actually improve the lives of farm animals in the UK? Yes, unquestionably. Veal crates were banned and eventually sweat-box piggeries too. In 2009 the Farm Animal Welfare Committee, which was set up as a result of the Brambell Report, reported on how far we have come: 'There is therefore strong evidence of significant improvements in livestock welfare since the Brambell Report of 1965,' it stated. 'However, further progress is needed, such that British citizens can be assured that each and every farm animal has had a life worth living.'

Sow crates, which do not allow a pregnant pig to move, were banned in the UK in 1999, but not until 2013 in the rest of Europe. Battery cages for hens were only outlawed in 2012 – but even after that cages can continue to be used as long as they leave room for movement and are 'enriched' with a nest box and perch. About half of the eggs eaten in Britain today, most often hidden in cakes and other processed foods, are from caged hens. Other recommendations, such as the prohibition of debeaking of chickens and tail-docking of pigs, have still not been carried out, 'primarily for economic reasons'.

Like free love and a lot of other good intentions that started in the 1960s, animal welfare never quite reached its potential. In fact one could argue that in 1965 the mass industrialisation of chickens was just beginning.

How did we get from a few chickens scratching around in the yard, to eating chicken at least twice a week? Come to think of it, how did the descendants of a South Asian jungle fowl become the second most consumed meat on Earth? Before the 1950s chicken was a treat. Our grandparents and parents will tell you poultry was eaten only on feast days, like the Easter spring chicken. Today the average consumer will eat at least 550 birds in a lifetime. It is the meat parents most often feed to their children – and I'm fairly certain this is not because kids like dinosaurs so much. In Britain, we eat five times as much chicken as we did 20 years ago.

One of the people who helped to lead this revolution was John Lloyd Maunder. I interview him in the VIP tent at the Devon County Show. As one of the livestock judges he is still wearing a smart suit and tie, and cufflinks decorated with farm animals. His bowler hat sits on the table near a cake stand full of cucumber sandwiches and cakes. It could not be a more English setting for an American Dream story.

John is a well-respected man in these parts. He not only ran the highly successful Lloyd Maunder chain of butchers' shops but also saved many farmers from bankruptcy. Over

Pimm's and scones he explains how he helped bring cheap chicken to Britain. Like fridges, milkshakes and rock 'n' roll, the whole thing started in the USA.

After the Depression, chicken was seen as the best way to feed a growing population with cheap protein. Just like the production of Ford motors, chicken could be mass produced by breaking down each stage into specialised, efficient parts. So instead of having a few hens in the backyard, sold at the market, you have a breeder, a hatchery, a grower, an abattoir, a processor and a retailer. This 'vertical integration' allowed the speedy production of chicken to be fed into the cities. As Herbert Hoover, the Republican presidential candidate, promised in 1928: 'A chicken in every pot and a car in every garage.'

Meanwhile, the variety of chickens in backyards was being replaced by a movement towards the meatier breeds. A competition for the chicken with the largest breasts was launched and the modern day 'broiler' was born, or rather, hatched.

In the UK it didn't take off until the 1950s when Sainsbury's brought back the idea of mass-produced chicken. The retailer basically divided the country up and asked a butcher like Lloyd Maunder to set up a processing plant for chickens in each region. John was one of the regional leaders. He looks back on it as an exciting time. He had to be truly innovative, persuading farmers to build poultry sheds, then working out how the chickens would be grown, transported and slaughtered. Soon he was sending thousands of chickens a day up to London and the British family could suddenly have their chicken and eat it, just like across the pond. Within a few decades chicken tikka masala – a dish unknown in a 1950s household – was a staple.

The poultry units also helped many small farmers stay afloat, especially through the foot and mouth crisis. As we chat many come over to say hello or doff their caps as they pass. But the golden period could not last. Gradually the small units on mixed farms began to be pushed out by bigger and bigger players. Greater and greater numbers of chickens were being packed into the sheds, despite the risk of overcrowding and disease.

John was beginning to get uncomfortable with what chicken farming had become. His biggest issue was 'this wretched business of getting heavier and heavier for fewer and fewer days. We had to take a step back.' John became a pioneer of free-range and organic chickens. But even that became an impossible business in the face of cheap intensive chicken. Finally, Lloyd Maunder washed its hands of chicken farming and went back to being a butcher.

'Everyone thought we were mad,' says John. Effectively they were going backwards just as the rest of the industry was diving headlong into further industrialisation. What worried him most was loss of reputation – if the public ever found out how their chicken was produced, which of course they eventually would … He puts his bowler hat back on and gets ready to go. 'Lose that and you have lost everything.'

In Britain we eat 15 million chickens a week. Have you ever wondered where they all are? There are certainly not millions of chickens scratching around in the open countryside. In the old days, you would at least see them transported in trucks, head and feathers peeping out the side of crates loaded onto lorries.

Mary McCartney recalled why her parents Paul and Linda McCartney became vegetarians. 'They'd been driving behind a lorry that had lots and lots of chickens crammed into it and obviously between the two of them they thought, "That's not right." I think Mum even took a picture of it …' she told the *Guardian* in 2010. I'd like to see that photo from the McCartney archive. I imagine Paul and Linda with their 1980s mullets, discussing it as they drove along with their young children in the back, and the more they spoke, the more uncomfortable they became.

Nowadays you would only see articulated lorries loaded with chickens if you knew what to look out for. They usually carry 6,000 or so chickens in blue or yellow crates. In wet weather there will be tarpaulin on the side. Perhaps you went past one the other day on the motorway?

What about the chicken farms themselves? As Ruth Harrison pointed out, they are no longer the pictures in storybooks we show our children, but a 'straggling factory' of long windowless barns with conical feed hoppers at the end. Around 95 per cent of the chickens we eat in this country are barn reared. Just 4.5 per cent are free-range and 0.5 per cent organic. There are around 2,500 poultry farmers, some small, some 'poultry magnates'. Around half are independent businesses that sell the birds to a processor, and half are contracted, or owned by the company in the more American 'vertical integration' style.

The chickens are usually from breed stock owned by two companies – Cobb in the USA or Aviagen in Europe. These companies have invested millions into developing the modern birds, directly descended from those competition winners in the 1930s. The only trouble is, birds designed to fly have weak bones and tend to topple over under the weight of their own huge breasts, a condition known as 'going off their legs'. Breeders claim this problem has been solved, but animal welfare experts are still unhappy with many of the breeds still used. The most common type in the UK is the Ross 308, a white bird with the ubiquitous big breasts.

The need for the birds to grow fast means that there are serious welfare concerns with breeding. The parent birds cannot be fed too much because they are genetically predisposed to build up flesh, so they are kept hungry most of the time to keep them lean enough to breed. Chicks arrive from hatcheries in the UK at a few days old and then are put into sheds lined with fresh sawdust. The flooring stays the same the whole time they are there, between 30 and 50 days.

The chickens are generally fed at least some GM soy, unless they are organic. Many environmentalists call this 'bringing in GM by the backdoor' and are concerned about clearance of rainforests in South America to grow the feed crop for cheap chickens. But even the more conscientious supermarkets have been unable to reject GM soy as the alternatives are so expensive.

Most sheds will house at least 25,000 birds. The biggest have 40,000 and some farms have up to ten sheds. As the technology keeping the barns maintained at the same temperature improves, they are likely to get even bigger, to save on costs. Stocking density or number of chickens per square metre cannot equate to more than 42kg per square metre (8.6lb per square foot) under EU rules. I struggle to imagine that until a source tells me 'basically you can't walk through them, or you'll step on a chicken; you have to shuffle'. Another describes them as a 'carpet of chickens'. The UK sets a slightly stricter limit of 39kg/sq m (8lb/sq ft) and the Red Tractor scheme, followed by 90 per cent of intensive chicken farms, states that farmers must not exceed 38kg/sq m (7.8lb/sq ft) – still barely a side of A4 paper for each mature chicken. The RSPCA keep it to 30kg/sq m (6.1lb/sq ft). Any type of intensive farming has a certain amount of collateral damage – with broiler chickens you will generally lose at least 5 per cent of the flock. It is someone's job to go through and pick up the dead birds. This is when you have to shuffle.

Because the chickens will be kept on the same bedding for their short lives, the sheds need to be ventilated, to suck out the gases from the dung. Hattie Ellis, author of *Planet Chicken*, tells me about visiting a chicken farm one day. In the course of the tour, there was an electricity blackout. 'I've never seen anyone move so fast,' she said. The farmer had to run to turn the generator on so the ventilator kept working and the chickens didn't die from heat stress or were not 'gassed by their own shit'.

The bedding also causes a problem called hock burn. This is when the chickens, tired of holding up their huge breasts, will 'go off their legs' and crouch down on the floor. The ammonia burns their knees. Look out for it next time you buy a chicken. Or worse, breast blisters, where they are actually resting their whole body on the floor.

The chickens are generally kept in dim lighting, because this encourages less movement and therefore faster growth. Under EU rules they need only a minimum of six hours of light per day.

The chickens live for an average of 40 to 50 days before being gathered by catching gangs. These come in the early hours, floating workers employed on low wages for what is considered to be a very tough job. Sometimes automatic chicken catchers hoover up the chickens and take them into the machine's belly. Awful as it sounds, I am told it is better than bad manual catching.

The chickens are loaded into crates and taken to the abattoir. Before it is light, the same crate is loaded into a chamber in the abattoir where carbon dioxide is gradually increased until the chickens are dead. The chickens are then shackled and their throats cut with a rotating blade and they are bled. The carcasses are dipped in scalding water to loosen the feathers and plucked in a machine. In some processing units the birds are also gutted and packaged by a machine.

A chicken could go through the whole process and the first time it touches a human is when it enters your mouth.

I have come to the mecca for conscientious foodies, Borough Market, to meet the man in charge of the industry getting the greatest rap right now from the foodie elite – Andrew

Large, Chief Executive of the British Poultry Council.
I arrive early to give myself enough time to stuff my face
with vegetarian dosas and other treats. I notice that every
single stall claims to be sourcing its meat from 'local, organic,
sustainable' sources; some even show the hunter with
the rifle.

'Ethical' is a word bandied around on most stalls and it's
one Andrew insists applies to industrially raised chickens.
He points out poultry has a low carbon footprint in terms
of its feed-to-protein ratio, is affordable for all, is packed
with nutrition, can employ local people as a 'home-grown'
product and is 'culturally neutral' across most religions.
'I think we are producing a meat that stands up very well to
ethical scrutiny. You also have to look at issues like food
security, national nutrition, affordability. It is part of UK's
food security that we have good sources of sustainable
protein.'

'But what about the sheer scale?' I ask. 'What about the
welfare issues?' Andrew stirs his coffee. He has a background
in trade and industry. He looks like a businessman, not a
farmer, but then poultry is big business. He says the latest
technology can help keep chickens healthy and happy. For
example, infrared cameras, necessary when there is no light,
will see if the chickens are gathering somewhere because
they are cold or if they are avoiding something. The
stockman can then resolve the problem.

In fact, argues Andrew, high welfare standards may be the
only way to ensure the British poultry industry survives.
Already around 10 per cent of the chicken meat we eat is
grown abroad – mostly in Brazil and Asia, where it can be
produced more cheaply because less heating is needed.
Ultimately British poultry will be more expensive. Why
would people pay extra, except for guaranteed welfare?

Andrew is calm and open. He doesn't flinch from telling
me about the whole process, although I am unable to see a
plant myself because of an ongoing avian flu outbreak.

There are about 30 poultry slaughterhouses in the UK. In the past most chickens were killed using the 'electric stun' method. This meant chickens were hung upside down on shackles and then stunned when their head hit a water bath. The stun should come within 90 seconds of being shackled and the cutting should be done immediately afterwards. The method was developed to process chickens faster in the USA and in that sense has been a great success. However, it can be problematic. If birds flap and struggle then they can miss the bath and even the cut. Birds scalded alive are called red skins and it is still a massive problem in the USA.

Gassing, the method used for around 70 per cent of chickens in the UK, is considered kinder because it minimises the handling of birds and therefore injury. Andrew says it is a 'calm and tranquil' process. 'The crates get slotted into the system, they rise up, and as they rise the concentration of carbon dioxide increases and they come out asleep,' he says. 'We have to accept that if we are going to eat meat we have to slaughter the birds and if that is the case then we need to make sure that slaughter process is as dignified and humane as possible and that is what we try and do.'

I wonder if anyone in Borough Market today has ever stopped to wonder how their chicken is actually raised or killed. Voicing their concerns, I say to Andrew, 'Shouldn't birds be outside, wouldn't it be nice for them to feel the sun on their backs, catch some grubs?'

He laughs. 'I think you are Disneyfying. I would not agree something has to give. You have to change how you view the process from a few brown chickens in a green pasture with roses around the door – what our grandparents and great-grandparents did – to reality. I would argue 40,000 birds in a shed are well cared for, they are under veterinary supervision, health monitored, environment monitored, by people properly trained. There is a real danger of anthropomorphising, transposing human feelings onto livestock, and I think it is a very dangerous route to go

down. I think we get good welfare when we focus on the
known feelings of the bird.'

There are no roses around the door, but there are flowers in
the hedgerows as I drive to Devonshire Poultry; I can see
greater stitchwort, lady's smock, bluebells, nettles and
cleavers. It is another bucolic countryside scene, until you
come to the chicken farm. Don't get me wrong, there is
nothing sinister about the farm. It is clean and neat. Mowed
lawns surround the long sheds and feed hoppers. But yes, it
does look more like a factory than a farm.

Just like in a factory, I have to go through the now
familiar process of changing into overalls and boots. Robert
Lanning, who owns the farm, explains that the main reason
he cannot show more people around is the biosecurity issue.
Diseases rip through chicken farms and anyone could bring
in a new virus on their feet or clothes. It is to his credit that
he is giving me a tour today and is keen on educating more
people about higher welfare chicken farming. Devonshire
Poultry is RSPCA Assured and is the only intensive chicken
farm in the UK to have a website.

Robert is rightly proud of the business he has built up
from scratch to seven farms housing 750,000 chickens. As
we suit up he explains the chickens are Hubbard JA87,
a flavoursome slow-growing breed that do not go 'off their
legs' and are slaughtered at 49 days.

We go into a shed. It is clean and smells like a hamster
cage, faintly of sawdust and shit but not overpowering
ammonia. I guess the chickens are only two weeks old and
half grown. There are windows and the chicks scratch
around in an 'enriched' environment with straw bales,
perches, knotted rope and CDs hung from string. There is
plenty of space to spar and dust bathe. I have to admit they
do look quite content. Chickens are descended from jungle

fowl; they like warmth and dry and shade and they have all this here.

'Intensive is used as an evil word; we go back to thinking of battery chickens,' says Robert. 'But intensive can be good. It means the birds get the best of everything – the best equipment, management, veterinary care. Think of intensive care in hospital – you get the best of everything – but when people talk about intensive farming it is evil. From a food security point of view, you have to do it on an intensive level.'

Each chicken has an animal health plan. They get a jab when they are born and 'starter medication' for three days. If any antibiotic medication is given, it is all recorded. There is no debeaking, caponising or despurring as the birds will not attack one another given enough space. The only trouble is that RSPCA Assured chickens are less than 1 per cent of the total amount we eat in this country. What happens to the rest?

The best way to focus on the 'known feelings of the bird' is to watch how chickens walk – or 'gait scoring'. Generally, if chickens are in pain they will stop walking and sit down – or 'go off their legs'. It is still a major problem on intensive farms. Robert picks up one of the chickens. A fierce little dinosaur. It quietens in his hand. He strokes its pink splayed feet. 'Feel this,' he says. 'So soft. It is a sign that the chicken is on good bedding.' There are no blisters on its feet; they are not even hard. It feels like the heel of my own hand. I am probably anthropomorphising again, 'Disneyfying', but I can't help feeling, what's the point of such nice soft feet if you can't feel the grass between your toes?

The charm of the Devon lanes soon fades when you are stuck for two hours in traffic on the M5. I stink. As my car gets hotter and hotter, the smell of the chickens intensifies; it is in my hair, my clothes. I need to find somewhere to swim, and fast, to cleanse myself of all this.

A friend has given me instructions on how to get to the Still Pool, a local swimming hole in Staverton near where I am staying. It is perfection. Red campion, cow parsley, spearwort and every shade of green in spring is reflected in the glassy black water. On the far bank a farmer is cutting the hay and as the machine turns away peace descends. I put on a swimsuit and wade into the pool. It is just the right temperature, cold enough to make you catch your breath but warm enough to stay under. I dive down and come up exultant, refreshed. The trees around the bank shimmer as if they are underwater. I am bathed in dappled sunlight and peaty shadows.

I sense someone looking at me and look up. A bird of prey so close I can see his yellow claws, his beak. I laugh – silly bird, I'm not a fish, I'm a predator too, just like you. He passes and a blackbird skims over from bank to bank. A wood pigeon crashes through the branches, and the surface of the water buzzes with mayflies and laps at my skin. For a moment I am suffused with joy.

To me 'joy' is the clearest emotion I see in animals. When I lived alone for a short time in the Scottish Highlands I had only Ruby, a loaned Jack Russell, for company. Every day, come rain or shine, we would tramp through the hills with no particular purpose, then come home and sit by the fire. Now whenever I see her, she explodes with joy. She associates me with one thing: long walks. She jumps over furniture, wags her tail, growls and gurgles in excitement. What is she experiencing? I can only describe it as joy. There is no food at the end. She is not chasing anything. She is merely taking joy in the feel of her legs, the wind, my company. The BBC presenter Chris Packham calls his two dogs his 'joy grenades', launched at the beach for a maximum surge of joy.

In the year I spent investigating intensive farming, I often found I was more convinced against factory farming by seeing pigs rooting in the dirt or chickens scratching for insects outside than I was by the stultifying boredom indoors.

I could see for myself that in the natural environment there was 'joy'. Ruth Harrison writes about this capacity for an animal to feel pleasure. It is a tricky thing to talk about without sounding like you are attributing human emotions to animals. But is it not a legitimate question when industry seems to be taking this capacity away from them? As Ruth writes: 'Is it not that in the surge towards poultry factories we have forgotten the bird is an individual living entity?'

Because of an illness Ruth never completed a project to write a sequel to *Animal Machines*. I'm quite sure she would be proud of what has been achieved so far. But is it time we went beyond the Five Freedoms? The FAWC, which she helped set up, think so. In the 2009 report mentioned earlier, the committee recommended that instead of simply the Five Freedoms, animals should have 'a life worth living' based on a new set of 'positive' welfare outcomes, rather than just avoiding the negative. This is based primarily on good stockmanship but also feed, movement and even 'play'. On the best farms, animals should have 'a good life' and farmers should advertise the fact so consumers can make a choice accordingly.

The FAWC were prompted in their concern by consumer feedback that found most people want to know animals are well looked after and want their food to be labelled accordingly. I sense this in the air myself. The movement towards bigger, cheaper, faster may be going on at industry level but on the consumer level, people choosing to shop at places like Borough Market are uncomfortable with the industrialisation of food. It is not a machine, it is an animal. It is something Ruth Harrison started. Animals have the right, she said, 'to feel God's own sun above their heads'.

I did not know chickens sunbathed until I saw it myself. I am peering over a stable door into a shed of young poults.

Evening sunshine slants into a corner of the barn and in this corner are gathered the young chickens, snoozing and wallowing in the sun.

Jacob Sykes, a handsome young farmer, leans on the door, admiring his crop. 'The funny thing is,' he says, 'until a few years ago, I knew absolutely nothing about chickens.' Jacob and his partner Nick Ball were a cosmopolitan couple living in London when they came up with the idea of becoming chicken farmers. 'We just saw a gap in the market,' says Jacob. 'There was no one selling chickens like they used to taste.'

The pair were looking to move to the countryside and start a business and chickens just fitted. Jacob was a property developer. Nick was brought up on a farm but had spent the last decade as a fashion designer in London for Gap and Fat Face. Neither of them had a clue what they were doing, but a sure sense that 'real chicken' would sell. 'Other farmers thought we were bonkers,' continues Jacob, 'when we said we were growing chickens slowly, and for flavour. When we said we were growing them for 81 days, they thought we were taking the piss.'

For decades farming had been trying to get more and more chickens out at a faster and faster rate. Now along came this couple from London intending to reverse the whole process. No wonder they raised a few eyebrows. But within months Jacob and Nick were proved right. Fosse Meadows chickens grown for 12 weeks and priced accordingly sold out at farmers' markets. The business began to expand.

In the meadows the chickens are ranging far and wide, despite the fact there is a cool wind blowing. As one poultry farmer told the Oxford Mail in 1962: 'The hens have the choice of snug indoor conditions on deep litter or the fresh air of grass range. But they have a preference for the rugged outdoor life even in winter. Not even a fall of snow daunts their determination to range over the ground.'

'Yes, they'll forage up to 200 metres,' says Jacob, indicating chickens picking through the ditches and under the hedgerows. The mobile sheds have just been moved onto a new patch of grass and so there is plenty for them to eat. They are also given cereals, including maize, which gives the meat yellow corn-fed fat. This varied diet and the marbling of fat is what makes them taste so good. There is more blood circulating, so the meat is darker and has a denser texture.

In France 30 per cent of chicken is free-range compared to 5 per cent here. Bless the French, but I think it's as much to do with flavour as welfare – a flavour we have forgotten. Fosse Meadows chickens do cost more, but they are considered a treat. A culmination of farming with care. 'The reaction we get at farmers' markets is extraordinary,' says Jacob. 'A lot of people have never tasted chicken like this before. It's changed their weekends.'

⟨⚶⟩

Of course, one can go too far. Whilst I am droning on one day about animal welfare and the right of a chicken to 'a life worth living', my friend Julie starts giggling. 'What are you laughing at?' I ask.

'Oh, it's nothing. Only you need to watch *Portlandia*.'

'What's that?'

'It's an American TV show taking the piss out of, well, um, out of self-righteous organic vegan hipsters.'

'Ah, I see.'

'It's in Portland, Oregon. It's not you! Well, not really …'

It is hilarious. I watch a now famous scene where a couple go to a restaurant for dinner. Every time the waitress comes up they have more questions about where the food comes from. 'Is it an organic chicken?' 'What was it fed? Non-GM? Local food?' 'How big was the area it was allowed to roam?' etc., etc. Eventually the waitress loses her rag and goes to get the chicken's résumé. It turns out he's called

Colin and he was raised on 1.6 hectares (4 acres) on a diet of sheep's milk, soya and corn. Still it's not good enough. The self-righteous pair make their excuses and leave the restaurant to go to see the farmer to find out for themselves whether Colin is good enough to eat. I wonder what they did when they got there?

I presume finding an 'ethical' chicken like Colin, which I can happily eat without losing my new 'holier-than-thou hipster' status, will be easy. Poultry is a national pastime nowadays. More than a quarter of a million people are keeping chickens in the UK, including many of my friends. But these are either laying hens or just kept to scratch around the yard and look pretty: breeds like Bluebells or Silver Laced Polish or Scots Dumpies. Unlike Hugh Fearnley-Whittingstall, who is an enthusiastic keeper of poultry, my friends do not 'take one for the pot' occasionally.

Finally, a friend who runs a campsite falls foul of his pet chickens on account of an 'aggressive rooster', who has been attacking the visiting children. He asks me to come and 'help out'. 'You can get yourself a Sunday roast while you're at it …' But I am outfoxed, several times, by a more experienced predator: the local fox. I bow to his superior cunning.

The next year, however, I am ready. Again there are too many roosters in the brood and two need to be taken out before the camping season begins again. Neck dislocation, or pulling chickens' necks, used to be the routine method of killing birds on farms. However, nowadays the Humane Slaughter Association (HSA) recommends that birds are stunned before slaughter. The charity states that neck dislocation should only be used for 'non-routine' slaughter for small numbers of birds when 'no better method is available'. On the campsite, where the chickens are a new addition and the male birds are causing a problem, it is decided neck dislocation by an expert would be less stressful than transporting the birds to the nearest abattoir more than an hour away. It is non-routine and we have an expert on hand to help. You probably could not get a greater expert than my Uncle Kenneth, who was taught by his grandfather, my great-grandfather. He is also, like my grandfather, a gentle man. On the phone, he is only surprised that I have not carried out this most basic of tasks before. Some farmer's daughter I turned out to be.

The morning before I watch HSA videos and practise with a small lemon in a sock. I write down my reasons for doing it over and over again. The chicken has had a good life, it is older, healthier and has been outside longer than any barn-reared chicken. When I turn up at Uncle Kenneth's I am in nerd mode, firing off statistics about broiler chickens to cover up my nerves: 'They only live an average of 43 days, you know. They grow so fast they go "off their legs". Do you know what that means? I can show you. I can show you hock marks next time you go to the supermarket.'

I am still counting down good reasons for free-range chicken on my fingers as we drive out to the farm. Kenneth steers the battered old pick-up, his woolly hat pulled over his eyes. Perhaps to calm me down, or perhaps to shut me up, he tells me about growing up on a farm by the sea. About running wild with my father, sneaking into the doo'cot to catch young squabs and selling them to a boy at school with a pet owl, just like Harry Potter.

It is low season and the campsite is quiet, the permanent tents, used for 'glamping', boarded up against a cold easterly. The wind flapping the boards and whistling through the canvas makes it feel like a ghost town. Kenneth and I are alone; no one else wants to be involved and we want to be quick so as not to stress out the other chickens.

The flock are in a pen for the evening; they are mostly females with just the two roosters strutting about. All of them are black, a glossy 'fighting cock' breed, but you can tell the males by their red wattles and bronze necks, and the fact they are already beginning to strut and preen. They remind me of the roosters on a Roman coin: a proud silhouette, all flowing feathers and spurs. A crowing, thrusting symbol of masculinity. No wonder the soldiers wore a cock's feather in their helmets. Yet the roosters are also surprisingly gentle.

Kenneth and I crawl into the pen and easily take one each by both their legs. Mine cackles and then immediately quietens when I lay his breast on my hand as I crawl out backwards in the cold mud. Uncle Kenneth is standing ready, a rooster laid diagonally upside down across his thigh. He gently takes the head between his two forefingers, his thumb under the beak – in a quick movement 'down and back' it is over and the chicken is limp, its wings flapping.

'Now you.' I need to be quick too. Being held by a human itself is a stressful situation, even though he lays across my knee, quite quiet. 'Back and down.' I feel the vertebrae click away. It is over. The chicken's wings are flapping but there is no movement of the eyes, the 'corneal reflex', just like in the HSA video. 'C'mon,' says Kenneth, laying his chicken gently into the back of the truck.

We pull over into a copse to pluck the birds. It is silent except for the trees rustling in the wind. Buckthorn creaks and groans, the Scots pine shivers and bamboo that has somehow made its way here rushes like a stream. A buzzard mews overhead, perhaps waiting for scraps. I hold the chicken by his legs and begin to pull out the black feathers. They are like scales, each feather laid geometrically, perfectly, across the other – like a dinosaur or a Roman soldier's armoured breastplate.

In Roman times the British did not eat chickens, we worshipped them, as fighters and foreseers. How things have changed. Nowadays many vegetarians eat white meat. It's as if chicken is no longer actually a meat. It's a convenience food. You can buy chicken nuggets at the garage as a snack.

Well, I can tell you that having killed, plucked and gutted a chicken, it most certainly is not convenient. It takes what seems like hours to get the last of the feathers out with my fingers. I try tweezers, feeling like an inept beautician, then finally burn off the remains with a candle. I cut off the wings, legs and neck, marvelling at the crop, still stuffed full of wheat.

A YouTube video shows me how to gut a chicken but I make a horrible mess of it. Blood spatters over my iPad as I scrape out the innards. I think of my ancestors, who treated the chicken as a sacrifice, a gamble, an oracle, rather than a mere convenience. Could I have cursed my enemies? Divined my own future in the chicken's entrails?

In the end it is worth it. My friends exclaim over the flavour of a slow-grown roast chicken, the crisp skin – even if it is peppered with the pigment of black feathers – and succulent brown meat. But what is even better is the stock. I bung in the 'giblets' – the neck, liver, heart – with the bones and carrots, onions, celery and whatever other vegetables are lying at the back of the fridge and leave it simmering for a few hours. It comes out lemon yellow and smells so rich even a sniff could ward off colds. It reminds me of the illustrations in self-help books, the ultimate comfort food, served with matzo balls and noodles. The chicken is still at the heart of our culture, even if it is no longer used for fighting and religious ceremonies. I feel like I am eating this amazing little animal slowly and with gratitude; true chicken soup for the soul.

CHAPTER TEN

Game Bird

Keep your place and silent be …
'A Father's Advice' by Mark Hanbury Beaufoy, 1902,
learnt by heart by every apprentice gun

As a child, I was a beater every winter on the annual farm shoot. I would pile into a trailer lined with straw bales and sit squeezed between the old men and the other children. Our job was to tramp through the woods tapping trees and calling 'up, up, up' and 'hey, hey, hey' to frighten the pheasants over the guns. I loved those frosty mornings. It was an opportunity to spend all day outside exploring parts of the farm I would never usually see. As a smaller person I was sent into the understorey of the most tangled coppices and crawling through the Christmas tree plantation. The old men told me stories about poaching during the war and sneaked me cough sweets. My feet froze in my wellies and the only way I could warm up was by cuddling the dogs when we all bundled back into the trailer for the next drive.

As an adult, pheasant shooting was a world I largely rejected. I chose friends from different backgrounds; I picked up their suspicion of the whole scene and felt slightly embarrassed to be associated with it. I grew dreadlocks then shaved them off, took up feminism and studied social anthropology. Like any normal teenager, I made a point of ignoring my father's sport. In fact I went further: I sneered at it.

As a journalist, I had the luxury of getting closer from a different angle. I wrote about the near extinction of the hen harrier, quoting extensively from those who blame driven grouse shooting, and at the same time cited reports showing the monetary value of shooting to the countryside. In a way, writing this book gave me an excuse to explore a world I had rejected, to try the boys' sport for the first time. It was also a chance to investigate the ethics of a world I had never questioned as a child crawling through those woods.

Learning to shoot pigeons, rabbits and roe deer for my Novice Macnab is the easy part. I find it simple to justify: these are animals that would be controlled by the farmer anyway. It is a sustainable and useful way to source meat. But pheasant shooting is more complex. The birds are raised specifically for shooting and driven over the guns by the beaters. No one could say that the pheasants are controlled as part of pest management. It is also complicated by class and money. The guns tend to be – though not always – richer people able to invest in guns and in learning to shoot them properly. The beaters tend to be farm workers, old men, women and children. They often have lunch separately.

It has shaped our countryside, encouraging farmers to leave field margins for wild birds and to feed wildlife over the winter. But also, in the past, driving gamekeepers to control raptors and raising questions of why many of those same raptors have failed to recover today. The dress code is compulsory, the language foreign to many people, and good manners essential. It is frankly a strange British social ritual, centuries old, riven by class and questions over the management of our countryside. As a social anthropologist it fascinates me; as an actual participant it terrifies me.

I want to start my investigation on 12th August, known as the 'Glorious 12th', the start of the grouse shooting season. The sport has only been around for a couple of hundred years, since the breech-loading gun was invented and railways allowed men from the city to get out to the moorland. It seemed like the perfect hobby. Grouse are a wild native bird that will breed in profusion if the numbers of predators – like raptors and foxes – are kept down. The guns could be placed in a line on the moorland in 'butts' dug out of the peat and lined with stones. Beaters would then drive the grouse over the guns, providing adrenaline-pumping sport. 'The cocaine of shooting', as one source described it to me.

Conveniently for the rich – perhaps portly – gentlemen, there was very little walking to do, and you did not need to understand the surrounding habitat. You just needed to be a good shot – sporting indeed. Queen Victoria got into it and the fate of grouse was sealed. Moorlands throughout the country started to be 'keepered' to keep up the numbers of grouse.

Today it hasn't changed much – and that's kind of the whole point; going up on a grouse moor is a bit like going back in time. Perhaps that's why people pay so much for it? Except nowadays birds of prey are protected by law, which begs the question – how come there are so few on grouse moors? In the UK there should be as many as 2,600 pairs of hen harriers or 'sky dancers', but the most anyone has counted in recent years is just over 800. Conservationists blame grouse moors for continuing to persecute hen harriers, although no one has ever been prosecuted for doing so.

Estates insist that they in fact protect rare moorland habitat
for a number of species and they are innocent of harming
birds of prey, but as the harriers' extinction looms in England
the government has intervened. The Hen Harrier Action
Plan aims to keep everybody happy by satellite tracking the
raptors, so they can be traced, and at the same time giving
estates the option to provide diversionary feeding and
ultimately move hen harrier chicks if grouse numbers go
below a certain point. It's the last chance saloon for the
driven grouse shooting industry. If they can't prove they are
behaving themselves then calls for a ban on the sport could
start to be taken very seriously indeed.

An estate on the Lammermuirs invites me to come along
on the Glorious 12th and see how they are providing the first
wild grouse of the season without harming birds of prey – as
long as I don't name the estate. I arrive early as the beaters are
congregating in the head keeper's yard. They come from all
walks of life: young men with pierced nostrils, retired
accountants, enthusiastic dog owners, old hands in the estate
tweed. We pile into the back of open Land Rovers, the guns
coming behind us in their own, more luxurious 4x4s.

I fall in with Petr Kicinko and Klara Zahradnikova,
a couple of musicians, over from the Czech Republic for
the summer. They enjoy it, they say, tramping over the hills
all day to make money. The moor is a patchwork of purple,
green and brown from muirburn, the cycle of burning the
heather to provide new shoots for the grouse and other
wildlife to feed on. We can hear the birds cackling happily
away and the bees buzzing. Then, just as we are enjoying the
peace of the moor, it starts. The flags made of old feed sacks
flap in the wind as we tumble down steep cleughs and up
laws, feeding the grouse over the stone butts. Mountain
hares or 'long lugs' lollop out of our path and meadow pipits
dash through the air. I hear the guns before I see them, pop
popping away, and then the silhouettes as we drive up to
within 90m (100 yards) of them.

The grouse take off with amazing speed, hugging the contours of the land like fighter jets, shouting their alarm call, 'get back, get back!' With apparent ease coveys escape the shots, turning as quickly as starfighters in *Star Wars*, the unlucky ones falling in an explosion of feathers and a flash of their smart white spats.

There is a moment of awkwardness as we approach the butts, once the shooting has stopped, like unexpectedly bumping into your boss. The guns are not necessarily wearing tweed. A beautiful young woman with long glossy hair and purple nails tells me she has shot 25 birds on this drive. 'You have to be a good pot shooter,' she says. It is true British privilege – understated, elegant and untouchable.

I follow the grouse back to the trailer where they are hung up ready to be transported back to posh hotels at lunchtime. I pick up a bird, still warm. The feathers are rich chestnut, mottled in dun. The dandy white feet give them their Latin name, *Lagopus lagopus* – *lago* meaning hare, and *pous* foot. The only 'red' on the red grouse is the shock of coral on the eyebrows – the colour of blooming geraniums. A gun feels the chest for meat and shows me how to tell a young tender bird by sinking his thumb into the skull.

The chef who has come to pick up the birds shows me where they store their food in 'the crop' before digesting it; I can feel the fresh heather shoots through the skin and soft feathers. He says grouse are delicious, best cooked rare with a bramble jus. Petr strokes the breast of a grouse as we stand there chatting. 'Tell me,' he asks. 'Does the meat taste of heather?'

The original game bird in Britain was not the grouse, but the grey partridge. An unassuming little bird, it rather neatly encapsulates the contradictions at the heart of game shooting. Bag records show that between 1870 and 1930 around two million grey partridges were killed annually. These fast-flying, dumpy birds thrived on farmland, eating insects and surviving the winter on seeds left lying on the fields after the harvest.

Then suddenly they disappeared – and it wasn't because we shot them all. On the contrary, it may be because of shooting that any survive at all. The grey partridges probably declined because the insects died out with the use of pesticides and the fields were ploughed up early to fit in another crop. The hedges and woods they nested in were rooted up to make bigger fields. At the same time the gamekeepers had all gone to war and predators like crows and foxes were no longer controlled. Unlike with pheasants or French partridges, you cannot release a huge number of grey partridges and expect them to thrive; they need certain conditions and without them they continued to die out. Between 1970 and 2010, grey partridges declined by 91 per cent.

The collapse of a game bird population was obviously of some concern to cartridge manufacturer Major HG Eley, who in 1931 started an organisation that was to become the Game and Wildlife Conservation Trust (GWCT). He was sponsored by ICI, the chemical company. Within decades an organisation kicked off by a cartridge manufacturer and initially sponsored by a chemical company was leading research into how to keep wild birds alive in our intensively farmed landscapes.

The GWCT has developed seed mixes to be sown on field margins that will keep birds alive and healthy over the winter. They have also shown how banks down the middle of fields can sustain beetle populations and undrilled patches in winter cereal can help nesting skylarks. Their advice has meant that many farms in Britain now have more wildlife on them than they otherwise would have – and probably because the owner shoots, and is rather sentimental about, grey partridges.

You will be surprised at how many grown men I have seen almost burst into tears at the site of a hen partridge running along a country road, her fluffball chicks bobbing and weaving behind her. In 2013 my colleague Michael McCarthy of *The Independent* described the Duke of

Norfolk's Arundel Estate in Sussex as 'bursting with birds' because the peer had restored the ecosystem to hold grey partridges. You will also be surprised at how many conservationists have copied the methods of the shooting industry to increase wildlife on their land, sharing information on cover crops and boosting insects. GWCT today is one of the most respected institutions leading research into British wildlife, and recently one of the few brave enough to point out the risk of certain pesticides to bees.

Nowadays, of course, the game bird of choice is pheasant. Although we think of them as part of the British landscape, the ring-necked pheasant is in fact from Asia and has been released by gamekeepers since the 19th century, especially since the decline of the grey partridge. Every season gamekeepers will release young birds or 'poults' around 40 days old (roughly when an eating chicken is slaughtered). The birds will be kept in release pens and fed for a few weeks to get them accustomed to their environment and even to certain flight paths, beneath which the guns will later stand. Around 35 million are released every year. Some will be shot, some will be killed by foxes and some will survive and breed. You may see such wily old cock pheasants returning to your bird table year after year.

As one beater said to me: 'At least pheasants live longer than them broiler chickens, at least they get a chance to fall in love …' It makes perfect sense to me as an argument, even though I am aware how tough life in the wild can be. As an experiment I question a few friends: 'Pheasant or broiler chicken?' All choose pheasant. We are anthropomorphising, of course, in the worst possible way, ignoring the fact pheasants often die of the cold, are maimed by foxes or shot by humans. Yet, what a very human response, to want to be given a chance.

I am familiar with the other side of the story, against pheasant shooting, because of the League Against Cruel Sports (LACS), who invite me to chair a talk at the Conservative party conference. The charity shows me grainy videos of pheasants raised in battery conditions abroad and brought over to the UK in cramped containers. The poults are kept in barren cages with uncomfortable 'bits' in their beaks to stop them feather pecking. The LACS is partly right – some shoots do import poults from abroad raised on battery farms, but most are raised in enriched cages governed by the same strict rules as poultry dealers. In a way it is no different from broiler hens, only the pheasants are released into the wild just when the chickens are 'put to sleep'.

Another video shows dead pheasants being ploughed into the ground. It is extremely rare, since pheasants are worth money to game dealers, but it has happened in the past when the market is so oversupplied it is impossible to sell pheasants for meat. An article in *The Countryman's Weekly* in 2001 complained of overstocked estates where 40 pheasants were being put down per acre, 'which must inevitably affect the environment into which they are released', and excess birds were disposed of.

The industry remains acutely embarrassed about these 'mega-shoots' that charge tens of thousands of pounds to shoot hundreds of birds per day. The pro-shooting organisations, including the British Association for Shooting and Conservation (BASC), GWCT and Countryside Alliance, have published a Code of Practice that counsels against high stocking density and advises boosting wild bird numbers by planting cover crops and managing the land for wildlife. It advises selling all the game to eat and promotes 'respect for the quarry' by ensuring shots are experienced and injured birds are retrieved immediately by dogs.

Off the record, many in the industry tell me about their disdain for a 'vulgar' interpretation of their sport, which encourages groups to come from the city to kill as many birds as possible without bothering to even take one brace home for the pot. Yet few will speak openly about it. I guess it is big money for Britain, a luxury business that is pumping money into the countryside and maintaining jobs. No one wants to be the person who speaks out, yet they all seem uncomfortable with this kind of shooting. It's giving the whole industry a bad name.

I'm not going to pretend that put-and-take game shooting is perfect. Even the best shots will miss sometimes, meaning the pheasant is injured. But there is a way of doing it that is, in my view, better for the countryside and the animals.

As with most things in life, there are good pheasant shoots and bad pheasant shoots. One of the best is George Eaton's farm in Buckinghamshire. Like many farmers he has a small shoot on his 61ha (150 acre) mixed farm, attended by local friends and family. It is an opportunity for everyone to enjoy a couple of social days at the end of a busy harvest and to enjoy the landscape they all manage.

Every year George releases around 100 pheasants, fewer than one per acre, and only half are shot. His latest bag shot this year was 69, of which only 10 were the tagged birds put down that year; the rest are wild. He encourages the birds to breed in the wild by planting cover crops like kale as feed and shelter around fields, and putting feed out in the winter. It also encourages insects, birds, bats, grass snakes and other species. A GWCT study showed shoots create or maintain 7,000 hectares (17,000 acres) of hedgerows and 100,000 hectares (250,000 acres) of copses. 'I want more wildlife on my farm and the best way to do that is to run a shoot,' George told the BBC Radio 4 *On Your Farm* programme. 'I see no contradiction in enjoying going to an RSPB reserve for the day and going shooting.'

George's farm has been given a conservation award by the gun manufacturer Purdey for conservation work and has been praised by the RSPB. Kirsty Brannan from the RSPB says the farm is an example of shooting encouraging farmers to manage the landscape for wildlife. 'Farmers do a great deal for the countryside. Not all of them are into shooting, but for many of them it is where their interest is first sparked,' she says. Martin Harper, the RSPB's Conservation Director, has said some shoots 'provide beneficial habitat management for wildlife' and often result in increased numbers of some birds.

Having reported on the environmental world for almost a decade, I find it a relief to see organisations finally working together. In the past, great conservationists, including Peter Scott, who set up the WWF, openly shot game and wildfowl. In other countries like Germany environmental scientists will openly admit going boar hunting at the weekend – an admission that would raise eyebrows in the UK.

I think the real reason the LACS hates pheasant shooting so much is that it is described as a 'sport'. Participants are not just killing animals to eat, they are doing it for 'fun'. That might be true but the enjoyment does not come from the killing, it comes from being outside in the countryside with your friends, seeing land well managed and eating the spoils. As Hugh Fearnley-Whittingstall says: 'It's almost impossible to explain to an "anti" that shooting does not make you a sadist. But that doesn't mean it's not worth a try …'

I decide if I am going to shoot a pheasant myself, I shall do it on a small shoot, and take the bird home to eat. My father has taught me the basics, with the Bos, but if I am to go shooting with other people watching, I need some lessons with strangers. I have seen adverts for ladies' shooting clubs but fear they are not for me. The pictures show gorgeous blondes in all the gear. It is not only intimidating but also perhaps a little patronising. Why do women have to shoot in tweed waistcoats lined with pink?

Despite all my reservations I book into a clay shooting lesson with the Shotgun and Chelsea Bun Club, a ladies' shooting group set up by Victoria Knowles-Lacks. I know what you are thinking: a club with Chelsea in the title run by a woman with a double-barrelled name. You could not be more wrong. Chelsea Bun refers to a cake – because we all like to eat lots of them – and Victoria is a self-made young businesswoman who has worked incredibly hard to create a safe space for women to learn to shoot.

We meet at England's oldest independent shooting school, the West London Shooting School. Yes, there are a few tweed waistcoats present, but what is so unusual about wanting to appropriate the finer clothes of the sport? I find most of the women are just like me: eager to have a go at a sport their fathers or husbands often enjoy, but determined to do it properly, to ensure the bird is killed cleanly. There is a mixture of backgrounds: stay-at-home mums, a stable hand and a lawyer. There are jeans and tattoos and shellac nails, and plenty of laughter.

The tutor Chris Douneen tells me I am a little slow and cautious at the moment. 'Be like Diana, the huntress,' he says. 'Be aggressive, confident, a predator.' But it doesn't work. I have no killer instinct. I struggle to move smoothly with so much to think about, so he tries another tack. 'Be graceful and elegant. Take a waltz with your gun.' Now I am listening. I think of those photographs of turn-of-the-century ladies in knickerbockers, their backs arched as they aim for the sky. If I am going to shoot, I want to look like them. I want to look elegant. My shooting improves.

It is the same north of the border. Glad Rags and Cartridge Bags also advertises with pictures of glamorous women in gorgeous tweed. We even use powder pink cartridges. In the historic grounds of the Raemoir House Hotel it is hard not to imagine a *Downton Abbey* style shooting party and all that goes with it. But although many of the women express an interest in game shooting eventually, I notice most are far too cautious about harming an animal with a bad shot to have a go before they are absolutely ready. Another positive side of female shooting perhaps?

At the end of the day we gather for a demonstration on how to pluck and gut a pheasant. We swap recipes on how to cook game the best way and even how to use the feathers for decorations in hats. I feel like I was a little unfair on the all-ladies shooting schools. I am much more comfortable learning how to shoot with people who seem to have a like-minded approach. Now I feel ready to go after real game.

I have no idea how to tie my garters, the woollen ties that hold up my new shooting socks, so in the end just tie them in a knot. I have dug out some breeks of my granny's. They are corduroy, so not strictly designed for shooting, but will have to do. I have a practical, waterproof new tweed coat that just happens to have a little bit of pink in the weave (not such a righteous feminist now), and my green wellies. I am ready for my first day's shooting.

As we drive through the grand entrance of a country house, beneath stone lions, I feel nervous. I think of the beaters piling into a truck, the dogs clambering over everyone as they pass around the sloe gin, and think, wouldn't I rather be there? But I've done my practice; I'm on the other side now, with the men. I have my loader or 'stuffer', my dad, to keep me right. We are given a pep talk by the head gamekeeper. 'Clear blue sky' shooting, meaning only aim into the sky rather than towards any cover or buildings – and 'no ground game' (that is, rabbits) – and 'enjoy yourself'. Dad and I look up at the grand house, the casement windows and ancient chimney pots, and giggle nervously.

Fortunately the drives are far away from the house, on valley floors beneath the woods or in fields fringed by copses. We separate and find our pegs, and I realise shooting is rather a lonely sport compared to the camaraderie of beating. As the beaters come towards us you can hear their tapping sticks, shouts and whistles. The songbirds come out first, the sparrows, chaffinches and blackbirds, twittering angrily. We stand with our guns broken, relaxed. Then come the wood pigeons, tumbling out of the woods. The better shots have a go at them as they are still considered game. Then finally come the pheasants; I hear their alarm cry and the distinctive whistle of their wings.

'It's yours!' I aim for a bird – clear blue sky, safe. But I was too slow, too nervous about remembering everything: gun barrels up, watch bird approach, lean forward, mount gun, cheek on stock, into shoulder, close left eye, safety catch off, focus on bird, swing through, pull the trigger … Oh, it's gone. A long elegant tail disappearing into the distance.

As the day progresses I start to lift my gun sooner, but I am stopping after I swing through, meaning the shot is aiming just past the retreating bird. The others are kind, giving me helpful hints, admiring the Bos, which is not the easiest gun for a beginner. But I feel their judgement.

On one drive an owl comes out of the trees. We all fall silent for a moment, guns broken, uplifted by the beautiful sight. His underside is snowy white, his flight soundless. We hang suspended in time and I wish it could last forever before the shots begin again.

On the fourth drive I am watching a sparrowhawk hunting through the beech wood; he moves through the trees as if the branches are not there. A buzzard is also there, waiting for wounded pheasants. He's learnt the drill. Then the drive comes and this time I am ready. I take a deep breath. Swing through, swing through, keep moving. 'Bum, belly, beak, bang!' A pheasant lifts up in a puff of feathers. I see his feet stick up in the air in an almost comical fashion before he comes somersaulting down and lands with a thump. Ignoring convention I hand my gun to Dad and run to the spot. The spaniel has got there before me. He wags his tail and proffers the pheasant for me, grinning, as if he killed it himself.

'Good shot,' says the picker-up. 'Here, so we know it's yours.' He takes one of the feathers and sticks it through the pheasant's beak, dislodging a little blood. 'Thank you.' I am not sure who I am addressing – him, the dog or the pheasant. I pick up my bird and take it back to the trailer. He really is beautiful, evergreen and russet brown, the colours of autumn. An older bird, his fighting spurs are sharp and blackened. I can feel his hollow bones as I search around inside me for how I feel. Yes, sad for the death of a beautiful animal, but, I have to admit, pleased I shot him well.

When I get back to the guns, they pat me on the back. A Norwegian lady, Anette, smears blood on one cheek. 'Here, it's what we do, it means respect for the animal.' I let her do it, hoping it will make me feel better for the death of the pheasant, but I don't feel any different. The pheasant is gone now; no ceremony will make it come back.

It is the last drive before lunch and we troop into the big house. I sit by the huge fireplace, waiting for the loo, admiring photo albums from 1897, around when my gun was made. Groups of Victorian ladies gather around picnic tables in elegant fitted tweed suits, the grey partridges laid out in the foreground. In the bathroom there is more of the country house ephemera – the green welly joke book, cartoons of men in checked shirts with labradors. It encompasses everything, I think: your weekends, your bog reading, your sense of humour. It's just another way of life. I look in the mirror and inspect my cheek. The blood has dribbled down onto my jaw. I wash it off before going in to lunch. My hands smell of expensive soap and gunpowder.

The best way to pluck a pheasant is to take it for a walk. I tramp through the autumn countryside. First the legs, short sharp pulls in the opposite direction to which the feathers are growing. His scaly feet, like those of a dinosaur, are the silver grey colour of the beech trees, his knickerbockers orange like the leaves. For the breast I sit down on a stone wall to do it carefully without tearing the skin. I watch the feathers fall; each is perfect, shades of peach and brown like the understorey of the winter woods. The most delicate part is where the breast meets the wing – I tear the skin revealing yellow fat and the red muscle underneath. The tortoiseshell wings are strong and versatile for flight – or a quill. I have to yank out the curving tail feathers with my fist; not very ladylike for a feather I intend to put in my hat.

What a magnificent creature. We used to cover ourselves in feathers. We still do, at Rio Carnival, on tattoos, on dresses. We used to know what we had. The tippet feathers are copper beech tipped with black, his back is the darker brown of the ploughed fields in the twilight – it shimmers purple like the bare birch trees. His neck is evergreen ringed with white, the vicar's dog collar. His eyebrows are rosehip red, the lid coming from the bottom, like a reptile. I finish with the downy feathers still clinging to his puckered skin; they lift into the air like a puff of smoke.

I draw the pheasant remotely. It's like an episode of *Casualty* when a child is left with an injured parent and takes medical instruction down the phone. My younger brother Hector William tells me what to do. 'Take a sharp pair of scissors and cut off the wings, feet and head. Yes? Excellent! Now, with a sharp knife cut up the neck and open it out to reveal the oesophagus and trachea. Hello? Weese! Have you got the trachea?'

'Yes.' It feels like a tiny plastic medical tube. I pull away the crop and the contents of his last meal spills out, gooey wheat.

'Now, for the other end. Have you got the cloaca?'

'The what?'

'The vent.'

'Sorry, the what?'

'The bum!'

'Ah yes, OK ...'

It is easy: I cut a large hole and scoop two fingers under the rib cage to pull out the intestines. The liver, guts and gizzard come slithering out neatly. 'My goodness, wow. I did it in one.' They don't say that on *Casualty*.

I share roast pheasant with my friends, none of whom have ever shot. I feel like I have blown in with the fallen leaves to present them with this dish. It smells of a farmhouse in winter and tastes like ... well, nothing like roast chicken anyway. The breast meat is much more dry but tastier, the bones harder but glazed in flavour – we suck on them afterwards.

The fact I have killed it myself adds excitement to the dinner party. People feel privileged and I feel excited to present them with something I have worked hard for. Inevitably it means discussing where the meat comes from, but no one ever complains. They tear into the meat and decry intensive chicken. They ask me what it was like and I describe the death, the blood on the cheek. I enjoy sharing the experience and people enjoy eating. It is a simple transaction: I have brought them back meat and they are grateful.

Roast pheasant with all the trimmings is my favourite dish, I admit. The one I would choose for my last meal on death row. It reminds me of childhood, picking lead pellets from the meat, cutting off the slightly bitter yellow fat, fighting over the parson's nose, setting the wishbone on the Aga to dry. A few hours later whoever remembered first would appear holding one end by the pinkie and proffering the other end for you to do the same. You pull, and snap! Someone gets a wish.

CHAPTER ELEVEN

Hunter–gatherer

Being a carnivore who's asleep at the wheel means someone else is driving. Being a carnivore who wakes up, looks around and engages means you're in charge. Being in charge is good.

Catherine Friend

You could hardly get a more suburban neighbourhood than Harrogate or a less suburban neighbour than Alison Brierley. I arrive on a rainy morning, walking past the neat terraced houses, filigree iron railings and wide parks of a Victorian spa town. Alison greets me in the doorway of her 'temporary' old stone house. Her 'real home', the Hymer mobile van, is parked out back. With her cloud of blonde dreads, black leather miniskirt and matching knee-high boots, she looks like a warrior from a manga cartoon; a character transported back in time to liven up a prim English town.

'Alright gorgeous!' She pulls me in for a big hug and a kiss. 'C'mon, let's go hunting.' Perhaps it's my imagination, but as we drive away I'm sure I see net curtains twitching.

The van is like an exhibition space for woodland taxidermy. Across the dashboard is a squirrel pelt; at first I think it is a red, but it's a grey faded to ginger in the sunlight. Every light switch in the living space is a rabbit's foot or a fluffy tail. Badger skins are draped across the seats, a fox tail hangs by the window. All of them are 'trophies' collected by Alison but they were not killed – they were 'roadkill recycled'.

I met Alison a few months before at the Edinburgh Science Festival, where she was busy shocking the residents of another civilised town by demonstrating her roadkill cookery skills. She immediately embraced my idea to only eat animals I kill myself, urging me to embrace my 'wild warrior woman', my 'archetypal Kali feminine psyche'. I'm not sure what this means, but I like it. A few days later she sent me an email: 'Dear Lady … So many carnivores bang on about the horrors of hunting when (barring blood sports) it is one of the most humane and intimate of activities. That and butchering, preparing and wearing your kill. When we give up those faceless proxy executioners in factory-style farms and take responsibility for the meat we eat food leaps to another level. It is beyond intimate. It is primal.

'Very rarely do I come across another woman who feels like I do and is ballsy enough, and caring enough, to follow this process through. It is essential to the planet and our humanity to reconnect with our food in this way. It would be an honour to help you …'

Alison is just as enthusiastic in person. The bones in her dreadlocks – python spine, fox, rooster leg, ram bones, cobra tail – clink as she drives along, swearing at the Monday traffic. Now is the best time to be out, she says, just after the rush of morning traffic when you can pick up animals freshly killed by a busy commuter.

'We'll head for the best hunting grounds,' says Alison. Roadkill tends to be most plentiful on country roads with high hedges or walls either side. You want to keep off the main roads, for the fumes,' she explains. Also places you can easily stop, jump out and sling a bloodied deer into the boot. Around sporting estates tends to be a good place, where they have released a lot of pheasants. There is one road that is so productive it's called 'Supermarket Sweep'. We head for Harewood House and I laugh to myself, remembering attending this year's Country Land and Business (CLA) Game Fair. The annual event is a gathering of agricultural folk to celebrate field sports and rather more expensive ways to get a pheasant than picking up roadkill.

Alison is warm and bubbly, chatting away constantly in her strong Leeds accent. A pair of baby booties made with her own placenta bounce around on the mirror; 'bump 'n' blink' lights hidden inside flash red, blue and green. 'To celebrate the birth of my son,' she says. The rest was eaten by Max's father and a few others at a Nomadic Art Gathering. As one German participant said: 'It tastes very good in zee mouth but very strange in zee head.'

Alison specialises in shock and awe. She is all about breaking down taboos. Every taboo she can find. How we dress, how we live, how we eat … Under the seat jars of bones rattle around: birds' feet, teeth, beaks, antlers, stoats' skulls with their tiny vicious fangs. It's like a witch's workshop because, frankly, that's what it is.

Alison wasn't always so 'in-your-face' wild. She has been a dental nurse, a graphic designer, a croupier, a performance artist and a teacher and has had many other 'normal' jobs. She started collecting roadkill seriously around a decade ago simply because she wanted the pretty objects for her artistic practice. But then she started thinking, why not eat it? The meat had nothing wrong with it. It was no different from the venison, rabbit or pheasant she paid for. And as she ate, she began to feel different. By collecting, altering and eating animals she was truly 'connecting to nature's food chain' for the first time.

'Now I am going to teach you.' Alison laughs. 'Urban foraging', she calls it. The grand villas of Harrogate are behind us now and we are driving into the Yorkshire Dales. The trees are skeletal, dropping the last of their leaves into the gutters and ditches. 'It's better in the winter,' says Alison. 'You can see more. Also, the meat keeps better.'

We are scanning the verges hungrily, looking for prey or the telltale sign of corvids, which usually find carrion first. 'It is like hunting,' says Alison. 'Your adrenaline is pumping, you want to find something. I am more alert than other people,' she adds, pointing out a pair of gloves and a child's toy with one eye by the side of the road. 'I have a stalker's eye.'

'Only it's better,' I say. In my small experience of stalking so far, there is always a part of me that secretly hopes we will find nothing, so that we don't have to kill. This kind of hunting doesn't have that dilemma; we can get on with it in the knowledge it is dead anyway – we are just doing the council's job for them. It is the perfect kind of stalking for the modern hipster, uncomfortable with killing animals themselves or too inexperienced to poach – or too broke to pay.

Alison has attracted lots of publicity from all over the world. People are fascinated by this woman who picks up meat from the roadside. But more than that, I think they are interested in someone who is not scared. Let's face it, what she is doing is not difficult. It's just a bit of common sense – and some balls.

For now we are looking for lunch. It is the kind of grey Monday morning when the commute becomes too much, the last slog before Christmas. Even the green fields are dulled by the drizzle, the dry stone walls shiny and slick in the rain. Only the dying leaves are bright, orange and black – like the colours of the tippet feathers on a pheasant's neck. 'Nothing, not even a squirrel,' says Alison as we drive down yet another lane, searching the wet, churned-up leaves by the side of the road. But the lesson is not over. We have a spare pheasant to use as a prop to teach me the art of roadkill recycling. 'OK,' says Alison. 'Do you remember the mnemonic?'

'Oh, umm …' I had not realised I would be tested on the Easy to Remember Roadside Roadkill Culinary Checklist she had sent me a few days earlier and instructed me to memorise. 'Ummm.' An Audi goes by, slowing slightly to scowl at these two strange women by the side of the road.

'Oh dear,' says Alison. 'You are not a very good pupil, are you? Don't. Eat. Flat. Furry. Roadside. Snacks. Before. Last. Diagnostic. Smell. Check. Got it?'

'Yes, I think so.'

'And D stands for?'

'Umm, umm …'

'Damage!' We inspect the bird. It is a beautiful hen pheasant, her patterning like a geometric wallpaper in shades of beige and brown. She has been 'bounced' off the road. Alison does not recommend animals that have been run over a couple of times – although the Americans call roadkill 'flatmeats'. Obviously if you see the animal killed, you know it is fresh. She recommends keeping some surgical gloves in the car and a plastic bag or tarp for storing roadkill.

'E?'

'Err …'

'Eyes!' We fold back the eyelid; it is clear, still glossy. 'A lot of roadkill will have already lost its eyes, since these are the juiciest, easiest morsels for any passing crows. Missing eyes are actually an indicator of time of death.

'F and F. Flat and Furry is …? Fleas and flies. Easy! Fleas good – she hasn't been here long. Flies bad … something else is living in there.' We inspect the pheasant. There appear to be tiny little mites living on her feathers, but no flies.

'R for rigor.'

'Oh yes, she's still floppy,' I say.

'But not necessarily fresh. That's something you have to learn,' says Alison. 'Rigor mortis will set in pretty quickly, maybe in an hour and a half, and last for maybe eight hours or so for a bird like this depending on climate and temperature, then it will relax again. This is called the resolution of rigor and is effectively what we do when we hang meat, to let it soften and become more tender.

'Snacks. Skin. Feel it.' I can feel the firm flesh under the pheasant's feathers. Like a plucked bird. 'It should be nice and supple,' says Alison. 'Not rigid, but sliding over the muscle. If it's rock hard then it's gone …

'B for blood. There shouldn't be much actually, just a little around the orifices. If there is you want it to be red not purple.' I gingerly lift the head; there is a smudge of red blood. This is where the gloves come in handy – wet wipes in the car are also useful.

'L is for law. Basically wild animals on the road are fair game. But not pets! Or livestock. Then you should alert the police, owner or farmer. Farmed game found on the road is also OK as the road is usually owned by the public, or the authority that maintains it. You can't run something over on purpose though – that is definitely illegal.

'Umm, what's next?' Even Alison is forgetting the mnemonic. 'Ah yes. Diagnostic: diseases. Do your homework. Rabbits can have myxomatosis, badgers TB. Almost anything can carry toxoplasmosis, but ultimately nothing can withstand boiling point. Venison and pheasants should be fine. Just make sure it was a healthy animal. Learn how to do the proper checks. Sometimes animals are poisoned by farmers and dumped to look like traffic accidents. If in doubt leave 'pest' animals alone.

'My favourite bit. Smell!' We both lean in for a good sniff, even though if it was bad I guess we would know by now. I'd go so far as to say the pheasant smelt nice, like a dog when it comes in from a walk in the rain. 'Trust your nose,' says Alison. 'It will tell you if you shouldn't be eating something.

'Check: climate and cooking. On a cold day like this, meat will keep longer, but in a warm country? Well, you probably have less chance. Also be careful cooking it. Use different knives and chopping boards to anything you are eating raw. And cook it well, minimum 75°C or 165°F, and if in doubt, boil the bugger …'

We wrap the pheasant in a bag. It feels lucky, like winning a fiver on a scratch card or a bargain in the sales. Suddenly I understand why there is no roadkill for Alison to pick up, because this is so much fun. She is a victim of her own success. Thanks to her website and instructions everyone knows how to pick up roadkill. People are not as scared of nature as the supermarkets would have us think. Maybe everyone is at it?

Only it is not that easy, as I realise when we get home and Alison tells me we are to going to 'taxi-dermy' – remove the skin. She throws her head back and draws a finger from her own breastbone to her chin. 'Then across the wings.' She slices at her own heart, like a crucifix.

Alison has some new blades for her scalpels but they are the wrong size so we have to stick them on with sticky tape. They wobble a little – though that could be my hands. I divide the feathers, finding the skin, and begin to cut up towards the beak. Slowly a feathered pelt is falling to the side, colours of autumn I can keep.

Next to me Alison works on a crow she foraged some months before and has taken out of the freezer. As we work we talk about the traditional role of women in hunting and gathering. 'We didn't just collect berries, you know,' says Alison. 'We did all the preparation. Taking objects from animals and wearing them close to our skin is something we have always done. It celebrates the animal and its life.'

It's not that women couldn't hunt: we are capable of stealth, and cunning and strength. I'm sure there were times and individual women who were very good at running and throwing spears. But hunting is dangerous, and you don't risk the most valuable people in the tribe – the life-givers – being trampled by a mammoth. Perhaps Alison is right and women are more connected to the delicate art of making an animal into food, clothes, instruments: bringing it back to life. 'Sometimes when I'm skinning or scraping, I lose myself,' she says. 'It is time to contemplate, to reflect about life and death – and to get your head around it. You have to some time. We are all going to die.'

We talk about 'the wild woman' and 'eco-feminism' as we work. I'm vaguely aware of these theories and even looked into them as part of my research. I've read bits of *Women Who Run With the Wolves*. I like some of the stories; they suggest women have a deeper connection to nature and animals. I don't feel I am absorbing the power of the animal or anything like that. But I think my sympathy is something powerful, whether it is masculine or feminine, and it is something that is silenced by modern life, when you have no connection to the animal.

'When the supermarkets close, we are eight meals away from total anarchy,' says Alison. 'At least I know how to look after myself.' Yes, with the help of certain herbs and spices, I think – bought from the supermarkets.

We cook the pheasant flesh with preserved pumpkin, nettles, ginger, turmeric and honey in a slow cooker. Every edible piece is kept, even the liver. We eat it off our knees in front of the TV. 'I have a much deeper association with food when I have sourced it and processed it from beginning to end,' says Alison. 'I respect meat much more, I don't take it for granted and I want to eat it as fresh and wild as possible.'

Tomorrow her little boy Max has to go to the dentist. She's got to pop out for milk. There is family stuff to attend to. The family live in a suburb of Harrogate, love their son and eat food from supermarkets. The fact they supplement it with some roadkill doesn't make that much difference. The fact is, Alison really isn't that odd. I'm sorry, but she's not. Not to me, not after the year I have had. Most of her theories are mainstream, already on the internet if you know where to look. What's odder? Eating a pheasant that smells of autumn rain and tastes of game and honey? Or eating a chicken that tastes of nothing and that's lived on its own shit for four short weeks? I know which I think is more peculiar.

A few weeks later, I find my own roadkill. It is a cock pheasant, turned black in the rain, just a bundle of feathers bounced off the A697 to Kelso. I jump out of the car, feeling a little embarrassed at first, checking furtively no one is around. I can't remember the mnemonic except for 'Damage'. Well, the pheasant is certainly damaged by a buzzard who has picked at the insides. But I can see the breasts are in one piece. I give them a poke – it is firm flesh – and have a sniff; it smells fine. I grab the pheasant by the legs and rush back to the car, before anyone sees. I don't feel empowered, I feel naughty.

When I get home I use an ordinary knife to slice along the bone and take out the breasts. It is far easier than dressing a chicken. Within minutes I have a couple of pink breasts that look like they came straight out of a packet. No skin or anything to remind you of where the meat might have come from. No breast blisters from ammonia burn.

It is months since I have had a chicken stir fry and that's exactly what it tastes like, a delicious, conventional, unthreatening ready meal you could get from the supermarket. Now I feel empowered. I text Alison excitedly. She replies: 'Nice one! Lol.' And lots of smiling emojis.

Alison is part of a tribe, a tribe of people taking control of their own food, whether they are picking it up from the road or shooting pests. I want to be like these 'hunter-gatherers', with their confidence and their skills, their freedom from the supermarket system. I realise I don't need to spend money, or receive a fancy invitation, or buy a set of tweeds to source my own meat; I just need to ask the right people, learn the right skills. In fact it feels better this way, more free and, frankly, more ethical.

I find these foragers I meet are more in connection with nature. Not because they are taking photographs or identifying it, writing about it, campaigning, complaining or tweeting, but because they are living it, understanding it. Eating it. It is a much more straightforward way to source meat than game shooting, which comes with so much social cachet but is in fact far more questionable in terms of ethics.

All over the country people are helping farmers and conservationists control pests; why not eat them? It's food for free, animals that despite their charm have become pests, vermin, fair game: squirrels, pigeons, roe deer, rabbits and signal crayfish.

My first attempt at a squirrel is stymied by the NHS and Her Majesty's Prison Service. I am staying with my friends Jonathan and Kirsten and their one-year-old twins while I attend the Oxford Farming Conference down the road. It is a bit of a mad house with two young children, very busy parents and a curious guest. As we eat breakfast in the morning before all rushing out to separate events, I admire the goldfinches on the bird feeder.

'Aren't they lovely?' says Jonathan, spooning porridge into a child's mouth. And then his voice changes; the spoon pauses in mid-air. 'But those bloody squirrels …' He begins to grow red and look angry – so does the hungry child. 'They eat all the food.'

'Jonathan shoots them,' says Kirsten, scooping up another child, a note of disapproval in her voice.

'Oh, you kill the squirrels?' I am a little shocked: hunting in the heart of suburbia. 'Umm, can I eat one?'

'Of course!' Jonathan shouts, as he rushes out the door to his two jobs as a doctor at a high security prison and a local GP surgery. Kirsten is rushing to drop the twins off at nursery and then catching the train into London and her job at *Channel 4 News*.

The next morning, I wake up at 5 am and sneak into the study. Jonathan is sitting in his dressing gown with his air rifle over his knees. I suspect he's been there for hours. 'He's just there,' he whispers, pointing out the window. 'Eating the food for my goldfinches.' He begins to look angry. I train the air rifle on the squirrel. 'The only trouble is, he's on the fence,' says Jonathan. 'And the neighbour might not be too happy if …'

I look at Jonathan in the early morning light. I'm not sure he's had a good night's sleep in about two years. He is currently under siege from the NHS, the prison service, two hyperactive infants and an equally exhausted wife. I don't think he needs to have an argument with his neighbour about a dead squirrel in the garden. 'Do you know what, Jonathan? It's alright. Maybe next time? Let's go and get pelted with porridge by the twins instead.'

Squirrels divide opinion. As they are one of the few mammals that live in the city, we are used to their cheeky little faces, their agile forms flying through the branches, a fluffy tail disappearing behind a tree trunk. We are fond of them. Others see them as 'tree rats', blaming the species for stealing birds' eggs and stripping the bark of native species like beech and oak.

Worst of all, they are blamed for pushing out the native red squirrel population by spreading disease. Grey squirrels carry a pox virus they are mostly immune to, but which kills their red cousins. Since the species was introduced to the UK in the late 19th century, it has pushed most of the red population further and further north into just a few pockets of northern England and Scotland. So far, most of Scotland has managed to remain pox-free, but in Dumfries and Galloway the first grey squirrels carrying the disease are beginning to show up. It is here, on the frontline of the battle to protect red squirrels, that I go to catch my supper.

Richard Thomson, a gamekeeper on the Hoddom and Kinmount Estate, has agreed to help me. On a spring morning, we meet in his office lined with newspaper cuttings and certificates from the Scottish Wildlife Trust thanking him for his work on the Saving Scotland's Red Squirrels programme. Richard is famous not only for being perhaps the most lethal controller of grey squirrels in Scotland but also for his secret weapon – the only dog in the country trained to tell the difference between a red and a grey squirrel. Rory, his black-and-white springer spaniel, will bark if a grey squirrel is in the trap and needs to be dispatched immediately. But if it is a red squirrel, Rory will remain silent while the animal is released. No one knows how he tells the difference; I guess it must be smell.

Richard and I set out to check the squirrel traps in the delightfully named Woodcock Air Wood. Perched on the back of the quad bike is Rory, wagging his tail, ready to help. As we drive through the beech and oak wood, Richard explains why it is so important to control certain species in order to keep balance in the countryside. 'We gamekeepers are not maniacs,' he says. 'We are custodians of the countryside.'

The traps, attached to trees, have been baited with whole maize and peanuts the day before. The squirrels should not be trapped for more than 24 hours but there have been problems with the public interfering, so many of the traps have signs explaining the purpose of the Scottish Wildlife Trust's red squirrel programme.

The wood is rank with summer growth; it almost blocks out the light. As soon as we get to the first trap Rory races to the bottom of the tree, barking excitedly. Sure enough, there is a whir of grey fur whizzing around the trap. Quickly Richard moves in, gently moving the animal to the end of the trap using a sheet of plastic. He has the Weihrauch HW45, a high-power single-shot air pistol, ready in his hand, positioned above the animal's head. It looks like a child's cap gun, with the brown plastic handle. Crack! It happens in seconds. I am expecting the smell of burning paper but there is just the squirrel, lying still.

Richard is fastidious about doing it right. He explains everything as he moves around the traps. He has even trained people from other environmental groups in the humane dispatch of squirrels. When it comes to my turn, I want to be just as quick. Richard gives me instructions, but other than that we work in silence. Crack! 'It is the most difficult part of my job,' he says quietly, moving the dead squirrel gently to a crate on the back of the bike.

As we check the other traps Richard points out the wild flowers in the wood, the germander speedwell, foxgloves and red and white campion. In the background we can hear the River Annan trickling through the valley below, and the occasional peep of oystercatchers. The tyres of the quad bike stir up the wood, releasing the dank green smell of crushed leaves as we drive out to our last trap. Rory sits waiting patiently, and sure enough it is a red. It is much smaller than the grey, except for the oversized tufted ears. I want to stop and watch him, a character from the storybooks of my childhood, here in this dark, dappled green wood. But he has to be released immediately. Richard opens the door. Watching the reds escape is a wonderful moment as they spring out of the trap and float an unfeasibly long distance, the tail like a sail, paws reaching out for the next tree. It is the first time I have ever seen this elusive species close up and it makes me smile.

The Scottish Wildlife Trust claims that reds in Dumfries and Galloway would be extinct by now if the grey population had been allowed to expand. Richard alone has stopped 600 greys 'moving north', possibly spreading the pox, in the last five years. Richard cheerfully admits that he's fighting a losing battle – the greys will come, they are the stronger species. But maybe, just maybe if he can hold them back until we get a vaccine, then we could have the reds as well.

We drive back to the estate deer larder, leaving the traps set for tomorrow. Usually Richard would only keep the squirrel tails for fishermen and sell the rest for further pest control or the pet trade. But occasionally he will keep the meat for a barbecue and he shows me how to skin the rodent. It is fiddly work, leaving me with a couple of meaty thighs and a saddle. Richard laughs at me cutting a minuscule fillet steak from the spine, not wanting to waste a scrap.

It is just about enough to make supper and I invite a couple of girlfriends over before a big night out on the town. I am not sure how squirrel will go down, especially before drinking, so I decide to mask the flavour a little with a tasty sauce. As always the cook Nigella Lawson comes to the rescue with a rich peanut butter satay sauce that sweetens the strong 'gamey' taste. Nevertheless, I take time to tell the girls about Richard, about his work saving the red squirrels, about killing the grey with an air pistol. Maybe it's the drink, but they don't bat a mascaraed eyelid. They are 'Women Who Run With the Wolves'; they can handle some satay squirrel.

Rabbit is of course the ultimate vermin for food. It is time to get back on the bike, get over my '*Watership Down* moment' with the first rabbit and try again.

This time, I am ready. When we go out to sight the rifle, Dad lets me do it alone, watching from the car. It is just turning to spring, I can feel it in the breeze; the warmth of the summer is coming. I do not flinch; the bullets fire straight and we set off to find our quarry.

It is a gorgeous evening. We see roe deer bouncing away into the barley that shimmers like a yellow sea, gulls swoop overhead, a hare disappears into the field. Dad says there used to be more wildlife, more hares especially. All the farmers say that. We drive over to a sandy bank where the rabbits come out. Sure enough, there they are looking like Flopsy, Mopsy and Cottontail. I can't get those talking animals out of my mind, they are so powerful, but it's not necessarily a bad thing. Sure, I remember Beatrix Potter and *Watership Down*, but I'm grown up now.

I roll under the fence Indiana-Jones-style and whisper to Dad. 'Is that close enough?' Now more to myself, 'Is that the safety off, yes, yes? OK, focus, focus.' I am feeling nervous, but I also know to be patient and I know Dad can be patient too. He hasn't always been. Maybe we've both mellowed.

It is a perfect woodland scene across the valley. The rabbits hop around outside the burrow, and there are a couple of grey partridges below. I wonder, would I see it all, in this detail, this sharp, if I wasn't shooting? The rabbit twitches every time the partridge calls; she grazes, looks up, a few more mouthfuls, looks up, always alert. I keep the sight steady on her, I stay calm and think in the direction of the bullet. I squeeze and watch the rabbit somersault in the air, its white belly flipping to the sky. Suddenly everything is huge through the scope, in slow motion; it fills my vision, it's all I can see.

I unload the gun and confirm it was a good shot by looking through the sight. I shot the rabbit behind the eye with a .17 at 140 metres, or 150 yards. 'Good shot,' says Dad, and I feel a glow of pride as I walk up the hill to where the rabbit is lying. The sand is turning orange as the sun sinks behind the hill, and molten gold is pouring through the clouds like the ceiling of a Renaissance chapel.

'Thank you,' I whisper to my rabbit, but it's not just for her, it's for the day, the roe deer, the sunset, the hares and the partridges, and my father.

I skin the rabbit with Dad. You cut around the middle and then pull the fur over the rabbit's head; it is like helping a child take off his sweatshirt. She is an old rabbit – her bones do not snap easily and she has bald patches beneath her eyes from a few fights – but even so her skin is beautifully soft, her flesh pink and muscled.

Alison is right: this really does bring you closer to your dinner. You get an appreciation of what you are eating when you have to do the whole thing yourself, from beginning to end. Certainly my friends all welcome wild rabbit as an acceptable dish when I invite them over for dinner. I cook the rabbit like they did in the Second World War, in a stew with carrots and turnips and anything else in season. There is an uncomfortable moment when one of my friends admits to breeding champion pet rabbits as a child, but most can't get enough. They pick up the bones and gnaw at the meat to get the last juicy scraps.

It's been a year since I started this crazy project. I feel a little insecure at times. Frightened by myself, the task I have set, the opinion of my friends. I probably worry too much about what other people think. I'm not like Alison, laughing in the face of convention. I like to win people's approval. I often worry that they think I'm 'sick' – and not in a cool way. So I'm surprised when my friend Cal suggests we have a 'hunter-gatherer' party to celebrate our birthdays. Will people get into it? Won't they think we are a bit odd?

On the morning of the party we gather wild strawberries by the Water of Leith for cocktails and put speedwell and alkanet from the verges in ice cubes. We make salads from colourful weeds we presume are edible, according to books published in the 1970s, and nettles we think we have crushed the sting out of, according to YouTube instructions.

I am in charge of the meat. Over the year, I have served my close friends satay squirrel, lamb, roast pheasant and rabbit stew and they seemed to enjoy it. But still I'm nervous about serving meat I've killed myself to more distant acquaintances.

We make marinades from Jamie Oliver recipes, safe in the knowledge he would approve of 'free-range' meat and wild garlic pesto that will make everyone's breath stink. Friends arrive bearing gifts. Dave brings along broad beans from his allotment and Verity bakes an elderflower cake. The tea lights are lit in the garden, the alcohol begins to flow, and suddenly everyone is talking at once about meat, and food, and nature.

I realise how deprived my generation is of all this. Our grandparents went to butchers' shops and pointed to the cuts of meat – and understood which part of the animal it came from. They saw flesh and blood and death, not just rows and rows of packaged pink meat. For many of us we are understanding how the animal died for the first time. Even the part-time vegans are eating the meat, tearing into it in fact, licking their sticky fingers. It is exciting for us to hunt and gather, because we have not done it before and we are bored, our senses dulled by computers and screens; this tastes real, smells real, is real.

In an article on picking up roadkill, George Monbiot refers to 'hunter's pride', 'the raw, feral thrill I have experienced only on the occasions when I have picked up a fresh dead animal I intend to eat'. I'm not sure it's when I pick up a dead animal but rather when I feed meat to my friends that I feel the strongest moment of 'hunter's pride'. It's not hunter's pride from killing. It's hunters pride from providing for others, providing for my friends. Just like my father has always provided for me. Just like Steve provided for his family. I understand this more than anything else quoted in the 'sporting literature' about 'bloodlust' or some gender-specific need to 'hunt' an animal. For me it is about the simple desire to provide for others.

I'm running around in my bare feet from the barbecue to the makeshift drinks table on my desk, to the melting ice in the sink, when I make myself stop and look around. None of my friends are disgusted. I'm happier than I've been in a long time. I wonder, is it because I'm reconnecting with my environment? Because I am sharing this crazy experience with my friends? It is starting to feel like a positive journey. I wonder if Alison is right and the wild woman in me is reawakened. Is it eco-feminism? Am I reconnecting with Diana? Learning to run with the wolves?

I have become a mildly proficient hunter, gatherer, scavenger, 'urban forager'. If Tesco was to close, like Alison says I'd be as screwed as everyone else, but I might have a chance. It is an empowering feeling.

I've learned skills. How to identify and find animals. And kill them and skin them. It's only the skills any young boy or girl should have; it's not much, but it's a long way from where I was. I feel more confident and free too. I have overcome challenges and proved what I can achieve outside of the supermarket system we are stuck in. I have made every decision all the way in the meat I eat. I have met some wonderful people.

But a wild woman? A warrior? The moon is in its last quarter. Maybe my power is waning. Or maybe it's a lot more simple than that. Maybe I just feel good seeing my friends eat the food I have prepared, dance and drink and laugh. It's not that complicated. It's simple really. I don't see the need to give it a mystical name, divide it by gender or look at the stars; we are just being perfectly natural. We dance around to Taylor Swift and all agree that, excepting my taste in music, I throw a damn good hunter-gatherer dinner party.

CHAPTER TWELVE

Tigers of the Sea

Third Fisherman: Master, I marvel how the fishes live in the Sea.
First Fisherman: Why as men do a-land, the great ones eat
up the little ones.
William Shakespeare, *Pericles* Act 2, Scene 1

The mackerel usually arrive in time for Wimbledon. I imagine them underwater, like a pulsating silver bullet moving around the coast of Britain. The flashing shoal is chasing the sand eels, which are in turn chasing the zooplankton, which are in turn chasing a green bloom of phytoplankton chasing the summer sun, arriving off the north-east coast of Scotland just as we are switching on our tellies to support our boy, Andy Murray.

They stay all summer, lighting up our lives with a brief glimpse of the riches of the ocean. In August, Dad decides to take out his two eldest grandsons for their first fishing expedition. The harvest is late up here, the combine is still working and the air is heavy with dust, though the sea is fresh. We troop down to the Ha'en, hauling buckets of kit to where the The Company Yacht is moored. The 'yacht' was christened after the one posh boat Dad got to go on during a trip through Hong Kong, but would more accurately be described as a floating bathtub with an engine attached. The Ha'en is Ethie Haven, a fishing hamlet north of Arbroath that is now mostly holiday cottages.

I have been assigned as lifeguard to the children, having survived a childhood myself regularly being put in mortal danger by my father. We tie extra string around the lifejackets, which are far too big, and there is a perfunctory lecture, which the boys seem to particularly enjoy, about how to remove a fish hook from the face by pushing it back in.

You can tell the mackerel are still in. Life above the waves is buzzing with excitement. That morning we saw porpoises off the rock pools and even now we can see the gannets dive-bombing shoals offshore. Rafts of puffins, though not as many as there used to be, drift offshore, spotted with razorbills and guillemots. On the rocks, the cormorants dry their wings, like Batman, ready for the next assault. Down below the water is seething with life, the seaweed pops and crabs scramble out of the way as we launch our boat. Dad throws in the children and the dog and I tumble in last, head first.

As usual with summer holidays in Scotland the weather is threatening. We are all bundled up in anoraks and waterproof trousers and the waves are splashing on the rocks as we motor out of the harbour. The prow of the boat rises and splashes down, leaving our stomachs behind. I look at the boys. Ewan has gone slightly green, Theo looks nervous. But neither lets out a squeak. They would follow their Papa anywhere.

Sometimes we find the day trippers out from Arbroath that have fish finders, so we can cheat, but today we are relying on the gannets. Dad takes us out beyond Doo Cove, where the water is a little calmer and we can see the birds feeding. 'Come on, get the lines down.' We have basic hand-held drop lines. I untangle the weights and drop them into the water, watching the hooks go whizzing down, decorated in feathers like my girlfriends' favourite eighties earrings.

'Hoick them up and down like this.' I show the boys how to lift their arms up and down, and keep the bait flashing. Pretty soon we have a bite. 'Quick, reel them in!' Dad staggers to the end of the boat, almost capsizing us all, and begins to reel in the lines hand over fist. There are three or four mackerel on each line. As they come out of the water, the boys roar in excitement, grabbing at the fish as I unhook them and throw them in a bucket.

'They're like tigers!' says Ewan, admiring their striped sides.

'They are like rainbow tigers!' I exclaim. 'Look at the colours.' I throw another dazzling creature into the bucket. Their iridescent green and golden and blue flanks glimmer like refracted light. 'Now, the kindest thing I can do ...' I pick up a mackerel and look around desperately for a heavy implement. My friend Alec dabs vodka in their mouths to lessen the blow; Hugh Fearnley-Whittingstall recommends pushing their heads back to break their necks.

The boys can see what I'm up to. 'Can I do it? Can I do it? Let me do it!'

'No.' I turn my back and hit a mackerel sharply on the head on the edge of the boat. They watch, fascinated. I am sprayed in blood.

'Ha, ha, Aunty Wouleeze has chicken pox!' crows Theo.

'Get those lines in again,' shouts Dad over his shoulder, steadying the boat. Hooks go whizzing past their perfect little faces as we scramble to get the lines back in the water, the boys leaning over the edge, willing more fish to come. Once again, I thank heavens their mothers are not around to demand we come back in immediately. It takes just a few minutes for the lines to quiver and pull with life and we are hauling up the bodies again.

It's not exceptional mackerel fishing; the shoal quickly pass and we are beginning to get cold and nervous, or at least I am. I believe the boys could stay out here all night. We chug back into the shore discussing the fish, picking them up again to admire their fading beauty, then splashing out of the boat, not caring this time if our wellies are full of water; everyone is soaking anyway.

A pack of small boys from the holiday cottages are waiting, ready to inspect the catch. Ewan and Theo stand by possessively, explaining loudly exactly how THEIR Papa is gutting THEIR fish that THEY caught. In the stomach of one mackerel Dad finds some whole sprats and puts them carefully aside to add to the feast. The blood pools on the black rocks and gulls come swooping in to grab at guts thrown up in the air.

We rinse the gutted fish and our hands in the rock pool and divide the loot into two buckets, one for each grandchild. Job done: young boys now obsessed with fishing. They troop into the kitchen carrying a bucket each in their scaly little hands, grins as wide as their catch.

Compared to almost any other food in my time only eating animals I killed myself, the animal I ate the most was fish from the sea. This reflects a wider trend: far more fish are killed for food than any other animal. It's easy, it's good for you and going fishing is enormous fun.

I know fish are magnificent creatures and quite capable of suffering. I have already mentioned the 2003 study conducted by the University of Edinburgh showing that trout feel 'pain'. In her book *Do Fish Feel Pain?* biologist Victoria Braithwaite says that 'there is as much evidence that fish feel pain and suffer as there is for birds and mammals'. PETA cites Dr Culum Brown of Macquarie University, who on Australian Broadcasting Corporation's *Counterpoint* programme explained that the stress fish experience when they are pulled out of the water into an environment in which they cannot breath is 'exactly the same as a person drowning'. In true PETA-style, a video shows the A-list actor and famous vegan, Joaquin Phoenix, 'drowning' in a swimming pool as his voiceover describes the burning pain of suffocation.

I do not dismiss these studies. After all, suffocating to death in the hold of a ship is how most of the one trillion fish we eat every year die. We should take it seriously. But there is another aspect to why we should eat less fish: the environmental impact of taking nature's last wild animal food. In this chapter I will put more emphasis on this element of the ethics because, frankly, it is at crisis point.

Also, we have more difficulty engaging with fish than with cute furry animals. Almost every vegetarian I know is in fact a 'pescatarian' who will eat fish. Veganomics, a study of the statistics of a plant-based diet, found that 'most people who say they're vegetarian eat meat', largely because they eat fish. I think people are more likely to respond to the frightening statistics on wild fish than an analysis of their nervous systems. It is also one of the few areas of life where consumers can make a difference, simply through understanding some basic labels on their fish.

I gained most of my knowledge about fishing from Charles Clover, my predecessor as the main Environment writer at the *Daily Telegraph*. I arrived at Buckingham Palace Road, where the *Telegraph* was based in 2008, as Charles was leaving, too big and too angry to remain in a modern newsroom. He had bigger fish to fry, investigating the state of global fish stocks.

Like a lot of fishermen, Charles is a gentle man at heart, much happier standing on the banks of the River Stour than roaring at hapless news editors. And like most fishermen, he is a force to be reckoned with when angry. After years of reporting on the state of the oceans, Charles was just about ready to explode. The poor man even got his head around the Common Fisheries Policy (CFP), a feat achieved by very few, including most of our ministers, yet still nothing changed. In the end he wrote a book setting out exactly what is happening. *The End of the Line* opened a lot of people's eyes to what is really happening in the fishing industry and to our oceans. Reading it, you gasp in surprise at our stupidity.

The statistics make for depressing reading. In Europe as a whole more than 80 per cent of fisheries are overfished and three-quarters of fish stocks around the world are being exploited at, or well beyond, sustainable limits. For me the most arresting image is to imagine if we did the same to the African savannah. If we dragged a massive weighted net over the Serengeti ploughing up the grassland and scooping up lions, elephants, antelopes, dung beetles – then throwing half of them away – there would be an outcry. Yet it is what we are doing every day to the bottom of the seabed.

It's not like it happened overnight, but it's only when it starts to hurt that we take notice. In *The Unnatural History of the Sea* Callum Roberts charts the decline of our oceans from the 'abundance' that saw economies built on herring and cod to the listing of cod as 'vulnerable' to extinction by the International Union for Conservation of Nature (IUCN). The decline began with the invention of bottom trawling at the beginning of the 19th century, the practice of dragging weighted nets across the seabed. In 1866 longline fishermen complained to a Royal Commission that already they were seeing a reduction in their catch because of the trawlers. But nothing was done.

During the Second World War, when fishing was impossible because the men were fighting, the stocks recovered. However, afterwards, thanks to the transfer of technology from weapons of mass destruction to fishing boats, we found we had the technology to hoover the surplus up. Radar, echo sounders (once used to locate enemy submarines) and navy-developed electronic navigation helped us to find the fish. Technology was also developing in the processing of fish. In the 1950s fish fingers were invented, allowing us to eat fish in a matter of minutes, rather than having to gut them and tweezer out the pin bones. It also made us forget there were any other fish than cod and haddock, leading to the target of single species. But nothing was done.

In 1992 the cod stocks on the Grand Banks of Canada collapsed. It is hard to express the significance of that. Where once cod were so plentiful 'a man could walk across their backs', there was now nothing, zero, zilch – except for a few pathetically small fish, and the shellfish at the bottom of the food chain. But nothing was done.

Callum Roberts estimates that today we probably have less than 5 per cent of the total mass of fish that once swam in Europe's seas. 'The sea has been put to the plough but we do not sow, we only reap,' he writes. In 2006, a controversial study by Boris Worm of Dalhousie University in Canada predicted there will be virtually nothing left to fish by 2050.

It was clear something needed to be done, so the Common Fisheries Policy (CFP) was set up. This set quotas for different countries, but it soon turned to horse trading. No country criticises another for failing to keep to the scientifically recommended level of fishing because, well, then they'd have to keep to it themselves.

On a global level, it is even worse. Rich countries trawl the oceans of poorer nations to feed their own people, leaving traditional coastal communities struggling to survive. The trawled fish is not even fed to humans, it is to feed the fish farms of the developed world. It's what *The Economist* calls 'the diversion of low-value fish from the mouths of people in developing countries into the mouths of well-fed fish in the developed world'. Or what Charles calls 'an obscenity on an imperial Roman scale'.

It's enough to put anyone off fish, but still we plunder the sea. Fish is more fashionable than ever because of the omega-3s that make us more clever – though apparently not brainy enough to work out how to manage the oceans.

Even in the sleepy hamlet of Ethie Haven, the Ha'en, we've managed to comprehensively screw things up. Off Arbroath later in the autumn, on a charter boat for anglers, I try sea angling with a rod. Seals lounge around the Bell Rock Lighthouse as we haul in dozens of mackerel. But where are the haddock the area is famous for?

The smokies, or smoked haddock, are still made the traditional way in cottages on the seafront. Indeed, the smoked haddock of Arbroath have been given a Protected Geographical Indication (PGI) status so that no one else can dare steal the name. But the haddock are not from Arbroath any more; they are trucked down from the fish market in Peterhead.

Jim Smith, the skipper, remembers when there were more than 20 boats out of Arbroath, just 25 years ago, delivering straight to the smokehouses. Now there are none fishing for white fish, only crustaceans, all that is left at the bottom of the food chain. Jim is one of the lucky ones, making a living from sea angling, but it's not the same; the old skills are being lost. As we chug home, I notice they still have the needles to mend the nets that will never be used again.

The British fishing fleet still exists. It may be a shadow of its former self with just 12,000 fishermen employed, compared to 50,000 in 1938, but it's not just a tourist attraction – not yet. My first fishing trip on a commercial boat is around the south-west coast in the summer. We sail out of Dartmouth while it is still dark, the pleasure yachts around us festooned with fairy lights. As we sail up the River Dart, the horizon begins to lighten, showing up the palm trees and the villas of the 'English Riviera'.

The crew of the *Britannia of Beesands* are silent. They may have seen this a hundred times before, but there is something about a sunrise that humbles a man. We lower our voices, pass around tea, spark up rollies and watch the sun come up. I think perhaps I will enjoy fishing after all.

I am just beginning to relax when Richard, my fellow crew member, pipes up: 'It was just like this before the 1987 Hurricane. Calm as a mill pond ...'

'And you know women are bad luck on a boat,' adds the skipper Stuart.

'Don't worry,' says Scott, the youngest member of the crew and my fellow rookie. 'It was my first trip last week. I was sick everywhere!' He neglects to mention that may be because the others forced him to eat a raw fish. I hope they don't put me through the same initiation. I don't think they will. Women are treated differently on a fishing boat. I am shown the bucket downstairs where I am to pee, though how I will squat in the tiny room is a mystery to me.

'Then chuck it.'

'Er, where?'

'In the sea of course.'

Despite the fact it is dead calm and it's only the English Channel, they have managed to make me feel nervous, but then I am a terrible seagoer, a real landlubber.

Nick Hutchings, the owner of the fishing boat, was practically born at sea, going out from Beesands, a fishing village just a few miles down the coast from where we are now, at only six months old. The village is now mostly holiday cottages and leisure boats. Like farmers forced to diversify, Nick and his family are the last fishermen holding on, converting the old petrol station to a shack where they sell fresh crab rolls and fish suppers. With his beard and canvas fisherman's smock, Nick looks at home on the sea. He lands mostly crabs and whatever he can get gill netting in the summer; it doesn't pay much. It's a struggle to get the crews and to maintain the kit, but he couldn't give it up. 'What can I do? It's in my blood.'

We romanticise fishing and fishermen. Perhaps because it is the last vestige of a hunter-gatherer lifestyle in Britain, the only job where you can make your money from hunting a wild animal. Unless you count poachers, and we probably shouldn't. *Trawlermen* on the BBC and *Trawler Wars* on the Discovery Channel have brought the lives of fishermen into our living rooms: the battles with the weather, the camaraderie on board and the competition with other vessels.

The reality is a little more prosaic. As the sun reaches its zenith we begin to haul in the gill net, a wall of netting with a 36cm (14in) mesh that hangs vertically in the water column catching rays, cod, haddock, crabs and anything else that is motoring along the channel. The net comes creaking up onto a conveyor belt, sloshing water and seaweed and life, like we have just been shopping at the supermarket of the sea. The first ray slips onto the deck, a gorgeous beast from another world, beating her wings and thrashing her tail to get away. It is a female blonde ray, her mottled leopard-skin back like a cheap fur coat. As the body is turned I can see the pale clown's face, the mouth gasping into an eery smile, the nostrils like eyes. Richard throws the body into a box and makes a grab for the next item on the belt.

I try to help untangle the crabs, as the rays, covered in spikes, are too dangerous for a novice. I struggle to keep my footing as the deck becomes slick with the mucus of the rays, oozing off each body. Nick shouts their names for me as they are hauled into boxes – 'a smutty-nosed, a small-eyed, a blonde' – as if describing regulars at the pub. Occasionally there is a turbot, its weird eyes all on one side of its face, as if trying to escape the flat body. Nick grins; that will get a good price at the market.

At one point I notice a lesser spotted dogfish come up in the nets. The beautiful creature lies to the side gasping, the slanted black eyes and pale skin making it look like an alien. I can see the rows of tiny sharp teeth. 'Can't we throw that one back?' I say to Stuart. 'You know it's a shark?'

'I know what it is.' I let it drop. It lies on the deck gasping for breath. Suffocating. I appeal to Nick. 'Crab bait,' he answers. I have learnt an important lesson: never, ever question the skipper. Not even the owner of the boat does that. That's how a crew works. Fishing is not a game.

Once the nets are in, the processing begins. Nick stands at a heavy wooden table at the centre of the deck, his legs akimbo, wielding a sharp knife. He hauls the rays up by their snouts and with two sharp swipes cuts off those powerful wings. The guts are thrown into the sea and soon we are at the centre of a cloud of herring gulls. They stalk the prow of the boat, blinking their cold yellow eyes.

Once the nets are packed up, the men join in the processing. For hours it goes on. Rita Ora and Ellie Goulding are blasting out of the radio as the fish are gutted and sliced, alive. Scott is singing along to the radio, Richard constantly has a damp fag hanging out of his mouth, Stu puffs away on his vape pipe that smells like air freshener. I wish it smelt of proper tobacco to drown out the smell of fish guts.

No one ever asks a fisherman what it's like to kill. 'Everyone has a conscience, you do feel bad, but then you get used to it,' says Richard.

'It's better than the crab processing factory where I used to work,' says Scott.

The men cut the tendons of the crabs, the bellies of the fish, the wings of the rays, taking away their superpowers. The adult gulls fight off the young birds trying to get in on the action. No one has time to eat or drink or watch the dolphins playing in the distance.

Yet this is nothing. I watch *Leviathan*, a documentary that shows the real life on a fishing boat. The film shows one trip on board a trawler out in the North Atlantic, where the men work 20-hour shifts for 18 days in a row. There is no dialogue, only the sound of the cranking metal of the nets, the slosh and slime of the unearthly creatures that come flowing on board, dredged up from the deep. Then the slice and slam of the knives as the meat is processed.

Is there any other commodity for which we take such little care to appreciate where it is from? The lives risked by the men, the brutality of processing the animals alive, the terrible beauty of the angry ocean? Depictions of fishing show the grand vistas, the jolly men singing their songs in bright yellow sou'westers. They don't show the straining, wriggling bodies of the fish as they suffocate and are crushed to death. But that's what happens on a boat.

The processing goes on until we are almost inshore again, back to the other side of Devon: the world of pasties and palm trees and a pint with your fish and chips – which is hopefully local but probably not, probably tilapia from China. It's certainly not these ray wings, which will be sold abroad, or in fancy London restaurants as 'skate wings'. In the UK we export most of our fish, and eat imported fish from Scandinavia or China.

A group of tourists has gathered on the quay to watch the fishing boat come in. Smeared in fish slime and blood, I jump out, running to the nearest pub loo. 'THAT'S fucking fishing,' I want to shout. 'Spit and hard work and blood and mucus. Not those pretty pictures you are taking of men in oilskins unpacking neat rows of white flesh packed in ice. And by the way, I haven't been to the loo for 12 hours!'

Later, I feel a little ashamed of my attitude. For Nick, the day is far from over. Now he has to sell the fish and make some money back – or no one gets paid. It's not an easy way to make a living. 'It's in my blood,' says Nick again and again. I know what he means. It's a precious gift, a skill passed down generation to generation; somehow he has managed to keep hold of it, keep it alive. Who wants to be the one to let it go? To watch it sink to the bottom of the ocean, a buried treasure.

I sit on the quay later, a stuck crab in my bag for my supper, looking through my photos. There is a sunrise and a dogfish – and because I left my camera unguarded for a moment, a lovely picture of Scott's arse. I hoot with laughter. What did I expect from a bunch of fishermen?

Fishermen are not all salty sea dogs – some come wearing suits. Mike Park, the Chief Executive of the Scottish White Fish Producers Association, is dressed in a smart shirt and chinos when I meet him at the Buchan Braes Hotel just outside Peterhead. It is an odd place, the expensive menu and conference rooms reflecting the big money around here from oil and renewables, while outside many of the houses around the harbour are boarded up for good.

Mike can remember the good old days when fishing was the industry that mattered. He was a top skipper for 30 years, including during the 'boom' years in the 1980s, when off Peterhead the fishermen were catching record-breaking hauls of cod and haddock thanks to advances in finding and catching the fish. But it couldn't last. Between 1996 and 2006, annual cod catches in the North Sea plummeted from 80,000 to 20,000 tonnes (88,000 to 22,000 US tons). Fishermen were having to go further and further afield to catch any fish, often straying into other territorial waters and causing the so-called 'cod wars' with Scandinavian countries. Mike himself was arrested twice by the Norwegian authorities for being in areas reserved for their fishing fleets.

It all came to an end in 2006 when a quota was imposed. The Scottish fishing fleet decommissioned most of its vessels – thousands lost their jobs. For Mike it was his 'mea culpa moment'. Like most fishermen I have met, he has a passion for the underwater environment. He could see what was happening to the North Sea. Now he is fighting to keep fishing alive as a 'sustainable' industry. 'I thought, I have caused this, and I feel it is my role in life to help it recover.'

Mike believes there is a way to bring back the fish. Since 2006 certain areas have been closed to protect spawning fish. Instead of using all the fancy new technology to catch fish, it is being used to monitor boats, making it much harder to go over quota – and get away with it. Discards, when unwanted species of fish are thrown overboard, have been banned. Already the haddock coming into Peterhead are certified by the Marine Stewardship Council (MSC), meaning the breeding population has hit a point where it is safe to take a certain amount of fish. There are rumours the cod stocks could soon be labelled MSC.

Mike is working with the WWF to try and educate fishermen on better ways to fish, including using less damaging equipment. The bottom trawlers that still exist are using barrels that go 'bouncing' over the bottom of the seabed, rather than ploughing it up. Mike is not just doing it for the fish; he's doing it for the people. When fishing collapsed in the 1990s, men moved into the oil industry. Now the oil is running out and the people are drifting back. He wants to see the next generation earn their money from the riches of the sea, not just take tourists out on a boat.

In the meantime, much of the labour has been sourced from abroad. Around a quarter of the crews sailing out of Peterhead are foreign, mostly from the Philippines, but also Sri Lanka and Ghana. In the fish processing factories I watch women from Eastern Europe fillet fish, where once it would have been local fishwives and herring girls. A screen monitors the filleting rate of Maureen, Stewart and Pat, and Jolanta, Jevgenija and Ivor. Prawns are sent abroad for processing and then bought back by Britain for scampi. Mike doesn't have a problem with this; it works well for everyone. But unless local young people are encouraged back into the industry there is a risk of losing local knowledge and a fishing culture that has been passed down for generations. 'We need to make it sustainable. For the sake of the next generation, we have to get this back into order.'

The next generation will work in a very different fishing industry. I go down to the quayside to see the kind of boats they are now using. Jess Sparks, the Technical Manager of Seafood Scotland, has agreed to show me around the harbour and give me an education in the boats. The first thing to understand is the different types of fishing: pelagic fish like mackerel and herring, which swim in the centre of the water column in vast shoals, are hoovered up by factory ships worth millions of pounds. These floating leviathans only need to go out a few times a year to fill their quota. Using echo-sounding to find out exactly where the fish are, they surround the fish with a purse seine net and pump whole shoals aboard. The fish are stored alive in the hold of the ship and pumped straight into processing plants when they get back to shore.

In contrast, the trawlers look more like the traditional idea of the fishing boat. These vessels target the demersal fish and shellfish that live at the bottom of the ocean: the haddock, cod and prawns. It is a much more Wild West approach to fishing. Trawlers will go out in heavy seas if the fishing is good and must process all the fish on board, just like the men in Devon, except they can be at sea for weeks on end. It's no wonder the industry has been targeted for reality TV; it's one of the few jobs left that pits humans against nature.

But for all their machismo, Jess insists the fishermen are much more aware of the need to manage a sustainable fishery. 'Fishermen are not here to rape the seas,' he says. 'They invest million and millions in their boats, they risk their lives. We want to make the North Sea sustainable – it's the only way we'll survive.'

The most surprising thing about fish markets is they don't smell of fish. Not the rich fishy smell you associate with the fishmonger or even cooking fish; when a haul comes in packed in ice it smells fresh, like the smell of the sea – the smell of money.

Peterhead has the largest fish market in Europe. Already the auctioneer has sold most of the 4,800 boxes of fish coming in this morning. He stands by a box of hake, a popular fish in Spain, reeling off numbers until deciding on the highest bidder. He moves on, plaice this time – I admire their lovely red spots – long ling, and gurnard with their peevish little mouths. It all looks strangely old-fashioned except for the fact most of the bids are being recorded on iPads. I am amazed by the choice: pollock, pouting, halibut, dab, witch, red mullet, grey mullet, monkfish.

I pose for a photograph with a John Dory, so ugly it can't help but make you smile. My favourite, though, is the haddock with their huge eyes and a thumb print on their cheeks. The mark of St Peter, they call it.

In this emporium of seafood riches, I can't believe that in the UK we eat just five: cod, salmon, haddock, prawns and tuna. Worse, they don't even come from our waters. The majority of our fish is imported, while we export most of the beautiful fish we catch. Around 95 per cent of the cod sold in chip shops is from Iceland or Norway. It doesn't make sense to me. Not only is it boring and probably nutritionally deficient – imagine if you only ate five types of vegetables – but how can you be expected to take an interest in fisheries all over the world? Surely the fish on our doorstep are the most interesting because they are fresh, seasonal and we can make sure they are sustainable. We are a seafaring nation. Isn't is time we got back in touch with fish?

I love sea angling but there is often a sadness behind it. In Arbroath the haddock are all gone from the bay, in the once great fishery of the English Channel they rely on crabs, off the west coast of Scotland there is nothing left and the east coast cod – once the most prolific of all – is not yet out of danger. Again and again the first thing people say to me is, oh Louise, if only you had seen it before, when there were more fish.

Jake Chalmers is no exception. The 63-year-old started fishing with a rod his uncle brought back from Japan. In those days they were made of cane with horse hair for leaders and braided silk for the fly line. The delicate magic wand that could bring creatures from the deep was enough to capture any small boy's heart.

Jake is now team manager of Scotland's sea fishing team, taking part in competitions around the British Isles to catch the biggest fish. Sea angling maybe less glamorous than fly fishing, but it is still an art practised with as much seriousness by its artists. The fishermen cast from the beach with heavy 12ft rods (3.7m), not like the flimsy wands you use for trout. There is a weight attached to the end and a big hook flung out to sea baited with stinking velvet crab or mackerel heads. The fishermen will go out in all weathers, even chaining themselves to rocks to catch the biggest fish. But for Jake it's more about being by the sea than catching the fish. 'You can switch off from everything,' he says. For his day job, Jake is a logistics and transport coordinator at Ninewells Hospital in Dundee. I imagine him at the heart of the NHS, keeping medicines and ambulances flowing, and longing for the sea.

On a sharp January morning, when the sea is more stirring than calming, I join Jake on the rocks beneath Red Head. It feels funny going fishing in winter, after so many summer days fishing mackerel out of the water. But beneath the surface this is when the biggest fish are coming in to the coast.

As we cast out spinning rods baited with crab we watch gulls circle the sandstone cliffs and a seal hunting through the waves. The cormorants are up on the rocks today, their wings closed, making them look more like Victorian ladies in their widow's weeds. It doesn't take long to get a bite. At this time of year the cod come inshore to feed up for spawning before returning to the cooler deep waters in the summer. Jake reels in the cod and I dispatch it on the sharp rocks. I feel a pang of regret but at least she has died quickly rather than suffocating in the nets or the hold of a commercial fishing boat.

I take time to consider the cod, a creature we eat in such abundance, yet rarely take a proper look at. She is over 35cm (14in, the minimum landing size) and probably around two years old. Cod can live up to 20 years and grow to 1.8m (6ft) long. With her powerful muscled body she may have swum as far as Greenland, exploring a world of kelp beds and mud, green seas and icebergs. She is grey, speckled in olive spots, with a neat white lateral line and a charming beard or 'barbel' under her chin which is used to look for food.

Jake says in the past, 12 or 13 of these beautiful fish could be caught in one day, but now you are lucky to get one or two. He blames the trawlers, who have damaged the sport of sea angling as well as the health of the world's oceans. 'What they catch in one net, we would not catch in a lifetime,' he says. I ask Jake about the return of the cod, the ban on discards, the new technology stopping fishermen from going over quota. He doesn't believe it. 'Ach, it's a fankle,' he says, using an old Scots word for a tangle. 'I can understand those boys need their jobs, but, well, where's the fish eh?'

Jake has nine grandchildren and two great-grandchildren but they don't like his freshly caught cod. 'They will not eat my fish – only battered or fish fingers,' he says as he takes out some sewing scissors and carefully cuts open my fish, taking out the egg sacks – raan, as they are called in north-east Scotland. I take my fish and set off home, with strict instructions on how to eat cod roe on toast, leaving Jake to try his luck with another cod. 'All fishermen are optimists,' he says. 'Because if you were a pessimist you would not do it; what keeps you going is hope.'

Charles Clover batters us with some pretty depressing facts but in the end, like a true fisherman, he seems to believe there is hope. Countries like Iceland have proved you can harvest the sea whilst maintaining a sustainable stock. The Scottish North Sea fishery has yet to prove it can do the same, but they are moving in the right direction. On the west coast of Britain the picture is a little more bleak. In a study published in 2010, Callum Roberts warned of an 'ecosystem meltdown' in the Firth of Clyde, mainly because of dredging for scallops and trawling for prawns.

Our best hope may be Marine Protected Areas (MPAs) currently being established around the UK. Originally the government promised 127; it remains to be seen whether enough funds will be put in to police any MPAs properly. The idea is to create a network of marine 'national parks' that will act as a nursery for commercial fisheries, as well as providing an opportunity to boost tourism from sea angling and activities like whale watching.

But ultimately we have to take responsibility for the seas ourselves. In the supermarket look out for the MSC label. It's the most reliable. Retailers are increasingly putting their own 'Responsibly Sourced' label on most fish. Their excuse is that MSC is too expensive or not available. I'm sorry, but that's not good enough. We cannot be expected to trust all of them. If a fish really is responsibly sourced it should be able to get MSC certification.

Eating out, check out Charles Clover's Fish2fork website that tells you whether restaurants are sourcing fish sustainably. You'll be surprised – expensive does not necessarily mean better. You can also order a wee booklet from the Marine Conservation Society (different from MSC – I know, confusing) that will tell you which fish are sustainable. It is very satisfying to bring this out with a flourish in the supermarket and/or restaurant. Do not be ashamed of being a fish geek.

Last of all, try to go sea angling yourself. It is the best way to learn about the amazing wild resources off our coasts, and in one afternoon in the summer you will catch enough mackerel to fill the freezer. Also, the more people start sea angling the more power behind the argument to protect our oceans for all.

My nephews eat the first fish they have caught with gusto, slicing down the spine and scraping off the juicy flesh. I dare them to eat an eyeball and they each pop one into their mouths – I don't even have to bribe them. 'What's the big deal?' they seem to say. Little boys are frightened of nothing. 'Look at these sprats Aunty Lou, they've been eaten twice!'

All the other children have gone to bed. They are up late, with the adults, and something of the occasion seems to have rubbed off on them. They sit quietly eating, absorbed in their supper: fresh roast mackerel with gooseberry sauce. For once, no one is shouting at one another. It feels calm, a rare special day in the summer holidays, a break in the storm of family life. Dad comes in, still in his wellies and wax gilet, splattered with fish scales. 'What happens when you go fishing with Aunty Lou?' he asks.

'Umm?' I try to look innocent.

'You capsize?'

'The boat sinks.'

Everyone has a suggestion. It's not very funny.

'The fishing gear gets in a fankle,' says Dad.

I follow him outside. It is a delicious evening, the soft pink light of Scottish summer. We sit on the bench outside. Dad sits on one end and I on the other, the tangle of lines in the middle. We work in silence, slowly unfankling the knots.

CHAPTER THIRTEEN

The Leaper

The charm of fishing is that it is the pursuit of what is elusive but
attainable, a perpetual series of occasions for hope.

John Buchan

The mists are rising off Birnam Wood, clinging to the tops
of the pine trees, as I drive up to Dunkeld. It is one of the
hottest days of the summer but the hay is still damp, stacked
in rows in one last desperate attempt to dry it before the
storm comes. Oystercatchers pick at the soft earth and a
buzzard hangs in the still air.

My first glimpse of the Tay under the Thomas Telford
Bridge is glassy black, not blue. The peat has turned the
water the colour of weak tea. It is one of my favourite parts
of Scotland, almost perpetually autumnal in a misty, Keatsian
sort of way. Beatrix Potter used to holiday here and you can

see why: there is a bosomy softness to Perthshire that is missing in the harsher environment of the true Highlands. It has been manicured, too, to suit the Victorian taste. Silver firs and beech trees line the drive to Dunkeld House, the ultimate sporting lodge.

I wander down to the fishing hut, surprising some American tourists on their way to tennis. 'Wellies? In this weather?' They clearly do not know Scotland. The hut is a refuge for stressed city folk, taking their time over this most laid-back of pastimes, discussing flies and techniques, the one that got away. No one is in a hurry; today is a day for stories, not fishing.

Simon Furniss, the ghillie, selects a garish fly compared to the delicate trout flies, and we get into a boat to drift down the river. It's really too hot for fishing and we both know it. The black water eddies and flows, speckled by foam, always going at just the right pace. The blossom drifts by. Usually I'd want to swim in the river on a day like this and in a way it pains me to be fully clothed and in a boat. But perhaps this is a better way to get to know the river? The wildlife doesn't seem to notice us. The alders and birch are wilting in the heat, trailing their branches in the river like fingers. The red campion, bluebell and cow parsley remind me of Devon lanes. Grey wagtails flash yellow, swallows dive and dart.

Simon says there aren't as many salmon as there used to be. By the end of the season he is proved right: Scotland suffers its lowest salmon rod catch for 63 years. The mystery of where they have all gone is complicated and my brain swirls like the water below. Climate change? Netting? Hydro schemes? Fish farming?

We go through different pools wishing for a fish. More for fun than in the hope of catching anything, we inspect Miss Ballantine's Pool where the UK's biggest salmon was caught in 1922. Georgina Ballantine's 29kg (64lb) record has been challenged a couple of times, but I don't think anyone wants to break it and break the link with that charming picture of a young woman on the banks of the river in her baggy tweed suit. It tells of a more innocent time, when the salmon kept running and the river was an endless source of food. So many other records have been set by women that it has led to speculation that the male fish may be attracted to female pheromones rubbed off on the bait as it is handled. Couldn't it just be because we are better at fishing? My Aunty Denise proved the rule one summer on the Carron. The men had given up early and she was fishing alone when she landed a huge fish. She had no one to help land it and no way of killing it so she whacked it on the back of the head with her mobile phone. Nowadays she could have taken a selfie with her mobile but this was in the day of the Nokia 'bricks' that had no camera. A photo taken with an old-fashioned SLR does hang on the wall of her kitchen showing Aunty Denise in her full wax waterproofs, the modern tweed, holding an enormous salmon, just a touch of Miss Ballantine in her triumphant smile.

I'm not very good at fishing – my casting needs improvement – but I'm good at listening. Simon tells me his story. He used to be a dairy farmer and gradually made his passion, fishing, his job. 'I think if you listen to the river, it tells you where to go,' he says.

The sun is high in the sky, the fish are at the bottom of the river. We drift down to the Cathedral Pool: surely here, surely? I remember a service my brother and I were forced to sit through at Dunkeld Cathedral one Easter. In furtive whispers we were discussing a KitKat I had bought that week which deliciously and surprisingly – like a magic Willy Wonka bar – had one solid chocolate finger. I recall nothing of the minister's words but something of the spirit of Easter must have entered our brains because we spoke about the KitKat sermon thereafter: the idea that one must have faith; your next KitKat could always be the one with the solid chocolate finger.

I think of faith drifting on the river. Fishermen have always had faith.

No one knows why a salmon takes a fly. He is not hungry; he does not feed in fresh water. In fact his intestines have shrivelled, making it impossible to eat. He is in the river for one reason and one reason only: to mate. Yet he will take a fly. It is a matter of irritating the fish, of catching his attention, getting 'a rise'. Like teasing your little brother until he cries – or thumps you. It is a pure example of human contrariness and curiosity.

The life cycle of the Atlantic salmon has mystified humans for millennia, perhaps because we know so little about it. We do know how the animals mate. You can watch them in a shallow moonlit stream: the female flicking her tail to make the nest or 'redd' then laying her perfect little pink eggs; the male joining her, pumped up on his own importance – he has turned red, his lips elongated into an aggressive hook shape or 'kype'. Lying alongside her he will fertilise the eggs, as together they shiver against the current.

The alevin, like little tadpoles, are born into burns and tributaries in spring, turning to fry, indistinguishable from the other tiny fish you will see darting away from the riverbank, and eventually into fatter, more fishy parr. I catch one on the River Ure. He has blackened marks along his golden body, as if someone with sooty fingers has picked him up, interspersed with smart red spots. I post a picture on Twitter of my 'brownie'. In a few seconds I am corrected. 'It's a salmon parr Louise!' Apparently you can tell by the streamlined body and lack of orange on the adipose fin, closest to the tail. Well, now I know. The wonders of social media.

Like the ugly duckling, the 'brownie' salmon parr will remain an unprepossessing inhabitant of the river for a

couple of years before turning into a beautiful smolt. He
will turn silver, growing a layer of guanine crystals that act
as mirrors, camouflaging the fish by reflecting its
surroundings, as if putting on Harry Potter's invisibility
cloak. Like the sea trout, the smolt also has a major
personality change, being suddenly seized with a courage
and sense of adventure that will take him to sea for who
knows how long, who knows where? Finally he is a salmon,
the king of fish, travelling thousands of miles to Greenland
to feed on krill and sardines, before returning to the river of
his birth. There are many theories as to how the salmon
navigates back to the exact place where he hatched. Is it
smell? Geomagnetic fields? One thing the fisherman knows
is that he will come back. No one can tell when or how, but
the salmon always return.

The mystery of salmon has always intrigued and inspired
our cultures. The Native Americans would handle the fish
pointing upstream so the soul could continue its journey.
The Celts associated eating salmon with wisdom, as if
digesting the meat would impart some of the mystery of its
survival. As with many myths, they weren't far wrong as the
omega-3s in salmon flesh are good for brain function and
mental health.

Is it any wonder salmon beliefs outnumber those of any
other fish? Salmon occupy salt water, fresh water, the air.
They are almost shape-shifters. Later in the summer I go to
watch the salmon I failed to catch leaping up the river at
Dunkeld. It is just after the Edinburgh Festival and we have
spent a month watching humans leap and tumble and fly in
the circus tents. But it is nothing compared to the salmon.
At Hermitage Waterfall we watch them leap and fall, and
leap and fall, again and again. I wonder whether they will
ever make it upstream, but still they keep trying. You can see
why the Victorians built a series of follies along the river,
a sort of shrine to these magnificent creatures. It is not just
the beauty of the fish flashing black in the white water, it is

the spirit of determination, to make it upstream to their birthplace, whatever the odds.

The word salmon comes from the Latin 'salar', to leap. Perhaps the greatest leap salmon have ever taken is from one of the most wild and free animals of our imagination to fish farming.

In the past salmon was seen as a luxury product, a fish one could only enjoy fresh during the salmon runs when the fish return from the sea, or if you were lucky enough to know a salmon fisherman (or poacher). The idea of farming such a wild creature seemed unthinkable. Fish farming of vegetarian species like carp has existed for thousands of years, especially in the Far East and in Britain around monasteries. But carnivorous migratory fish were never seriously considered, until the 20th century when people realised a luxury item could be grown on the scraps of the fishing industry.

Salmon farming started in the fjords of Norway and soon spread to Scotland. The first farms in the 1960s were bodged out of planks and nets in sea lochs. It seemed the perfect industry. Scots already knew how to breed salmon and there was little else to do in terms of industry. The government jumped on the bandwagon, keen to encourage revenue and employment in remote areas suffering from depopulation and poverty. Grants were handed out and little attention was paid to environmental regulation. By 2015 salmon had become the largest food export in Britain. In comparison to sheep and pigs, which took thousands of years to domesticate, salmon became a 'farm animal' within a few decades. What could possibly go wrong?

If you thought the life cycle of the wild salmon was complicated, wait until you hear about the farmed salmon. The eggs used in Scotland are generally from Norwegian broodstock. Our own salmon has not been selectively bred to produce the kind of 'domesticated' salmon that are best suited to farming. Like pigs, where most of the genetics are owned by the Danes, and chickens, where most of the genetics are owned by the Americans, most of the genetics of salmon are owned by the Norwegians.

The eggs are placed in temperature-controlled tanks in a freshwater hatchery, where they turn into the tiny little alevins. Once they 'smoltify' they are transferred to a freshwater loch to be grown in cages or bigger tanks in a recirculation plant.

Like babies, after a few weeks the smolts are given their vaccinations against the three main diseases. I presumed this would be done through the feed, but no, salmon get their jabs. In Scotland it is mostly done by hand: the smolts are emptied onto a giant tray and one by one held against the side and injected with a device like a staple gun. In Norway, where the industry is more developed, the smolts are pushed through a machine that holds and injects each individual fish. If you don't vaccinate fish, you could lose half the crop.

After about a year smolts are transported to sea in well-boats, or slung in containers beneath a helicopter. You can see them sometimes, hovering over the lochs like military food aid. Once in the sea, the smolts will do their magic and turn into salmon, but instead of swimming to Greenland, they swim round, and round, and round, and round …

Fish farming is big business in Scotland. Still, it's hard to get my head around it, without swimming in circles. In the end I decide to follow a salmon from farm to fork with the world's largest fish-farming company, Marine Harvest, a Norwegian multinational that produces around a third of Scotland's farmed salmon.

I visit a fish farm on Loch Leven. The cages floating on deep black water look out towards Glen Coe. You could not get a more spectacular setting, but it's still a factory farm: the animals are in cages where they must defecate and urinate in the same water. Scotland's salmon aquaculture industry is estimated to produce the same amount of nitrogen waste as the untreated sewage of 3.2 million people, just over half the country's population. The twelve cages, 24m square (258 sq ft) and 15m (49ft) deep, hold around 20,000 salmon each. I am told they have a lot of space, officially taking up just 1 per cent of the caged water. Occasionally one leaps out, but mostly they swim in thick shoals at the surface.

The salmon are fed pellets that rain down in regular intervals from an automated rotator; it makes the clear Highland air smell slightly musty rather than fishy. The pellets are made up of vegetable oils, including soya, and fish meal including oils. The fish oil is necessary to produce the omega-3s the consumer demands and is the most controversial aspect of salmon farming. Marine Harvest insists it has got the proportion of fish meal down to a quarter, made up of scraps from the processing industry and 'sustainable' wild stocks. But concern remains about the hoovering up of anchovies and herring to provide fish meal to feed to salmon. Is it really an efficient way to use our fast-diminishing wild stocks? To feed them to caged predator fish? Experimentation is ongoing to see if omega-3s can be introduced into plants through genetic engineering, or if salmon can be fed algae. In the meantime, eating a carnivorous fish produced in Scotland may have far-reaching consequences in oceans across the world.

The most expensive component in the feed is perhaps the most important, other than the fish oil to retain the omega-3s – the yeast extract to retain the colour. In the wild the salmon would eat crustaceans that make their flesh pink, but on this diet the flesh is white. The producers once tried to sell 'ivory' salmon but it did not go down well. To produce the same carotenoids, astaxanthin is added to the feed, a derivation of yeast. On this mega-diet, the fish are fully grown in three years, some reaching the length of two arms. In comparison, during the same time a wild salmon may still be swimming around in the burn of his birth wondering when to go to sea.

Nowadays CCTV will watch the animals to monitor when they need feed so that protein is not wasted in the sludge under the cages. We walk into the control room, like a security centre in a multistorey car park; CCTV watches each and every corner. The screens flash up showing salmon dashing and gliding as the pellets fall from the sky. Alarms go off if the carbon dioxide, oxygen, pH or anything else go beyond a certain level. It reminds me more of an intensive chicken farm than anything I have seen so far in the fishing world. Everything is controlled.

Under the nets I hear a faint bleeping sound, like an old-fashioned computer connecting or faint Morse code. It's the 'seal scrammer'. Seals have been a huge problem for fish farmers in the past. Like foxes around a hen coop, they can't quite resist these seemingly easy pickings. Marine Harvest claims the problem can be solved by the so-called 'seal blinds' that send out noise to scare the seals when they come close. It is also about properly tensioned nets and making sure dead fish are not rotting at the bottom of the nets, to reduce temptation. In the worst-case scenario, when you have a seal who just gets it into his head and keeps coming back, the company applies for a licence and an appointed marksman will kill the seal. It's just like the fox control that a farmer would do every day, but because we are less used to losing the wonderful seal it attracts greater protest.

It's not just seals eating the salmon, it's also sea lice. As with pigs and chickens, when salmon are put in a cage together disease spreads. The little sea lice, like tiny blood-sucking crabs, eat the salmon alive. A few is OK, perhaps even healthy, but a thick covering will kill a fish. Mortality on fish farms can be as high as 20 per cent, much higher than on terrestrial farms.

Since the 1990s vaccines have reduced the need for so many antibiotics but still, throughout their lives in the cages, salmon will be 'treated' for a number of illnesses, mostly sea lice. Strong chemicals are also used to clean the nets of shellfish. In 2011, 35 medicines were licensed to keep salmon clean and 25 anti-fouling substances were available to unclog nets and cages. Many are similar to hydrogen peroxide and there are concerns that chemicals designed to target sea lice will also kill baby prawns and other shellfish, damaging another important industry in Scotland.

I am told on Loch Leven there are just three sea lice on each salmon on average. Marine Harvest attributes the cleanliness of its fish to another little fish, the wrasse. We watch the punctilious cleaner fish darting out of its 'hide' within the salmon cages. Wrasse eat sea lice and have helped to clean up the problem. But it is not quite a panacea. The wild wrasse population itself is under threat and the species cannot possibly eat all the sea lice.

An online report on the Marine Harvest fish farm in Torridon shows an outbreak of sea lice 20 times the recommended limit in the spring of 2015 – just near where George Monbiot and I were fishing on Loch Dughaill. Once released, that little trout caught by his tail had to negotiate a cloud of sea lice. Unlike wild salmon that continue out into the ocean, sea trout stick around feeding by the coast, which is why they are so susceptible to the sea lice problem. Is it any wonder the sea trout population in Scotland has collapsed? Anti-fish farm protesters say that sea lice are damaging wild stocks of both sea trout and wild salmon, and in Norway farms suffering outbreaks are closed down. In Scotland the advertising suggests salmon is farmed in a pristine environment. Salmon is certainly farmed in a beautiful setting, but after they have been vaccinated and treated for sea lice, I'm left wondering how natural they really are?

Mallaig Harbour at night cranks and gurgles, kids mess around with an old shopping trolley and the last of the tourists depart the ferry from Skye. A mural on one of the old warehouses shows scenes from the fishing industry. It is almost Soviet in style, showing strong men steering boats and netting fish. It's what fishing is really about – what it's still about – the brutality and bravery, the skill.

The Marine Harvest harvesting station, lit up like a Christmas tree, is easy to find. Alongside it is moored the *Ronja Atlantic*, ready to pump in fish collected from the farms that day via a giant pipe. The well-boat, crewed by Norwegians, has a Jacuzzi and a sauna on board and all the latest technology. Television screens show the salmon swimming round and round in the 'well' at the bottom of the ship. It is all much more civilised than the old days when the salmon would simply be emptied onto old carpet spread out on the quay and killed one by one by lines of men with priests. 'Back-breaking work it was,' one old boy told me, 'and you should have smelt those carpets …' Now the salmon come into a pristine factory. The hygiene swabs have been done and the aluminium steel shines like a bar of silver.

Martin Boyce, the manager tonight, was a fisherman for 20 years. He skippered trawlers, dredgers, creel boats. Now he skippers a factory. 'This is a better lifestyle,' he says. 'A lot healthier'. On the boats you could be out of work for much of the winter, then when the weather was right it was 18-hour shifts processing fish in gale-force winds. 'This is regular work,' says Martin, 'making something we can be proud of.'

It is all fishing families employed at the plant, 18 in total. According to the Scotland Salmon Producers' Organisation

(SSPO), over 2,500 people are employed in salmon production in Scotland. The Scottish government estimates that over 8,000 jobs are generated directly or indirectly by the aquaculture industry. I had gone into this cynical about Marine Harvest's claims of keeping local areas alive. It is so often an excuse to pollute the environment. But the people I meet on the west coast of Scotland say it is a good employer, it can be fitted in with crofting, and it's kept the fishing families in the area. After all, the fish are all gone, except for the crustaceans at the bottom of the food chain. I know many an environmentalist who has moved to the west coast and found their resistance against fish farms crumble in the face of the economic argument and the death stares down the pub.

At midnight on the dot, the fish start coming. They slide down the metal chute, at first one or two, then dozens, ranging from the length of one arm to two. They should leap, but they slide, unstoppable towards death. It is a noisy chaos that will go on for about 90 minutes, up to 115 fish a minute, before the men get a break. By the end of the night, they can do a small fish farm's worth: 45,000 fish.

What strikes me about the fish is how alive they are. How they wriggle and move and thrash. Yet it is nothing like when you land a fish: there is no reverence, there is no time. Fishing, they have the advantage. They are underwater and we are on land. Here we have turned the tables. On land, they are ours. As they slide to the bottom the fish are directed through a tunnel where a percussive stun knocks them out and then their gills are cut from the bottom. Men in yellow anoraks direct the salmon towards the tunnel and check the gills are properly cut. Blood splatters up the walls. Martin points out the inspector looking out for 'misshapes': like intensively farmed pigs with hernias, there are animals with hunchbacks and other abnormalities.

The priests are still there for the killing. Occasionally a leaper will jump off the table and have to be killed on the floor with the wooden stick. I watch it happen more than once. It is just as brutal as a fishing boat, noisy and slimy and bloody. But as Martin points out, the fish will only spend 20 seconds in the harvesting station, whereas on a trawler they would suffocate to death. This is the RSPCA-accredited way of doing things – a percussive stun, as quickly as possible.

Martin tells me the story of the RSPCA inspector who liked to 'get right in there' and check the salmon are being processed properly. 'Of course by the end of the night, he was covered in blood ... He went back to his hotel at 3 am and gave the nightwatchman an 'affie fright'. I imagine the empty hotel corridor, already reminiscent of *The Shining*, and a man wandering down it in his blood-splattered suit. No wonder the poor man nearly had a heart attack.

I see what the RSPCA is trying to do with high-welfare salmon. But for me it's not just the killing of these magnificent creatures, it is the diminution of their wildness. We have brought these magical fish, which can swim for tens of thousands of miles, change colour and shape, dive down and swim up, to this? Compared to the salmon hauled out by Georgina Ballantine and others, admired and eaten with gratitude, it seems a very different death.

Tankers full of snow are ready to take the fish away; the ice soon turns pink with blood, like a strawberry slush puppy. There is a Gaelic saying: only a child, a woodcock or a salmon looks beautiful in death. The tankers become just another one of those lorries you see on the motorway and have no idea what it is. The fish that die on Sunday night could be on our shelves by Wednesday or in China, one of the main customers, by Thursday.

Martin says the plant is due to expand, there is such demand for fresh, farmed fish. As he tells me about his salmon tikka masala – a favourite in his house – I notice the blood in his hairnet.

On the way back I take a closer look at the mural on the harbour wall. It shows the men and women on the processing line. It also shows the fish floating above, as if in heaven. It was a hard, harsh business and it has been replaced by another one. They should be proud. We should be grateful.

The processing at Fort William is different. Most of the workers are from Eastern Europe or Russia, just like the processing of sea fish at Peterhead. Unlike in Mallaig, where there are few other jobs, in Fort William the Scots work in tourism and the food processing industry once again relies on a migrant workforce.

When I arrive the female receptionist is chatting away in Polish. Workers wander past in tracksuit bottoms and T-shirts decorated with SpongeBob SquarePants or Disney characters to have a smoke outside. There is a shinty shirt on display, worn by a team Marine Harvest sponsor, and posters of the 'pure' environment where salmon comes from. Golden eagles soar over the pristine lochs and wild mountains: the 'Scottish Premium' that adds value to products.

Marine Harvest wants to talk about the 'blue revolution'. Already the amount of farmed fish has doubled in the last decade to 70 million tonnes (77 million US tons) and is expected to increase by an additional 70 per cent by 2030. Fish farming is the fastest growing animal-based food-producing sector in the world. Fish are cold-blooded, so do not waste energy keeping warm. As a result, their feed-to-protein ratio is much lower than a lot of meats.

There is also the argument that fish farming takes pressure off the seas. Already aquaculture is providing more than half of the fish we eat and is expected to grow. It seems like the perfect solution to overfishing the oceans, as long as we respect the 'biological limits'. Like sea fishing, fish farming has recently been forced to admit that 'the industry has become too large for the receiving environment'. Certainly in the developed world, where use of antibiotics, escapes and sea lice are now well known, they are having to clean up their act. Scotland raises 163,000 tonnes (180,000 US tons) of salmon at the moment but Marine Harvest itself admits the maximum that could be produced within environmental limits is 210,000 tonnes (231,000 US tons) by 2020 and 300,000 by 2030.

Led by Norway, fish farming is changing. It has had to. Use of antibiotics on farmed fish in Norway in the 1980s was more than in all farmed animals and humans combined. It is now a fraction of what it was because of vaccines, although they are still used. In the same way, use of fish stocks under threat has been reduced by replacing fish meal with other proteins and finding alternatives. Sea lice remain a running sore, with the use of treatments greatly reduced and salmon farms sited away from river mouths, but the lice still pose a threat to the greater environment.

Marine Harvest Scotland already operates four hatcheries, four freshwater loch sites and 49 sea farms situated in Lochaber, Skye, Lochalsh, Wester Ross, Argyll and the Western Isles. In the future farms are going to be based more around the islands and the company insist they will only be built with the blessing of the community. About five years ago a referendum on the Isle of Canna refused a Marine Harvest farm, but on Colonsay and Muck they voted in favour.

In future salmon farming could become much cleaner by 'recirculating' both the water and the energy produced. The smolts could be raised on land, while the salmon farmed offshore are out of the way of river entrances where sea trout and other salmon swim. The dead fish and waste from the farms could be used to produce energy in anaerobic digesters. I expect you will still have those pristine lochs on the label, but how salmon is farmed will be very far from that bucolic image – as far as an intensively farmed pig is from the fields and barns on its packaging.

There is a way to judge how sustainable fish farms are: in the same way the Marine Stewardship Council gives the MSC label, the Aquaculture Stewardship Council or ASC label denotes sustainably farmed fish. There is only one problem. At the time of writing, only two farms in Scotland have an ASC label. By 2020 Marine Harvest wants all its fish farms to be ASC.

I watch the salmon being gutted and packaged in the busy plant. Some 50,000 fish are processed a day by around 100 staff. Men and women direct the salmon, arrived this morning from the harvesting station, through machines where they are automatically gutted. The filleting is fast and furious. I lean in close. 'Wash your hair with lemon juice,' recommends the friendly Polish receptionist as I leave. 'For the smell.'

The idea of 'sustainable' fish farming is a nice one. But is it too late? Is the genie – or more precisely the gene – already out of the bottle?

Domesticated salmon regularly escape the cages. They are slightly slobbish animals that can't be bothered to migrate, and grow at twice the rate of a wild salmon. But they can mate with the wild population. Gradually, like domestic cats mating with wildcats in Scotland, the farmed salmon are entering the native gene pool. In a process of hybridisation, known as the 'extinction vortex', they are slowly diluting the 'pure' native breed in many areas.

An even greater threat to the salmon gene pool is GM salmon escaping. An article in the *Daily Telegraph* in 2010 by one Louise Gray predicted GM salmon would be on the shelves 'within a year'. It now looks like it will take a little longer, but it is increasingly likely that it will happen. The US food authorities have authorised a GM salmon that could enter the food chain as soon as 2018. The

GM salmon not only grows faster but also in colder climates, opening up new areas of the world to aquaculture.

Will 'The Leaper' make the ultimate leap and become the first genetically engineered domestic animal? I can't help wondering if it has already come this far because we can handle the idea of a 'Frankenstein fish' more easily than a pig, which is just that little bit closer to ourselves. The companies developing GM salmon insist the animals would be sterile and unable to escape from cages on land, and the meat would be safe to eat. Perhaps the consumer will accept it as part of the reality of raising protein for nine billion people, but I can't help thinking that perhaps we should try and work out how to farm fish sustainably – or at least find ways to feed the fish without plundering the oceans – before filling the cages with GM fish.

Only time will tell how science will change this great, wild, sparkling fish. But at the rate I am going, by the time I catch an Atlantic salmon, I wonder if it will even be a proper wild salmon at all.

If anyone can save the salmon, it's the anglers who catch them. I know that sounds dangerous – the hunter protecting the hunted – but in the case of fishing it is true. Anglers will generally put fish back. They don't have to, they choose to. They hunt the fish because of a fascination with and love of the environment.

It is an environment that is increasingly under threat. Like the canaries in the coal mine, fishermen were the first to notice a change in the riparian environment. The salmon they wait so patiently for have hit record low numbers around the world, including in Scotland. Salmon are under threat from a number of causes. The most persistent and difficult to understand is climate change. Warmer temperatures are pushing the krill that salmon feed on

further north, but they still have to come back to the same
natal stream, making it a longer, more dangerous journey.
There is also the threat of fishing at sea. Although salmon
are not targeted, they are often caught up in the 'by-catch'.

Netting, the traditional way of catching salmon as they
return to river mouths from the sea, has been going on for
centuries. Fishermen have always protested but in recent
years have had success in persuading salmon netters and
those fishing with drift nets to leave the salmon to spawn.
Often this has been done out of the anglers' own pockets –
with no help from government – by fundraising to pay
the salmon netters off. Netting has fallen from 100,000
salmon a year in 1990 to 13,000 twenty years later in the
UK. Embarrassingly, one of the few places where salmon
netting survives is off Scotland just north of Arbroath.

Anglers also bring money in for the maintenance and care
of rivers. In Scotland angling is worth £123m (US$172m).
OK, it's hardly the £500m (US$700m) earned from the
salmon farming industry, but money from angling stays with
local people through hotels and ghillies. Fishing also has a
role to play in looking after the nation's mental health. I have
lost count of the number of people who told me stepping
into a river for that annual meditation helped them recover
from grief, trauma or just the everyday stress of modern life.

Anglers are as much part of the ecosystem as the salmon;
a link to a vibrant, strong, living animal, to a hunting past.
Often they wear tweeds and could be described as toffs, but
more often they are ordinary people who care about their
rivers and fight hard to keep them alive. The fishermen
understand all the threats to the salmon but still they have
faith the salmon will always come back.

Stepping into a river is like stepping into a different world.
On the Spey winter is holding on, even though it is March.

I can feel the snow rushing down from the Cairngorms through my waders. The cold gets into your bones and never leaves. Compared to the soft peaty Tay it is a hard, unforgiving environment.

Yet still the salmon come. We are here to catch springers, salmon returning from the sea to spawn, silver from swimming in the cool blue depths and fat from feeding on the riches of the ocean. Perhaps Scotland seems warm after the Arctic temperatures of Greenland. I practise my Spey cast again and again, trying to make a figure of eight. Sunshine sparkles on the black river and the songbirds promise spring.

Steve Harrod, my 'fishing buddy' and a much more experienced fisherman, is further up the bank casting beautifully, letting the fly fall like thistle down, rather than my unsubtle splash. Steve is good at fishing for the same reason any of us are good at anything: it is a necessary part of his life, his meditation, what keeps him sane. I think I am beginning to understand why. I cast out, let the line drift down with the current, move a step along, repeat. Even if we catch nothing, I feel lucky to be here on this beautiful river. The swallows are just returning, martins collect mud for their nests and sandpipers see-saw along the rocks. Red squirrels knock the last of the snow from the branches, chased by Steve's Jack Russell Ernie.

The Castle Grant beat used to be full of family parties fishing together throughout the year, but it's quiet now. The salmon have gone and families today have other things to do. It's a shame. I can hardly think of a nicer thing to do than meditate together on the banks of a river.

A flumpf of falling snow makes me look up and then Steve shouts. I see a flash of silver; it must be a real springer. Steve lets the line run out in order to exhaust the animal before reeling it in. I fall out of the river and trip up the bank in waders too big for me, grabbing the net. It's a striking fish, flashing purple and blue as it is reeled in. As we

bring the net to the bank we realise it is not a salmon at all;
it is a rainbow trout escaped from a nearby fish farm. That is
the nature of fishing, I guess. You never get quite what
you expect.

As a true sportsman Steve is disappointed, but I am
thrilled. Supper! I kill it quickly and cleanly with a blow to
the head. Government agencies specifically asks anglers to
net escapees from fish farms if they find them as, like farmed
salmon, they can spread disease. It feels like it was meant to
be. A fine fish I can take back and share with my friends.

It is my cousin's birthday and I rightly assume she would
love a 2.9kg (6.5lb) trout for her dinner party. Sure enough,
the next day a group of doctors tuck into trout grilled with
lemon and butter. Not including me we manage to feed five
– though not quite five thousand – with the help of a
supplementary farmed rainbow trout from the supermarket.
I notice the farmed fish is flabby in comparison to the sleek
rainbow trout that must have spent at least two years free in
the river. The 'chubby trout' also has a blunt tail and barely
any fin, as if he has never had to truly swim.

Just like when I have served other meat, the diners are
eager to know where their dinner came from and I am keen
to tell them. After all, I am a fisherman now, I am allowed
to exaggerate.

CHAPTER FOURTEEN

Damh

For wildlife lives in balance, where nothing kills for joy,
With man the one offender to this old survival law.
Where nature in her wisdom does every beast employ,
Man, so wise, yet ignorant, seeks only to destroy.
'The Barren Hill' by Hugh MacNally,
featured in *Highland Deer Forest*

The aspen turn first. I notice them, not because of the bright yellow leaves against the green birch and rowan, but because of the sound. Even in the slightest breeze they quake and quiver – hence the Latin name, *Populus tremula*. The distinctive rustling was thought to be the voices of the spirits, singing to anyone patient enough to listen. I walk beneath the silver trunks growing straight out of a rocky gorge by the River Balgy, listening.

An aspen clone might be thousands of years old, a root system waiting patiently in the rocks to send out trees that last a mere 150 years. A stand is a sign of ancient woodland, along with the cow-wheat, finished bluebells and fading foxgloves dotted along the path. I follow the river down towards evidence of human habitation, ruined crofts and beneath that middens full of discarded bones and shellfish. People have lived here for thousands of years too, harvesting the sea and bringing back deer from the mountain.

As usual I am looking for otters on Loch Torridon, and, as usual, not having much luck. I find their own midden: conch shells with satisfying tooth marks on them, mussels and oysters and the spines of fish broken up into neat little platelets. I crumble the spraint in my fingers, and sure enough, it smells like jasmine tea.

I sit down to wait – perhaps they will come. A huge blue and silver dragonfly motors over to investigate me, bumping against my shoulder like a sniffing dog. I can hear the stags bellowing behind me on Ben Shieldaig. Ahead in the distance Ben Alligin, the Jewel, still glints green, and beyond her the mountains are hazy blue. It is the soft end of the summer; everything is wilted but not quite yet dead, just about ready to turn. Even the late salmon in the river, waiting for the rains to come so they can leap up the burns to spawn – or die in the attempt – are slowly turning red.

I am coming to the end of my year too, one more task to go. I am nervous about it, my heart fluttering like the aspen leaves. This is my last attempt at a red deer stag, having gone stalking up here before and deciding not to shoot. I stare out to sea trying to work out how I feel. I should enjoy it – this is a privilege, to go on a stalk with my father. I know what I am doing now, I can say no, I am in control of this. My feelings see-saw with the call of the oystercatchers, between excitement and fear.

A nose emerges and some ears. An otter? A selkie? No, a young seal. He bobs about, watching me curiously, not sure what to make of this legless beast: a wolf? A mermaid? I lean over and crawl forward. See? I'm not a human. Look, four legs. I'm just another animal. I came from the sea, just like you. I can swim. I like fish. I won't hurt you. I hear a derisive snort as he goes back underwater. 'I know exactly what you are.'

I pick over the stones and find a piece of driftwood shaped like a stag's antlers. It fits into my hand, smooth as bone, pressing against my fingers like the grip of a friend; a talisman. I slip it into my pocket. Perhaps it will bring me luck? For what, I'm not sure.

The base rock in Torridon, Lewisian gneiss, is some of the oldest on Earth, dating back a couple of billion years. Laid over the top, the Torridonian sandstone, which gives many of the mountains their red peaks, is 900 million years old. And over the top of that, the grey or white Cambrian quartz is just 500 million years old. Yet nothing stays still for long: the mountains are rising, and have risen 70m (230ft) since the end of the Ice Age 10,000 years ago when sea levels separated Britain from mainland Europe.

Humans only got here 7,000 years ago and that is because we were following the deer, which were in turn following the retreating ice. Mesolithic humans hunted the deer for their meat and their skins, also using the antlers and bones for tools. How he – or she – managed to catch the ancient red deer is a matter of conjecture. The most likely method was probably digging pits or climbing trees and hurling down heavy stones or spears.

Red deer in those days were twice the size they are today because the ancient Caledonian Forest covering the mountains provided better feeding. As the forest retreated because of climate change and felling by man, the deer also shrank.

As people developed tools, they were used to catch the deer, and celebrate the hunt. Some of the earliest evidence of humans in Scotland are Pictish carvings of deer in the rocks. The Celts saw the stag as the God of Plenty, bringing meat and skins, antlers to carve jewellery and shamanic powers to whoever could control it. In medieval times, as the land was enclosed, deer became an animal preserved for kings and hunting forests. Dogs drove deer through the glens into circles of men known as 'tinchels' who would kill the deer with spears and daggers.

The role of the deer as the ultimate hunting trophy in a way saved it, making sure that at least some of the deer forests were preserved as the land was cleared for sheep farming in the 18th century. While the rest of Britain became increasingly urban, the deer forests, although in fact land now largely bare of trees, managed to survive. The deer remained a staple for the people left living in the Highlands and a source of pride in songs and poems to this day. Gaelic songs celebrate the stalking of the deer before the southerners came and made it into a very different pursuit.

In the 19th century the Victorians elevated the 'sport' of hunting deer to a pastime to be enjoyed by the rich and leisured. A season was established in late summer/early autumn when the stags are rutting; they are high on the hill, at their most glorious, tastiest and easiest to identify. It was also an opportunity, perhaps, for a new breed of industrialised men and women, unfamiliar with the hunt, to accompany a stalker and bring back the greatest, most testosterone-pumped trophy of all, a stag. A famous painting of the time by Edwin Landseer, the *Monarch of the Glen*, shows a 'royal' stag with 12 points to his antlers gazing out across the glens. The image is so popular it is used to this day to sell everything from soap to financial services.

Today we still revere the deer. It isn't necessary to go stalking. There are aftershaves with stags on the bottle, cufflinks and ties embossed with the trophy heads. We still associate the stag with the most aristocratic and male of beasts.

The social anthropologist, Lévi-Strauss said we think in animals: salmon to inspire determination, a pig intelligence, a chicken motherhood – and the deer? Nobility, the wild. Can you blame us if we look to the largest surviving mammal we have left on this island? Deer flicker through our collective imaginations, appearing on billboards, jewellery, clothing. I lose count of the number of times I note an antler motif in a trendy bar whilst discussing 'rewilding' the soul over my gin cocktail. I wonder, are we looking for something? A connection back to when we brought the animal back down from the hill?

Stalking today is quite different from its heyday in the late 19th century. In many ways it has improved. It is carried out more for management of the countryside, as the number of deer has risen exponentially. Since the removal of natural predators like wolves and the coming of cheap food, meaning people no longer needed to poach, deer have had it pretty easy. The native populations of red deer and roe deer have exploded. Also fallow deer, introduced by the Romans, and the little 'dog deers' or muntjac, escaped from safari parks, are increasingly common.

The Deer Initiative, a government quango set up to manage the deer population, estimates that there could be as many as one million deer in the UK, the highest number since the Ice Age. While that is a wonderful sign of biodiversity and we all love to see the deer bouncing over the fields or jumping into our gardens, it can be a nuisance. The most serious problem is road accidents. Deer are involved in up to 74,000 accidents every year and cause many human fatalities, not to mention the painful injuries and death of the deer. Around the UK, local councils, the Forestry Commission and other official bodies are dispatching 350,000 deer a year to try and manage the problem.

The most serious environmental problem is the impact the deer are having on the landscape. Although red deer are

a native species, they would never usually have existed in
such high numbers. Tree regeneration is suffering as a result
of their browsing. In the Highlands, the clearing of trees –
and the people – for sheep has already killed most of the
ancient Caledonian Forest, and it can't spring back because
of the deer.

Alan Watson Featherstone, founder of the charity Trees
for Life, calls it the 'geriatric forest', with granny pines still
surviving in the gullies and cliff faces, but no young 'uns
able to come up and create the next generation because
they have been nibbled down by the deer. His charity is
trying to replant the forests to bridge the gap. Another
option is to fence off areas to deer so the trees can regenerate,
or most controversially reintroduce wolves, to keep the deer
moving over the hill. The rewilding argument has hit the
headlines recently because of George Monbiot's book *Feral*,
but really the conversation has been going on in Scotland
for decades. Even Prince Charles has got involved, ordering
'ecological restoration' on Balmoral, the Royal Estate. The
debate is building because some estates want to get rid of
the deer completely, to allow the trees to regrow, while
others run a profitable business taking out paying stalkers.
Often, they are next door to one another.

Ben Damph* is a relatively small estate in Torridon managing
deer sustainably. It has almost 250 hectares (620 acres) of
woodland, much of which is fenced off for regeneration or
replanting. As in all Highland estates the deer are managed in
conjunction with neighbouring estates and the approval of

---

*A note on spellings: technically it should be Beinn Damh. I have
always spelt it Ben Damph and it's the name of the estate. I have
left them interchangeable because that's how it is in the Highlands.
I guess in the past, before the Gaelic language was 'official', the
spellings were interpreted as they sounded. Now there is an effort
to make it more consistent, but being the Highlands everyone
does as they damn well please.

the government. In fact, if enough deer are not culled then landowners will be required to take action. Ben Damph will usually take off around a dozen stags every year. A small number of deer are taken off by paying clients but it's tough ground and only fit stalkers would enjoy a day out – they also have to be willing to drag the beast off the hill themselves. The rest are taken off by family and friends.

Most of the venison is sent to game dealers. I pop into Highland Game, the biggest processor of venison in Scotland, to see the great shaggy carcasses of red deer being broken down into products the modern consumer can handle. Christian Nissen, a Danish entrepreneur, spotted a gap in the market in the 1990s. He saw all this high-quality meat coming off the hill and realised he could sell it simply by putting it in a ready meal, a sausage or a burger and labelling it as 'low fat, wild game'. But still he struggles to sell all the venison to the UK because it tastes too much of, well, deer. Half of the venison we consume comes from farmed deer in New Zealand as that has a much milder – one could say bland – taste. Most of the venison from our own mountains goes to Europe, especially Germany, where they enjoy the gamey taste.

After failing to get a roe deer, I decide to go after a red deer on Ben Damph, a hill famous for its stags, hence its Gaelic name. I have been going on holidays to the estate since I was a child and lived there for a few months in the winter of 2014. I take time over the decision. I have always admired the beauty of the red deer, I feel close to them and I will have to take responsibility for a death. But I have been going there all my life and watching others manage the stags. I would like to understand that work and be part of this ancient process.

I could have gone with someone else – there are plenty of stalkers I know who would be happy to take me out on the hill – but I wanted to go with my dad. It's not because

I feel it is some kind of coming of age experience. It's more for the honour of it, the privilege. I am aware my father is a good stalker; he knows Ben Damph intimately. It is a side of him that I would like to see and I would like to learn from.

We never discuss it; that would be dangerous, possibly emotional, and we don't really do that in my family. I just tell him when I am coming up to Ben Damph and hope he realises this is important to me. It is treated as perfectly normal, as if I have done this before, though I am in fact extremely nervous.

I don't trust myself with just Dad. It is too loaded. I fear I cannot take his criticism, or even advice, so I ask my friend Ed if he will come along on the stalk. He's a former soldier, knows the hill well and more importantly knows me and my father and how to handle the situation if we start bickering. He has brought his own gun. It's a modern .270 Blaser rifle with a hole behind the trigger, designed for an opposable thumb. It will kill the deer instantly, but it's heavy. We practise on the target and I'm surprised by the lightness of the trigger and how quiet it is with the silencer on, almost as if nothing has happened. I insist on carrying it, at least part of the way.

We start by the shores of Loch Torridon. I can hear the bubbling call of the curlews as we strike up the hill. We are passing through Celtic rainforest now. Trees cling to the gully, dripping with bryophytes and lichens. At the waterfall the trees peter out to a few granny pines and a view over the Torridon hills. The water is Mediterranean blue from up here; you can see the old fish traps, an arc of stones in the bay, where they used to catch so many sea trout you could see them jumping out of the sea. We are heading for the Ben Damph saddle along a popular footpath. I'm sure the deer can tell the difference between a friendly walking party in brightly coloured anoraks and stalkers in tweeds and green turning off the path. Every so often Dad will stop and 'glass the hill', spying with binoculars, and once he is sure get into position, the classic stalker's pose, lying down with the glass, a battered old telescope, on his knees.

Dad is excited, like a wee boy. He loves being on the hill and will stride up mountain paths with men decades younger, though his gear is shocking. His breeks are almost worn through at the seat and his elbows are patched with old leather. He sneers at my new breathable waterproof trousers and fleece. He is all in wool: tweed plus fours and a woollen shirt – warm in the rain, breathes in the heat. It means he never smells of human sweat, but like a wet sheep; perhaps it disguises him a little from the deer.

We can see a stag holding some hinds in Tol Ban, a green bowl to the east side of Ben Damph. It's good safe ground; the wind swirls around so the deer can smell danger and it is sheltered from the rain. The stag has a harem of 30 hinds, which is unusual. Usually he would only hold 15 or 20. He has ten points, far too good to kill, especially if he is holding all those girls. It's poor land in Wester Ross; the deer will only get up to 12 points, 14 rarely, but more likely ten. The estate only culls stags with fewer points and 'narrow tops', antlers that are closer together and considered dangerous when the stags fight because of the risk of maiming. Trophy heads are frowned upon.

It is just the beginning of 'the rut', when the groups of hinds, who have been grazing peacefully with their babies on the summer greens, are joined by the males. Now the battle begins. The stags must fight to establish who will be this year's dominant male. The hinds are only fertile for a few days during the year, so it's a short window and competition is fierce. It's a pumped-up, testosterone-fuelled time, like a city centre after a rugby match or, come to think of it, a 'stag do'.

As we climb over the saddle and down onto the west side of Ben Damph we enter that world. Even though we are up in the clouds now and visibility is bad we know the stags are there by the smell. We are passing wallows where the stags have urinated and then rolled, covering themselves in unctuous black mud. They will piss on themselves as well, blackening their fur, to attract the ladies and warn off other stags. Funny, not something that you can see on the *Monarch of the Glen*, even though he is in the height of the rut.

We can hear the stags too. I am surprised by how different they sound. One has a deep resonant roar like a foghorn, another is high-pitched. I wonder if it corresponds to their size or if the biggest, bravest stag on the hill in fact has a squeaky roar like David Beckham.

As the mist begins to clear we can see glimpses of Loch Damph below, a wheatear rises above us and we can hear a ptarmigan fussing in the rocks. We nestle down into a gully, peeping over the top. Dad spots a young male or 'staggy', not yet big enough to win any battles but ranging around the edge of the herd to try his luck anyway. We watch him through the binoculars as we eat our pieces, the Scots term for our sandwiches.

Dad knows there will be stags on this ground, Creag Liathad Saoghal, a series of steep turrets and gullies; it is just a matter of moving against the wind, coming up gradually on the skyline so they can't see us. Dad checks the wind every now and then. The old stalkers used to do this by sparking up a fag or a pipe; he seems to sniff the wind. I throw grass in the air, but it confuses me. Eventually I find a much better method is to pluck a strand of my hair and watch the way the wind blows it.

We start stalking the mountain, Dad moving first, inch by inch over the skyline so the deer don't see him. It is movement they detect. He finds a switch, a stag with just one point on each antler and a danger in fights. Dad beckons me forward by waving his hands behind his back, not turning round. I can see the tip of the switch but I'll have to inch head first on my belly to get into position properly. I start sliding down, digging my elbows into the heather, wishing now I was in scratchy tweed not slidy gortex. Ed comes behind me, holding on to my foot for extra anchorage. I can see the stag now; the sight is wobbling though. I am wobbling. The stag moves and I get into position again but it's no good. I'm scared. I can't regulate my breathing. I signal to Dad that I can't shoot. I don't look at him.

I try not to feel a stab of shame. Why should I? I did nothing wrong. It was my call and I wasn't comfortable. Perhaps I care about what Dad thinks more than I admit. Perhaps I should let that go. It's between me and the stag, no one else. We walk back down the hill, and by the time we get home evening has fallen and the curlews are silent.

The next day is Sunday and stalking is not allowed or at least would not do, certainly not in the God-fearing West Highlands. I take the opportunity to practise getting into position with a gun. Dad gives me his 7mm-08 unloaded, a lighter rifle, designed for stalking. It is not as powerful as the Blaser, but that just means you have to be more accurate. An inexperienced stalker will always go for the 'boiler room', the area around the heart and lungs, as it is an easy target and it will kill the animal quickly. More experienced stalkers will go for the head, as it kills the animal outright, but you have to be sure, as it is a much smaller area so there is more likelihood you will miss. A marksman should be so comfortable taking a shot, he or she could fall asleep in that position. I slide over the heather, getting splinters in my hands, practising taking a shot from a rock, down a hill, up a slope. I take the time to think about the philosophical arguments for hunting that I've read during my research.

José Ortega y Gasset, the Spanish philosopher, who wrote the most quoted book in sporting literature, *Meditations on Hunting*, argues that stalking is a way of connecting with nature. 'One does not hunt in order to kill,' he wrote. 'On the contrary, one kills in order to have hunted ... [For] the immersion in the countryside, the healthfulness of the exercise.' I prefer a less famous passage, one that makes sense to me now I have decided to do this for myself. It is about the 'solitude' of hunting the animal without the need for an audience other than 'the sharp peaks of the mountain, the stern oak, and the passing animal.'

As we set off for a second time Dad is already noticing things: a tree guard that needs replacing, rhododendrons that need spraying. This time as my 'dragger', I take my friend Dan, who is a complete newbie on the hill, but keen to try stalking and fit enough to help drag down a fully grown stag. Dad is different too. Less excitable, more focused. I realise with a tightening of my chest that he wants to help me; he doesn't want to let me down. He has to consider everything: the wind, the terrain, where the hinds graze, where the stags travel, where they lie up.

We are heading down the other side of the hill today, taking a boat over to the far banks of Loch Damph. We glass the hill repeatedly. On Ben Damph – hill of the stag – there should be lots of them, just like last time. But we have left home late, taking time to sight the rifle again – the sun is high and the light is bright and flat; it's difficult to see shapes on the hill. Even Dad is struggling. I don't stand a chance – every dead tree looks like an antler, every patch of sphagnum moss a deer.

We beach the boat on the Caribbean. I know this patch of land well, having spent many happy hours on this beach I named for its white sands. The biggest and most beautiful oak on the estate is here too. In English parkland you wouldn't look twice, but here it stands out. It is constantly wreathed in lichen and moss, as if decorated. Dad says I must collect acorns on this oak if it ever comes into mast. 'I shan't forget,' I say.

We set off up the pony track inside the deer exclosure. The removal of ungulates has led to an explosion of growth.

There is sessile oak, downy birch, holly, Scots pine, alder. It buzzes and sings with life. I rub bog myrtle on my neck to keep the midges off. As we come through the gate, it's silent, open hill once more. There are no trees where the deer can nibble the first signs of growth. We are up on Meall na Saobhaidhe, the plateau of the fox's den. It is broken ground, a series of rocks scattered by glaciers over the hill. It's a completely different world to the other side of Ben Damph. A place to lie low, and wait – perfect for a fox.

The stags are bellowing on the other side of the loch, but not here. It's quiet ground. This is where the young stags come to wait before picking a fight where the hinds are. There are plenty of cosy nooks and crannies to lie up and snooze. Dad is crouching, whispering. It is ground you sneak over; a deer could be anywhere. There are footprints and droppings everywhere: stories, if only I could read them. The deer grass is tricolour at this time of year, turning from green, to gold, to red. The ling heather has faded to peach, the bell heather to mauve. The bog cotton is tired and scrappy after the long summer. The landscape is in a state of flux, the sweet grass is dying, the stags are moving, the colours are changing. Everything is changing.

The wind is difficult to predict. We can see from the whirlpools on the loch below it is constantly changing direction, swirling around the rocks. A puff of wind carries our human scent and we startle a couple of stags, watching their bounding antlers disappear into the distance. Dad swears at us and instead of being upset I just laugh and suggest we have lunch. I don't care whether we get a stag or not, I'm just happy to be up here. We enjoy our pieces looking over Loch Damph, sharing a few shrivelled blaeberries I have found, admiring the frogs under the rocks.

Like the good ghillie he is, Dad soon disappears around the corner to glass the hill. He comes back. There is a young stag with narrow tops lying down – just about shootable. I go to have a look, balancing the glass on a rock.

Yes, I see him, and take time to admire him, his gorgeous antlers, eight points, holding up the sky. He is lying in the lee of a crag for his midday snooze. Dad explains the stalk to us first. We are going to have to move a long way without him seeing us. We'll go back on ourselves to cross the dead ground in front of the stag. Then we will follow the burn up to the lochan and crawl the last few yards. We set off, silently running across the corrie; the light is fading and we don't have much time. I am carrying the gun, binoculars banging at my chest, my heart pumping. The burn is dry enough to spring up it. Once we get to the lochan we must creep around the edge, at one point a ledge a few inches deep around the water. The wind is making little white horses on the surface.

We come over the top and Dan holds back. I leopard-crawl behind Dad. My knees scrape the rocks and heather digs into my thighs. I can smell the dry earth. The rifle is heavy on my back and Dad takes it for the end of the stalk. 'Your hair,' he says. I tuck it up in my woolly hat. I lie up while he goes ahead to get the gun in position, then he beckons me forward.

The rifle is steady on a rock. I have to come forward without moving it, without raising my head. Lean into the stock, cheek on wood. I can see the deer clearly 80m (90 yards) away. I brace my legs, steady. 'He's lying down,' whispers Dad. 'You'll have to go for his neck.' The stag is quite calm, his head turned towards us, almost resting his chin on the ground. The neck is hidden.

'No, I can go for his head,' I say. 'Between the eyes.'

'If you think you can do it.'

'I can do it.' I am staring so hard at that stag, focus unblinking, I feel my mind detach and travel forward with the bullet. The deer falls straight down off the ledge, his antlers first, in slow motion, leaving the sky bare. 'Did I do it? Is he dead?'

'Yes, he's dead.'

I pull the bolt, let the bullets fall. Nothing, no Gaelic songs, shooting literature, philosophy, nothing, can give you the answer. People ask: what was going through your head? What were you thinking? I know what I wasn't thinking. There is no testosterone surge, no primordial hit, no elation. A gun is not about freedom, it is not about being wild; it is about being absolutely in control. It is neither male nor female. You are either in control or you are not. You either hit or you miss.

We make sure the gun is safe and set out towards the stag. 'It could not have been a better shot,' says Dad, taking out his knife and bleeding the beast, a torrent of blood over the heather. There is no blooding, when people smear blood over their faces. We have no tradition for it. It's not about me, a Facebook photo, or this moment. It's about the stag, the immense gratitude I feel, all three of us feel, in silence. The celebration will come later, with the eating.

We get on with the job. Dad cuts open the belly for the gralloch and I insist on scooping out the guts, but my arm is not quite long enough. Dad ties a knot in the oesophagus and heaves. Steam rises in the cold air as the glistening grey, blue, red entrails roll onto the hill. They call the blood paint, it is so red; the hairs are called pins, the intestines, the gralloch. Words to make it less gory? Or words that have always been there and we have simply forgotten? The crows are already circling, the mediators between life and death. I've watched a murder of crows mob a golden eagle before for the privilege of the gralloch. The fox has probably smelled it too and is awaiting nightfall to trot over here for a feast; it is his mountain after all.

After removing the gralloch we wash our hands in a nearby burn, slooshing the water up to our elbows again and again, the blood turning the water a deeper, peaty red. The men tie ropes through the back hocks and front legs and we start hauling the animal down the hill. I try to help but it soon becomes clear the weight difference is too much, so I take the gun and sticks instead. The mood has changed again, the sky has darkened, the deer grass is flattening against the wind and the lochan swirls and boils.

I realise I left the glass behind and run back to get it, over the rough ground, to the point where the stag was shot, my stag now. The ground is stained with blood. Suddenly I am alone but for the 'sharp peaks of the mountain'. I feel the other Louise, the person who pulled the trigger, who was in absolute control, lift and retreat. I allow my imagination back in. I see Nature is angry with me, growling, lashing my cheeks with rain. Yet I don't feel afraid. I dig my feet into the soil and feel my bones reverberate with the earth. I feel defiant. After all that control, a moment of wildness, a square-off with Nature. No matter, She'll win in the end. I start running down the mountain, bouncing over the heather, the gun crashing into my back.

Dan and Dad are falling down Cadha Laum-Dharaich, the leap of the oak. There is plenty of leaping alright. There is always a good reason behind a Gaelic name – perhaps this is it? I catch up with them in the regeneration. Dan has already done a couple of 'half pikes with double somersault'. The deer is so heavy it is dragging them down the mountain. I follow with the gun, falling into gullies and holes. I notice I am looking at the flowers again. Orchids, self-heal, lousewort, bog asphodel. I am coming back to the real me. The antler talisman has crumbled in my pocket, squashed by leopard-crawling, mixed in with cake and clingfilm.

At the foot of the hill, we haul the deer into the boat. Its tongue lolls out, grey, and its eyes have a green sheen like the surface of the water. Dad takes the engine and we float home over the deep loch.

It's getting dark by the time we get back. In a rare admission of tiredness, Dad lets us drop him off at the house while we take the deer to the larder. I watch him walk down the road, hunched forward a little, hands crossed at the wrist,

just like Grandpa. He doesn't go inside immediately, he goes
to collect logs for the fire.

The National Trust for Scotland (NTS) larder is the same
white-washed stone as the bothy next door, but inside it
has the rubberised floor of an abattoir, with a hook to
hang the beast and a cold room in the back to store the
carcasses.

We hang up the stag and I start skinning. There is a scene
in *Game of Thrones* where Charles Dance, playing the
patriarchal warrior, is butchering a stag. Watching it, I was
appalled. 'But that's not how you skin a deer!'

'Shut up Louise, this is a major plot development.'

'But he's doing it all wrong!'

Charles Dance hacked and sawed away, as much to
dramatise his latest speech on who to rape and murder next
as to remove the skin of the animal. What a waste. In fact
skinning a deer is a delicate art. You start on the hind leg,
cutting around the bone like a bottle top. Then you slice a
line from the bottle neck to the inside of the crotch, and
begin to peel. With a few cuts, crossways, to the fascia,
the white substance that binds muscle and skin like dry glue,
the skin should open up. The knife should never dig into the
meat; the skin will come away quite easily, leaving firm pink
muscle and eventually its coat, pooled at your feet.

We do the basics on my deer and leave the rest for later. It
would be impossible for us to butcher such a large animal
without the correct equipment and I want to cook it as
mince, stewing steak and burgers, rather than huge haunches
that will not fit into my oven. We share the larder so it must
be moved on in a few days anyway. I take out the kidneys
for my breakfast and the liver, to be made into paté with
local herbs: mountain thyme and juniper. On the side is a
tray with the cheek bones of other deer recently brought

down from the hill, which will show the age and health of animals and help monitor the population. Seamus MacNally, the local NTS warden, pops his head in to inspect the teeth and see how we got on. The deer was young, maybe five or six years old. Seamus tells me about the Germans who put 'just a wee bit of heather' between the teeth of their kill, to comfort it, to almost send it to the next world with something. I think, should I have done that? But I wouldn't have done anything differently.

A week or so later I pick up the deer – venison now – and begin to distribute it among friends and family, because I cannot fit it all in my freezer. It is good meat. The young stag was fat from feeding over the summer and, because it was early in the season, he was not quite yet rutting. Yet it is still strong meat, so I do not want to eat it more than once or twice a week, taking my time to cook and eat it slowly.

I make rowan jelly from berries picked on my street in Edinburgh. They are the red of oxygenated blood and make a sharp sauce that smells of wet fallen leaves. Mixed with sugar and strained it makes a gorgeous jelly, the colour of stained glass.

Over a long winter of writing I serve it alongside venison chilli, venison and ale pie, venison heart stew, sausages, burgers, stalker's pie and steak. Every time I eat the meat I remember the day on the hill. I feel a connection to my father, and all those stalkers who have gone before. Most of all I taste a deep satisfaction in what I have achieved, in providing food from such a special place – it is better than any trophy.

CHAPTER FIFTEEN

Beyond Meat

Progress is the realisation of Utopias.

Oscar Wilde

Vegan cheese destroys the soul. It tastes of the orange powder that flavours cheap 'cheesy' crisps, the texture is like rubber, and it smells of a cold fridge. I try to like it, I really do, I'm sure it's made by an ethical company doing their bit for the planet and the lactose intolerant, but really? In comparison to real cheese, which often has a history spanning hundreds of years, a connection to a specific place and people, even to the soil – the 'terroir' – vegan cheese feels like cultural vandalism.

We are sitting on the green at Finchingfield waiting for the cyclists to come by on the Tour de France. It's the morning before I go after my first rabbit and Le Tour is passing through Essex. If they only knew, those French cyclists, that I was displacing their national dish with this pale imitation, they would swerve off their million-dollar bikes and end up in a ditch.

Everyone is munching happily on their ham and real cheese sandwiches. 'What do you have, Lou?' asks my brother James.

'Er, it's vegan cheese.'

'Good God.'

'I know.'

'I'll get you a pint.'

I am trying hard to not only be vegetarian, when not eating animals I have killed myself, but also vegan. Like most converts, at the beginning, I am extreme – hence the vegan cheese. Veganism is attractive to me. Let's face it, everyone who ever lived who was cool was a vegetarian – Plato, Voltaire, Tony Benn. In the modern age an increasing number of the beautiful people are vegan: Joaquin Phoenix, Russell Brand, Michelle Pfeiffer.

I was entirely vegetarian throughout writing this book, except for the animals I killed myself. At first I put on weight as I was travelling a lot and seldom cooking for myself, so often had to suffice with bread and cheese – and chocolate. But once I got home and settled into a routine and began to cook properly again, I lost the weight and actually dropped a few pounds. I felt lighter and full of energy. A diet of nuts and vegetables and pulses, when I have time for it, suits me. To quote all the fashionable websites and cookery books, when you do it properly – which for most of us is infrequently – it does make you glow.

In fact, learning how to cook more vegetarian meals and dishes and changing my lifestyle to eat less meat and fewer animal products turns out to be one of the most valuable things I have learned. I now see meat as a treat to be eaten with the reverence and respect it deserves. Even with a lot of venison in the freezer, I eat meat perhaps once or twice a week at the most. In future I think it will be much less. I would like to go to a butcher occasionally and buy meat I can trust has come from a good source. I would also like to try new cuts and dishes. But I have no desire to eat chicken breasts midweek. What's the point? There are cheaper proteins that are just as satisfying. I walk into a supermarket and I see animals, not just meat. I smell them too. It makes meat a much more visceral experience and makes me want to eat less of it. And if I am going to eat an animal, it has to be worth it.

A meat reductionist message may seem like a strange juxtaposition with killing animals but stay with me. Many of the problems vegans have with the current food system relate to the factory environment in which animals are raised. I meet more than one 'vegan' or 'paleo-vegan' who will eat roadkill or even what they kill themselves. If there is anything that killing and processing animals has taught me, it is the huge amount of energy and skill that goes into raising animals. It has not made me want to eat more meat, it has made me want to eat less. Also fewer eggs and less dairy, having been given an insight into how other animals are raised as well.

In a way I have come full circle, from being a 'blind omnivore' with no idea where my meat comes from, to being a 'smug vegetarian' appalled by the treatment of animals, to an 'ethical carnivore' comfortable with meat raised and slaughtered humanely. As I will set out below, there are many good reasons to eat less meat. The 'vegan revolution' does not have to be extreme – or involve vegan cheese. There is, I believe, a strong – and growing – argument for the sake of the planet, your health and wallet that if you can't quite manage to be vegan, at least eat less meat and be 'vegan curious'.

Vegetarianism has been around since the dawn of man, whether you are a Creationist or an Evolutionist. Most interpretations of the Garden of Eden have us only eating vegetables. It was only when the Serpent came along that we discovered meat. Interestingly, it probably mirrors our evolution from a largely vegetarian ape to an upright meat-eating ape.

In England the history of vegetarianism began with religious ascetics and a desire for this prelapsarian perfect world. It was particularly popular during the English Civil War when perhaps the death and destruction around them led people to long for a more peaceful way of life. Travellers were also returning from abroad and reporting on Indian vegetarianism and a land where people lived healthily and happily without needing meat. Curious folk looked further, back to the ancient Greeks like Pythagoras who argued for a return or indeed a progression to a more civilised world where people live in harmony with nature. 'As long as men massacre animals, they will kill each other. Indeed, he who sows the seeds of murder and pain cannot reap joy and love,' he wrote.

We imagine our Puritan forebears surviving on oxtail and lard but in fact, just like today, many were concerned with the well-being of animals. For example, even though he thought animals were machines, Descartes did not want to eat them. In the industrial age abstinence from meat became more about getting back to nature. Some of the greatest minds of the age advocated vegetarianism – and running around naked. Writers like Shelley formed communes where they ate 'nothing but potatoes and boiled cabbage', according to contemporary accounts, and 'lived as nature intended'. Awkwardly this idea of 'purity' was taken up by Hitler, who believed that eating only vegetables was good for health. It has since been questioned whether he was totally vegetarian and vegetarians tend to distance themselves from a person whose other theories are so abhorrent.

George Bernard Shaw, the playwright, was perhaps the greatest wit the vegetarian movement has ever had, fond of skewering his hostesses at society dinners for eating 'corpses'.

Visiting London, Gandhi considered the city's vegetarians 'among London's most eccentric idealists', yet he was also inspired by the social reform movement in Britain and writers like Henry Salt.

In the late 20th century vegetarianism became part of a movement again as the hippies adopted it as part of peace and love. The achingly cool Paul and Linda McCartney promoted vegetarianism, also influenced by Indian philosophies and the anti-war stance.

Vegetarianism was often led by women, from the suffragettes onwards. In *The Sexual Politics of Meat*, Carol J. Adams argues that meat-eating is associated with masculine dominance over weaker creatures and is therefore part of sustaining the patriarchy. She makes some very interesting points about how meat is objectified in the same way as women – for example, 'Double D Cup' turkey breasts advertised in restaurants. She argues that ultimately all of us are 'blocked vegetarians', prevented by the patriarchal and carnivorous society we live in from eating as we naturally would. In a wonderful scene she describes the 'predatory' meat-eaters attacking vegetarians at a dinner party for their views, rather like they would have attacked an animal in the past. Having sat through more than one dinner party repeatedly having to explain why I have chosen the vegetarian dish, I can understand her point on aggressive omnivores.

Lately veganism rather than vegetarianism has hit the fashion pages, becoming the diet of the beautiful and the slim. The biggest selling cookery book in 2015 was Ella Henderson's *Deliciously Ella*, promoting a totally vegan diet. In the UK between 7 and 11 per cent of the population are vegetarian – a growing number of whom are vegan – while in the USA it is just 2 per cent.

Perhaps the most famous vegetarian of all is Lisa Simpson. In a now cult episode of *The Simpsons* in 1995 she befriends a lamb from the petting zoo and decides she no longer wants to eat animals. Presented with lamb chops at the family table, she refuses to eat. 'This is lamb,' Homer responds in a moment of typical logic. 'Not *a* lamb.' Marge suggests other carnivorous food options, but Lisa can no longer think of meat without imagining the animal it comes from – I know *that* feeling.

Just as Pythagoras had wished for a better future, modern vegetarians and today's vegans believe cutting out the killing and farming of animals will save the planet. 'I have no doubt that it is a part of the destiny of the human race, in its gradual improvement, to leave off eating animals, as surely as the savage tribes have left off eating each other when they came in contact with the more civilized,' wrote Henry David Thoreau.

Despite being promoted by the most clever, beautiful and cool people, vegetarianism was always considered to be the preserve of cranks and people who wear socks and sandals without any hipster irony. Only now is it becoming mainstream – because the argument is reaching crisis point. During the writing of this book two major reports have, I believe, pushed us onto the path of a reduced-meat future, and there is no turning back.

Firstly, meat is killing us, just as many of those early vegetarians predicted. The links between eating red meat and cancer have been around for decades, but again it was considered the opinion of cranks until a report was published by the World Health Organization in October 2015. It said 50g (1.8oz) of processed meat a day – less than two slices of bacon – increased the chance of developing colorectal cancer by 18 per cent. Processed meat includes products like salami or bacon or sausages that have been cured and smoked.

It is hard to emphasise how important the report was in terms of how we see processed meat. The only comparison I can think of is when we finally realised smoking was bad for us after decades of puffing away in cinemas and aeroplanes. In fact the WHO report put processed meat up there with smoking on the 'causes cancer' chart. Red meat 'probably causes cancer' and we should not eat more than 500g (19oz) a week, the report said. For most people that would mean one good-sized portion of meat a day on five out of seven days.

Of course there was instant outrage. *The Sun* newspaper launched a 'Butty Battle' to 'Save our Bacon' from those interfering doctors. Bacon lovers 'fought back' on Twitter by posting photos of themselves eating their favourite full breakfast. They kind of had a point. The statistics are not quite as scary as they sound. In the UK we are only eating 17g (0.6oz) of processed meat a day on average. So we would have to eat three times the amount of processed meat to increase the risk. On average we eat about 70g (2.5oz) of red meat per day, within the recommended amount.

However, a third of us eat 100g (3.5oz) a day, and some eat even more – after all, an English breakfast with all the trimmings can contain up to 90g (3.2oz) of red meat alone. If you take out the vegetarians, children and the elderly, many of the rest of us really are eating too much meat. Some 58 per cent of men in the UK exceed 70g (2.5oz) of red meat per day. Meat consumption in the UK is approximately twice the global average. If everyone in the world followed suit the situation would simply be unsustainable.

It is laudable that journalists took the time to break down the statistics, but I'm not sure they do that for every cancer scare. It was because our bacon sandwiches and more importantly a key aspect of our culture – perhaps a culture at times obsessed with boobs and 'meat' – really is at risk. The real reason the report frightened people was because it was suggesting a much bigger change is on the way.

I'm afraid it warrants another *Simpsons* quote. David Mirkin, the *Simpsons* executive who created 'Lisa the Vegetarian' – and in a cultural coup got the McCartneys to do a voiceover – describes the reaction of carnivores to suggestions they should eat less meat. 'It's like taking a dog's bowl away from a dog, the way that he'll growl at you,' he told *Slate* magazine. 'It's exactly that. When you talk to people about not eating meat, if they could, they would make that sound.'

The Sun newspaper was growling like a British Bulldog deprived of its processed sausage.

It's not just the doctors coming for our bacon, it's those pesky scientists too – or 'Warmists' as one UK Independence Party (UKIP) MEP likes to call them. In November 2015 a respected British think tank, Chatham House, stated unequivocally that if we want to do something about climate change then cutting down on meat is a good place to start. Again, it is hard to emphasise how significant this was. We have known for decades that livestock is a big contributor to emissions but few academic institutions had stood up to say that the industry should be targeted for cuts.

The report itself, *Changing Climate, Changing Diets*, put emissions from livestock at a conservative 15 per cent, still more than all the planes, cars and trains of the world combined. And it warned the problem could get a lot worse as global meat consumption is set to rise by more than 75 per cent by 2050. But what was more surprising is that the report suggested that the government should be doing something about it. The report pointed out that meat production has been almost entirely forgotten in the fight to stop climate change, despite being one of the easiest wins. It accused politicians worldwide of 'inertia' in the face of one of the easiest ways to tackle the biggest threat to humanity. If meat consumption could be cut, it argued, it could provide one-quarter of the further emissions cuts needed to limit global warming to 2°C (36°F), the minimum level scientists believe is safe.

Chatham House points out that monogastric animals such as chickens or pigs produce less methane. They can also be kept on less land if farmed intensively and therefore have a lower carbon footprint. But ultimately the report argues for less meat, rather than a switch to more intensive farming methods. None of the report's authors are vegetarians, but questioned by the *Guardian*, Rob Bailey from Chatham House said: 'Having worked on this project, I have drastically reduced my meat consumption – I now eat it once a month.'

In December 2015 the United Nations finally agreed to keep global warming below the limit of 2°C. For once, meat-eating was included in the discussions as one of the main ways that could be achieved, a glaring omission in previous talks. It was helped by Arnold Schwarzenegger, the Hollywood actor, appearing at the talks to call on the world to stop eating meat. Ever the consummate politician, the former Governor of California pointed out that no one is taking away your bacon butty, merely suggesting cutting out meat one or two days a week. He urged the world to go 'part-time vegetarian', not only to help the planet but also to alleviate world hunger. No doubt the backing of 'The Terminator' and former body builder helped to end for good any claim vegetarians can't be macho.

With all this growing evidence, the question is why aren't we already eating less meat? In 2014 a young American, inspired by Al Gore's film *An Inconvenient Truth* to fight climate change, asked the same question.

Kip Anderson is a conscientious Californian. He cycles or takes public transport, he recycles, he turns off lights, he even showers less to reduce his carbon footprint. He describes himself as an OCE (obsessive compulsive environmentalist). But as he began to read more about climate change he noticed a glaring omission. Why weren't any of the environmental groups talking about the carbon footprint of livestock, the use of water, the species extinction, the ocean dead zones, the destruction of the rainforest? 'Why didn't the world's largest environmental groups, who are supposed to be saving our planet, have this as their main focus?' he asks.

He blames a conspiracy or 'cowspiracy' for the failure of non-governmental organisations (NGOs) like Greenpeace to attack animal agriculture because of the power and even violence of the animal agriculture lobby. He also suggests an unwillingness for NGOs to address behaviour change because it could affect fundraising.

In late 2014 Kip and his co-director Keegan Kuhn launched an independent documentary called *Cowspiracy*. It was crowd-funded, released on the internet and featured worthy environmentalists and some cows. It was an unexpected underground hit thanks to recommendations on Facebook and Twitter. A year later it was streamed live on Netflix because of the number of people keying in the title to the search box. Leonardo DiCaprio featured in a new introduction. All over the internet, there are stories of teenagers forcing their parents to watch it, and of whole families turning vegan, or at least vegetarian, as a result. All I can say is parents must have changed since my day.

I watched it to see what all the fuss was about. It is certainly an affecting film. It's great to see an angry young man in a baseball cap go for sacred cows like Greenpeace and Rainforest Action Network, angrily confronting their public relations teams about the failure of such organisations to stop one of the biggest destroyers of rainforests: cattle farming, or more precisely, burgers.

Kip considers organic agriculture instead. He watches a duck being slaughtered and afterwards, contemplating a Tibetan prayer flag, comes to the noble decision that 'If I can't do it, I don't want someone else doing it for me.' He takes it to the extreme, arguing that the only way to save the planet is 'veganic' farming: a new method of farming without animal manure and minimising destruction of any other living creature.

It certainly made me think. A few weeks later I am invited along to a conference on the Future of Food as part of the Festival of Ideas at York University. The conference's message is simple: eat less meat. The lectures are all convincing. Joyce D'Silva of Compassion in World Farming thumps eight bags of flour onto the table – that is how much it takes to produce one steak. Oh, and 30,000 bottles of water. 'Is that right in a world where people are starving?' she asks. She goes on to point out that half the world's antibiotics go into factory farming, leading to antibiotic-resistant strains of bacteria. Some 94 per cent of global soya production is destined not for tofu-eating vegans but for cattle, pigs and poultry. There are the carbon emissions from methane, not to mention the nitrous oxide from fertiliser and further pollution from slurry pits. 'Excreta from billions of farm animals has to go somewhere,' she says.

The unpalatable facts go on and on. I know most of them, but sitting in a lecture theatre watching the appalled faces of the students I wonder, is it really sinking in? Will it ever sink in? At the interval delegates chat earnestly over their Quorn sausage rolls and vegetarian canapés. But I feel a surge of anger. I am having my 'cowspiracy moment'. If all this is true, then why the hell aren't we doing something about it?

Who was behind this conference? I looked up the supporters of the Eating Better alliance: the WWF, Friends of the Earth, the RSPB, Greenpeace, Oxfam, etc. These organisations have had decades to promote this message individually, yet they haven't, or not very loudly anyway when you compare it to other campaigns on climate change. I wonder why they have to hide behind this new organisation Eating Better? Is it because it would put off potential funders? The idea that the organisation that you want to save pandas also wants you to eat less steak could be rather off-putting. And the idea that the NGO you rely on to save birds might lecture you on what to have for dinner is frankly a little irritating. No thanks.

The NGOs have not been entirely silent. In 2009 Friends of the Earth released a report showing that it will be possible to feed the predicted human population in 2050 both humanely and sustainably – but only if the major meat-eating nations reduce their consumption. They claim eating less meat could prevent 45,000 early deaths in the UK every year and save the NHS £1.2bn (US$1.7bn). The WWF has quietly issued reports that recommend eating red meat only three times a week. The WWF Livewell Plate recommends cutting the proportion of meat in our diet from 16 per cent now to 4 per cent by 2020.

Smaller NGOs like Meat Free Mondays, set up by Paul McCartney and his daughters Stella and Mary, campaign solely on trying to persuade the public to cut out meat at least once a week, pointing out it is cheaper, healthier and better for the environment. It is supported by Jamie Oliver, Joanna Lumley, Leona Lewis and a host of other celebrities.

Maybe it's not the NGOs holding back on the less meat message but the government? In May 2015 the peer-reviewed report *UK Principles of Healthy and Sustainable Eating Patterns* was finally 'published'. Produced by a group of experts convened by the government's Department for Environment, Food and Rural Affairs (DEFRA), it sets out clear advice on how to eat healthily and sustainably, including advice on eating more plant-based food and eating less meat. Yet DEFRA declined to endorse or publish the report. Instead it sits gathering dust on the website of the Global Food Security programme – largely invisible and lacking government ownership.

The facts and figures are all there, in expensive and glossy reports. But no one is shouting them from the rooftops. Why? My own personal theory is this: no one wants to be the person to tell the British Bulldog to its face it ought to be cutting down on meat. They are not saying meat-free Mondays, they are saying meat-free Tuesdays and Wednesdays, perhaps a meat-free working week. Meat-free months, even.

It's not quite a conspiracy, or even a 'cowspiracy', but it's not entirely open either. The NGOs and the health industry and even the government are all quietly working towards you eating less meat. You just don't know it yet.

Perhaps one of the reasons people like *Cowspiracy* so much is that it is hopeful. It offers a relatively simple answer to climate change and ill health – just cut out animal products – and job done. Planet saved! It is one of the main reasons I started out on this journey. I could see that being a vegetarian or vegan was the best thing for the planet, but I didn't want to stop eating meat I felt had been raised in a humane way, or controlled as part of pest management.

Deciding to investigate how animals are raised and where possible kill them myself was a much more difficult path to follow, but I discovered all the messy, complex reasons I would rather be an ethical carnivore than a vegan. I think the farmers and the animals I have met have a role in maintaining the countryside and in feeding us. I guess, when I looked at Tibetan prayer flags and thought about killing a chicken, and life, death and the universe, I still thought I could do it, and I did.

I realise I have a message. It's not quite as clean and clear-cut as *Cowspiracy*. It is this: you don't have to kill animals yourself, but you should go to the effort to find out where they come from. I believe that when people see how animals are raised and processed on their behalf, it will naturally encourage them to eat less meat.

I tried so hard to think of a name for this way of eating I have invented: only eating animals you kill yourself, or even just eating animals with a known provenance. I toyed with existing names like flexitarian, part-time vegetarian, feastarian, blocked vegetarian. Then I realised it is simple: this is the human way to eat. We are the only species who can think deeply about what we eat. Therefore, we could choose to eat less meat based on how it is raised. It is a natural way to be and I believe pretty soon everyone will be doing it. We certainly cannot sustain a future population of nine billion by 2050 continuing to eat the amount of meat we currently do.

A common concern is that even if small countries like the UK reduce meat consumption, the overall increase as developing countries like China increase their meat-eating will negate any benefit. I do not agree with this. For one, it is slightly patronising. India has had decades to eat more meat, but the cultural attachment to a vegetarian diet is much too strong to be overturned. China will certainly eat more protein, but it will not necessarily be from farm animals. One of the fastest developing countries in the world, China, is looking at much more efficient ways to feed its population with lab-grown meat and plant-based proteins, as well as meat. Also, why should developing countries necessarily follow our food habits? The cultural exchange cuts both ways. We are eating far more delicious vegetarian dishes inspired by India and other countries. Also, we are showing the way to a healthier low-meat diet by already reducing our own consumption.

In the USA, one of the world's biggest meat-eating countries, meat consumption is falling, plummeting by 12 per cent in just five years from 2007 to 2012. Beef sales have been falling for the last 20 years and now even chicken and pork consumption is falling. In the UK, consumption of meat fell 13 per cent between 2007 and 2013. Much of the change has, like most eating fads, been driven by celebrity chefs. Hugh Fearnley-Whittingstall, Jack Monroe, Jamie Oliver and Yotam Ottolenghi all argue for less and better meat. Yes, high-quality meat can be expensive, but unusual cuts are cheaper and if you are buying less the money will go further. A recent study published in the *British Journal of Nutrition* found more of certain nutrients, including omega-3s, in organic meat and dairy. In addition, vegetarian foods such as dried beans are cheap and incredibly nutritious. You just have to think a little more and take a bit more time – the most precious commodity in this day and age.

The argument that eating less meat will leave you nutritionally deficient has been dismissed. Yes, a certain amount of meat is good for you, full of protein and minerals. But with careful planning they can be replaced. An adult needs very little protein (a woman needs no more than 45g or 1.6oz a day and a man 55g or 1.9oz) and it is quite possible to get it all from plant products.

It's not 1950 any more, when the best vegetarian meal you could get was a feta cheese parcel – well, it is still like that in many places, but it is changing. Eating vegetarian or vegan food does not mean having to miss out on protein. Nutrients found in meat and fish, such as protein, iron, calcium, zinc, vitamin B12 and vitamin D, can be found in beans, lentils, pulses, green leafy veg like kale and spinach, and oils such as flax and rapeseed. If you go to the supermarket there are already plenty of vegetarian options, from falafel burgers to tofu, driven by middle-class demand.

In the future we will undoubtedly have less meat on our plates. The question is, what will it be replaced with?

Why not eat insects? Why not indeed. It was the question posed in 1885 by eccentric Victorian Vincent M. Holt. He suggested we eat slug soup, curried cockchafers and stag beetle larvae on toast. 'While I am confident that they will never condescend to eat us, I am equally confident that, on finding out how good they are, we shall some day right gladly cook and eat them,' he wrote in his avant-garde essay. It never really caught on. However, his little pamphlet does resurface every few decades. It is telling that it was reprinted in the sixties and seventies, when alternative ideas were again emerging.

Holt was a radical. Not only in culinary terms, but also social. One of the main reasons he wanted people to eat insects was to provide a cheap source of protein to the poor. It happened in other countries all over the world, he pointed out; all that was stopping us here was a ridiculous prudishness, a refusal to try something new. 'We imitate the savage nations in their use of numberless drugs, spice and condiments,' he writes. 'Why not go a step further?'

Today, mainstream food companies and academics are thinking the same way, except with even more urgency. In 2013 the UN released a report that recommended eating more insects to combat world hunger. There are 40 tonnes (44 US tons) of insects per person in the world. They do not need a lot of space, water or heating. They survive on waste and produce huge amounts of protein. There are 1,900 insects edible to humans. What's not to like?

Unlike beef or chicken, insects have a light carbon footprint and there are fewer welfare concerns. Crickets, for example, need 12 times less feed than cattle to produce the same amount of protein. Insects don't burp – or produce methane. Already in other countries, two billion people eat insects to supplement their diets. In Thailand children catch the crickets in the fields before school and take them in to be cooked at lunchtime – much more nutritious than turkey twizzlers – with the added bonus of contributing to the local farmers' pest control.

Already insect farming is taking off in Europe, with mealworm farms established in the Netherlands and France and the first insect farm to open in the UK soon. There are also maggot or 'mag' farms opening in South Africa to produce high-protein meal both for humans and to feed to other animals such as chickens and pigs. Could this be the perfect solution to feeding the growing human population, especially as countries crave more protein?

I have a confession. In my year eating only animals I kill myself, there has been one exception: I have eaten dead animals with six legs – or no legs at all. Actually, I probably ate insects more than once in processed foods as they are regularly used for food colouring. Carmine (E120) is made from cochineal bugs and can be found in some red food colouring.

Shami Radia is one of the many young entrepreneurs looking to take advantage of the emerging market in insects. He first came across insect eating in Malawi, where flying termites are a great delicacy served with your evening beer. It seemed like the perfect solution to him, a nutritious food that took up less land than meat. We meet at Borough Market to discuss his start-up company, Grub. He offers me a mealworm. There is no attempt to disguise what they are. I can see the eyes, or are they bottoms? I'm not sure I really want to know. But I have to admit they are tasty. Crunchy and salty, like pork scratchings. Certainly a satisfying accompaniment to a drink – especially for an Essex girl. 'They are packed with protein,' points out Shami. 'They have a 45 per cent protein content.'

Shami also lets me try the crickets roasted in chilli and lime. I try not to think of my favourite character in *James and the Giant Peach* as I chow down on the snack. They are delicious, like a husky, chewy, salty peanut. The crickets are killed by freezing them, then dehydrated and processed. 'We need to get over the *I'm a Celebrity Get Me Out of Here* mentality,' says Shami. 'Insects are delicious and it's a sustainable way to eat protein.'

Grub is now building an insect farm in Cumbria to create a UK supply of cricket flour. One of the wonderful things is that the crickets could live off vegetable peelings, creating a new food out of waste. The 'mini-livestock' can be kept in urban environments in a small space, reducing the need for transportation.

Insect eating is not a new idea. Even before Vincent Holt, John the Baptist was living off locusts and honey, and ancient Greek texts mention entomophagy. But we do struggle to get over the 'yuck factor'. Perhaps this is because there is a genuine risk insects could be raised on unsanitary wastes, and, just like with other foodstuffs, there is a chance, especially over the internet, of rogue suppliers. Much of the delay in supplying insects to the mainstream market is because of the risk of contamination, both of insects in the wild and from fungus getting into the waste they are fed.

Personally, I think insects make really nice bar snacks and I'd buy processed food 'enriched' with insect protein such as cricket flour. Soon, I suspect you will be able to buy both in the supermarket – in fact Grub are working on a snack bar. Restaurants will also serve insects that are difficult to source and prepare them as a novelty. But probably not with the legs attached or as 'slug soup'. We've had more than 100 years to think about it. I'm afraid we are as stuck-up as we were in the Victorian age. I suspect we will opt for a different alternative to meat.

'Plant-based meat protein' is the future as far as the creators of Google and Twitter are concerned. And they should know; their job is predicting the future, or at least the next easy buck.

Among the geeks and beanbags, Silicon Valley has a number of 'alternative meat' start-ups. All are trying to create a plant-based substance that looks and tastes like meat. They all want to be the next Steve Jobs or 'Tesla' of the food industry. You would have thought this is easy. We already have fungi-based substitutes like Quorn, soya burgers and vegetarian sausages. But these will no longer cut the mustard. The holy grail – targeting the millions of Americans who actually want to cut down on meat – is an alternative that really tastes like an animal.

Meat is simply water and long chains of amino acids or proteins. Of course, many plants contain proteins too. So in theory it should be easy to 'rebuild' something similar to meat by isolating proteins in plants and building them up again into a 'meat-like' substance. This is essentially what most of the start-ups are doing. The difficulty is making those proteins behave like meat – to react to cooking in the same way and to sizzle on the barbecue.

Beyond Meat is being backed by Twitter co-founder and confirmed vegan Biz Stone. They have had the most success in creating 'meatless chicken strips'. The flavour of the chicken was easy to fake, but it took years of experimentation to find the right combination of heating and cooling and pressurising soya so it created the right 'fibrous' texture. The beefburger created by Beyond Meats is called The Beast. They are not only trying to replicate meat but also the feeling somehow that it makes a person stronger, more macho. The burger is also – reputedly – better for you with less fat, more protein and possibly in the future the addition of omega-3s and other nutrients. Beyond Meat uses non-GM soya, and although this obviously requires land, they argue it still requires fewer resources than feeding a chicken or pig.

Impossible Foods, another start-up company, has gone one step further by trying to create a burger that is 'bloody' by including 'haem', the substance found in our haemoglobin and also found in plants, to create blood. The founder of the company, Stanford biochemistry professor Patrick Brown, is a bit different to the Silicon Valley entrepreneurs – he refused to be bought out by Google – but he has the same motivation. He wants to save and even replace the forests of the world by removing the need for pastures and feedlots. He says he knew he had the perfect meat-free burger when he tasted the blood created out of plants and remembered what it was like to be punched in the face.

San Francisco-based company Hampton Creek Foods, backed by Bill Gates, has investigated more than 1,500 plants to come up with a combination that tastes just like real eggs. It can be used in anything from mayonnaise to scrambled eggs.

In Silicon Valley, where everyone who is anyone is a vegan, the race to become the 'inventor' of the most convincing fake meat will bring millions. But I can't help thinking that just like the most clever tech start-ups, it won't be a billionaire-backed company that cracks the code – it will be a couple of geeks in a rented studio somewhere quite unexpected.

Not all the meat alternatives are plant-based. Biofabrication – or growing cellular structures from stem cells – is also possible. In a way we have been doing it for centuries, growing yeast cultures for bread and beer. Winston Churchill suggested in 1931 that 'We shall escape the absurdity of growing a whole chicken in order to eat the breast or wing, by growing these parts separately under a suitable medium.' He thought it would take 50 years, but we're not there yet.

In 2008 the animal welfare charity PETA offered a US$1m (£715,000) reward to anyone who could produce chicken from a Petri dish. By 2013 the first 'frankenburger' was created. Using blood from foetal calves, a Dutch team from Maastricht University managed to 'grow' the world's first lab burger. The stem cells, which have the power to turn into any cell, were incubated in a nutrient 'broth' until they multiplied many times over three months. The gooey pink mess was then 'exercised' by being stretched back and forth. Finally the strips of 'muscle' were minced and turned into the world's most expensive burger at £250,000 (US$350,000). The burgers were cooked live on television and tested by food critics who agreed they tasted quite like meat but required more fat.

'I haven't eaten meat for 40 years, but if in vitro meat becomes commercially available, I will be pleased to try it,' said Peter Singer, the author of *Animal Liberation* and godfather of the vegan movement. Cultured meat is a 'natural evolution' for humans: environmentally responsible, humane, flexible. It sounds like the perfect solution. The sheet of meat or 'shmeat' is expected to be on shelves within a decade.

Yet I don't like it. I'd almost rather have a soya alternative – or a mushroom. I hate the idea of a pink gooey mass growing exponentially underground, like a 1950s, horror B movie. Eating a burger is not just about the taste and flavour – otherwise why would you call it The Beast or bother about fake blood? It is about where it came from.

And it's about the smell. I am wandering around Edinburgh Farmers' Market, trying to ignore the wafts of roasting meat, when I notice a sign that says 'mheat' rather than meat. Strange. I queue behind other curious shoppers then accept a cocktail stick holding a piece of brown 'steak'. It's good, so good I can't quite believe it. This is no vegan cheese.

The stallholders Hilary and Alberto fit perfectly into the market; they have piercings, ethnic woolly hats, bright eyes and red noses. The 'mheat', they explain, is all made entirely of plant-based products. The Sgaia food range, named after a Venetian word for someone who is cheerful, animated and positive, is stacked up on the stall: vegan smoked sausage, burgers and different types of steak. I can't quite get my head around it. 'Can I come and see how the steak is, er, processed?' 'Of course!' I note down their address and rush off to get a chocolate brownie – well, if I'm not allowed a burger ...

A few days later I turn up at Carlton Die Castings, an industrial estate in Paisley. At first I can't find Hilary and Alberto, so enjoy wandering through the metalworks. There is a sense of old-school industry with huge bits of freshly cast moulds lying in heaps like collapsed robots, and the flash of furnaces. It smells of dust. Eventually I find Hilary and Alberto in their rented studio. It is a totally different world: a cooker, sink and fridges, bags of flour and rows and rows of spices squashed into a tiny space beneath cooling pipes wrapped in foil. It smells delicious.

The pair are hard at work creating their latest range of 'mheats'. On the side is a plate of speck, usually a type of ham. It actually looks like meat – it is exactly the right purplish red with a yellowing fat rind and peppercorns sprinkled through the 'flesh'.

Hilary Masin and Alberto Casotto are both in their early twenties and full of idealism to change the world. They became vegan to reduce their impact on the planet and reduce animal suffering. But they are also Italian. They understand food. If they were going to create a plant-based alternative to meat it had to taste good. It also had to come from the heart. They understand food as more than fuel – as something you make from scratch, with love and integrity.

'Food is a serious business,' says Alberto. 'Food is memories, smells, comfort, safety, cultural heritage, recipes, traditions.'

'We wanted something fresh and artisanal, not from a packet,' adds Hilary. 'Not processed. It's like in Italy: pasta handmade with love to share with people is completely different to dried pasta from the supermarket.'

The pair started experimenting a few months after becoming vegan as they were bored of tofu, beans and chickpeas – 'although we love them' – and craved a more satisfying flavour and texture. Wheat proteins, or seitan, made by washing the starch out of ordinary flour, has been around for centuries. Indeed, it was fed by monks in 6th-century China to the emperor. Like many vegans, Hilary and Alberto experimented at home and found with a bit of creativity they could make different dishes by mixing flavours and adding texture with soya. 'We wanted to preserve taste and texture and traditional cuisine, but make it tasty.'

They were inspired to set up Sgaia Foods by a wider worldwide movement of 'vegan butchers'. In Amsterdam there is a 'Vegetarian Butcher' and in Minneapolis a 'Herbivorous Butcher' set up by Aubry and Kale Walch – yes, his name really is Kale. Eventually, Alberto and Hilary hope to open the first vegan butcher in the UK – in Glasgow. Yes, in the city of Scotch pies and battered sausages. But also a city full of art students.

Hilary and Alberto are from a digital generation. They not only know how meat is made, from watching films like *Cowspiracy*, but they are comfortable with virtual reality. 'Nothing is real any more,' says Hilary. 'Why should meat be real?' She realises that vegans, just like omnivores, want food that has a story. Why shouldn't a vegan butcher have the same principles as a good meat butcher – of knowing where the raw ingredients come from, the best recipes, the best way to prepare and cook the products? 'We want to create something as valid as meat in people's lives. To do that we have to create something from scratch that is delicious, tasty, real.'

Their biggest challenge is texture and the 'barbecue problem' of the 'mheat' falling through the grill. But in terms of flavour they have had some great success, with recipes such as peach and rosemary burgers and smoked steak. Abertay University are working with them to try to create a gluten-free meat alternative that is made out of something other than wheat.

'Vegan food does not have to be about denial, but about adding stuff in,' says Hilary. Alberto has the air of a mad scientist as he throws in wheat protein flour, adds soya for texture, beetroot extract for colour, garlic powder, paprika, molasses and chilli for flavour and yeast for vitamin B12.

He measures out exact amounts of water and kneads. I am thinking this is ridiculous, it looks like a cake, but then it starts looking, well, like meat, bouncy and chewy. We put it in the pressure cooker for 20 minutes and when it comes out, steaming hot, it does taste delicious. I haven't eaten anything like this for months and I'm taken aback at how much I enjoy the 'meaty' texture, how we do indeed perhaps crave it.

Some vegans object to making any plant-based dish that looks and tastes like meat. But Alberto is a realist. He believes that if it helps even some people reduce their meat intake or 'transition' to being a vegan, then it will help. It's like a way of tricking our bodies into being more civilised, even though we are still apes. 'If you are helping people reduce meat intake that is a win,' he says. 'Even if it's just one in 100 going veggie.'

Sometimes Hilary will pop downstairs with a tray of new mheats and try them out on the ultimate carnivores – the metal workers. 'They *quite* like them.' I question Alberto about it: doesn't this 'craving' show that we are designed to eat meat? 'Perhaps our bodies want it,' he concedes. 'But our minds have evolved beyond killing animals. We are evolving beyond meat. In the wild no animal kills unless it needs it – we don't need meat any more.'

It seems like a crazy way to make food, but when I think about it no less crazy than growing a pig, feeding it, slaughtering it, butchering it, hanging it, brining it and spicing it. In fact a part of me wonders why that sort of thing has not died out earlier. Why they are not already offering a plant-based pepperoni alternative at pizza restaurants rather than often cheap meats. Alberto thinks the revolution will come, that in future there will be vegan meat aisles as well as baked goods. Sounds strange, but I don't suppose anyone in the past would have imagined the array of goods we currently have on supermarket shelves in the 'Free From' or 'Exotic Food' aisles. Why not more plant-based products? OK, a few people will still go to butchers, but as a treat. 'I think it will have to happen if we want to keep on living on this planet,' says Hilary.

While multimillionaires set up labs to find the vegan meat of the future, these two Italians, with their sense of food culture and taste, may beat them all to it. 'You know that quote?' says Hilary. 'Progress is the effort towards Utopia or something like that?' I look it up later. It is an Oscar Wilde quote: 'A map of the world that does not include Utopia is not worth even glancing at, for it leaves out the one country at which Humanity is always landing. And when Humanity lands there, it looks out, and, seeing a better country, sets sail. Progress is the realisation of Utopias.'

The appeal of the vegan world is that it is neat – you don't kill any living thing, you are perfect. But of course life is not neat. It is chaotic and messy – and that is what makes it real. A few weeks after meeting Hilary and Alberto, I go back to the farmers' market. It is a busy Sunday afternoon. The hungover students are queuing up for paella and the young professionals are already on the coffee and brownies. It is a noisy, messy, diverse mix of people and foods. Plenty of vegetarian fare is on offer as well as high-quality meat and hot food from around the world.

I wander around the stalls overhearing conversations and thinking back on the experiences I have had sourcing my own meat to eat. At Ridley's Fish and Game a sign urges 'Eat a Grey Squirrel! Save a Red!' The stallholder is describing pheasant as an 'oriental' dish, best used in curries, and how to cook venison. At the Going Native Heritage Breeds stall viewers are admiring the intramuscular fat on Galloway beef steaks. There is an argument going on about whether to grow more trees in the uplands or run livestock that sustains communities. At Peelham Farm Shop, Denise Walton, the farmer, is explaining the joys of meditation and the origins of ruby veal, which is from young cattle kept outside and slaughtered before a year old. She is telling the customer how the animals are taken to the slaughterhouse in Durham, rather than Shotts, as it is a nice straight road down the A1 and more comfortable for the cattle.

People are not just interested in food but also where it is from – even the grisly details. As ethical carnivores they have made a decision to eat meat, and they want to make sure it is from a good source. You might think this is just a small part of the population, but statistics show that we are all eating less meat and many more of us are going to farmers' markets, enjoying the diversity of food culture.

Perhaps this is our new religion? Food. Perhaps it always was. There is the same sort of atmosphere here as any human gathering. A hubbub of conversation, plenty of flirting, laughing, and lots and lots of eating. It's hardly Utopia, but it's a start.

Epilogue

Some hae meat and canna eat,
And some wad eat that want it,
But we hae meat and we can eat,
Sae let the Lord be thankit.
The Selkirk Grace attributed to Robert Burns

The rabbit with the white blaze sits at the bottom of my brother's freezer in a thick brown paper bag while I try to decide what to do with him. Of course I mean to eat him, but he almost seems too special. In the end 'The Ethical Taxidermist' comes to my aid. Sammy Cockhill has seen my blog and wants to help. She is just in time. A storm has cut off the electricity at my brother's house and the freezer is emptied. I rush the rabbit down to Hackney.

Sammy has an achingly cool studio in the East End stuffed with, well, stuffed animals. There are mice in teacups and a

raven hanging from the ceiling. There is a jackdaw with a
beaded beak, a sly fox and various squirrels. Sammy has
made fabulous hats for weddings, including her own,
featuring dove wings. Taxidermy is all the rage now and she
has workshops every afternoon to teach hipsters how to
stuff squirrels. All the animals are sourced ethically from pest
controllers or were roadkill.

I am dreading seeing the rabbit with the white blaze
again but as soon as he slips out of the bag we both exclaim
at how beautiful he is. We sit there drinking coffee and
stroking the rabbit as I explain how I shot him. On closer
inspection we find 'he' is a she, a young doe. Her ears are
soft, like a child's toy.

Sammy and I share our stories. She has been skinning
animals since she was a child, fascinated by their anatomy
and beauty. After a fashion degree she wanted to improve
her skills and perhaps also bring a new perspective to the
taxidermy world, which tends to be populated by rather
gruff older men unwilling to discuss the origins of their
material. Sammy only ever wanted to work with animals
from an ethical origin. She loves my angle, fitting in as it
does with her own views, and agrees to stuff the rabbit as
soon as she can find the time. I pop back in later to collect
the little bag of meat; she is a small rabbit and there is not
much. The skin sits pooled on the desk, ready for curing.

It is almost a year since I shot her. I take her back to my
brother's house. Everyone is busy so I raid the fridge for
olive oil, tomatoes, peppers, the leftovers of some rosé wine.
I cook it slowly, chatting to my sister-in-law, letting the
flavours deepen. We have the usual discussions over my
book but this time it is calmer. I am growing in confidence,
both in shooting and stating my conclusions. I no longer
expect a revelation or a sign by the moon. I have seen
animals die and taken on the responsibility. I have seen how
they are farmed and processed and I have made my own
decisions.

I eat the rabbit all to myself, rosé rabbit ragu, alone in the kitchen, while the children are put to bed. It is cooked in the kind of red orange sauce that stains your chin when you slurp the spaghetti. It tastes like a dish served on a Sicilian mountaintop, rich and tasty.

A few weeks later the stuffed rabbit appears at my publishers. She sits on the bookshelves watching the mostly vegetarian editors do their work. Waiting for me to come and pick her up. Her whiskers still quiver.

Author's Note

The Ethical Carnivore is about my year only eating animals I killed myself. In the event, it ended up being rather more than a year. As I stated in the beginning, I quickly realised that learning to fish, shoot and stalk was not something I wanted to rush. I was also limited by the game seasons, which state by law certain times when animals can be killed in the UK. The investigation of how domestic animals are raised and slaughtered also took a little longer than expected since I was frankly traumatised by my first sight of an abattoir and it took many months to recover. It also took a long time to set up the interviews with abattoirs and to research some of the science and technology behind the process.

All the events in this book are factual, though they are not all described in chronological order.

Now the book is finished, I expect many readers will be interested in how I intend to eat in the future. I would never tell anyone else how to eat; however, I hope my book can inspire people to take an interest in where their meat is from.

I do enjoy eating game and I would like to be able to source it for myself in the future. I don't think I will ever be one of those people who wake up on 12th August with trigger finger itching. If I ever do take it up, I will take the time to be a decent shot. To me it is a lifelong choice, about learning how to identify and stalk the animals of our countryside and, where necessary, butcher and eat them.

It would not be realistic to continue sourcing my own domestic animals. Writing this book has made me aware of what the labels mean in the supermarket and taught me to appreciate butchers and buying meat direct from the farmer. I expect to eat very little meat in future, and where I do source it as ethically as I can.

I realise meat from sources like this is much more expensive. Where possible I have tried to suggest affordable alternatives: an RSPCA Assured chicken costs just pennies extra, though an organic chicken is twice as expensive. Arguably some of the more expensive sausages and processed meats are nutritionally better, so you get more for your money. I hope you are inspired to try different cuts of meat such as liver and heart, which are cheaper, and to find game dealers and butchers who can offer affordable quality meat. Of course, meat sourced yourself in the countryside, once you have learnt the skills, is free. And there are plenty of ways of getting pests such as squirrels and rabbits from gamekeepers and others for a small price – or a pint. Roadkill is always free.

I understand that for many people, the use of animal products is as big an ethical issue as eating meat. I absolutely agree, I just ran out of room for it in this book. I did, however, visit both laying hens and dairy cows during the course of my research.

We are already eating mostly free-range eggs when we buy them fresh, but half the eggs we eat are from caged birds because that is what is used in processed food. The only way to change this is to put pressure on retailers to change. When buying eggs, organic or RSPCA Assured mean the hens are more likely to have had actual free-ranging space, rather than just a door, which they seldom use.

Dairy farming, for me, is a people story. Over the years as an environmental journalist I have interviewed countless dairy farmers going out of business. It is a heartbreaking story and already affecting our countryside as the mixed farms die out. I don't want to see this happen and, where I can, I take the opportunity to buy dairy products direct from smaller dairy farms. In my opinion, larger units do not necessarily mean cattle are suffering more. But there is a limit, a point where both the cattle and the people become 'machines'. Like most consumers I am frustrated by the behaviour of the supermarkets and dairy corporations in pushing down the price and forcing smaller farmers out of business. I'm sure we would all agree that a few more pence on milk from cows grazing outdoors in our countryside would be worth it.

Learning how to cook vegan food has been one of the unexpected joys of writing this book. I have learnt to reduce the use of animal products significantly in my diet and hope to keep those habits. It has made me healthier, and richer. I do think this is the overwhelming trend in the modern diet. As a society I believe we have hit a philosophical wall in terms of accepting factory farming and we crave connection with the meat we eat.

I have kept to my 'kill-to-eat' diet for two years, from July 2014 to July 2016. Everyone knows diets don't work, but habits do. I am now in the habit of eating food that makes me feel good and is from a source I am comfortable with. I hope I am not too annoying at dinner parties. I make mistakes – I am greedy and inconsistent – but I am trying. To me, that is being an ethical carnivore – or, to give it another word, human.

Louise Gray
Edinburgh, July 2016

Appendix

Animals killed and eaten July 2014 to July 2016

3 x oysters

12 x mussels

1 x hand-dived scallop

4 x creel-caught langoustines

2 x creel-caught brown crabs

1 x creel-caught lobster

6 x creel-caught American signal crayfish

1 x brown trout

1 x rainbow trout

1 x cod

1 x pollock

12 x mackerel

1 x pigeon

3 x pheasant (one roadkill)

1 x chicken

3 x rabbits

1 x squirrel

1 x sheep

Half a Berkshire pig (the owner of the animal kept the other half)

1 x red deer (at least half gifted to friends and family; still quite a lot left over)

Not killed myself

A handful of mealworms and crickets

A vegan steak

NB: Each Briton, on average, eats about 85kg (187lb) of meat a year, which roughly translates into 33 chickens, one pig, three-quarters of a sheep and a fifth of a cow (*Independent*, July 2013).

Acknowledgements

A number of animals helped make this book happen, some of them human. I cannot possibly mention everyone, so please consider this a thank you to all the people who have given me tips on stalking, shooting, fishing and writing, introduced me to farmers, opened doors at abattoirs, recommended books, provided advice on cooking game, fed me delicious vegan food and been a shoulder to cry on when it all became too much.

Steve Reynolds is a true English countryman, perhaps one of the last. I owe him a huge debt of thanks for teaching me the most important lesson of all: to respect the quarry. I have much to learn and I hope that one day I can provide some of the joy he has brought to so many people, by learning to source and cook the food of the great British countryside.

Steve Harrod is the perfect gentleman and fishing buddy, and Gerald Stubbs, George Monbiot, Simon Furniss, Oli Hallam, Sheena Goode, Andy Richardson, Peter Cunningham: you are my 21st century Piscators! Thanks to Jack and Robbie Dale for the delicious lobsters, Bram and Richard Haward for the oysters, Spider for the langoustines.

Fishermen of the sea tend to be a salty lot. Nick Hutchings and the crew of the *Britannia of Beesands*, thanks for not making me eat raw fish. I'm sorry I was so rude about the toilet arrangements. Charles Clover for *The End of the Line* and Callum Roberts for *The Unnatural History of the Sea*. Jake Chalmers, Jim and Alex Smith, Ian Burret, and the Professor of Fishing for your knowledge of the oceans.

Mike Park, Jess Sparks and the men and women of Peterhead fish market, thanks for letting me pose kissing that John Dory, before selling it.

Farmers are incredibly busy people, yet many gave up their time to talk to me, including Ross Mackenzie, Denis Rankine, Adrian Ivory, Robert Lanning, Nick Ball and Jacob Sykes, John Gray and Kenneth Gray. There is a new generation of farmers out there and I am excited about what you are all doing to improve and regenerate our shared landscape. Most especially Jade Bartlett and Oli Parsons, Roly and Camilla Puzey, James Rebanks and Nicola Bulgin. If anyone is looking to mail order good meat, look up their websites or Farmdrop.

Fred Berkmiller is a great chef and has helped me contact farmers, abattoirs and butchers to find out how meat is produced.

Abattoirs are supposed to be dark and difficult places. I was always treated politely and, considering all the questions I asked, with a good deal of patience. Special thanks to Philip Goodwin and everyone at Wishaw, St Merryn Foods in Cornwall, Dovecote Park in Yorkshire and Humphrey's in Essex. Slaughtermen and women are not given enough thanks. I watched many at work and I believe you deserve respect from all meat-eaters. You are not dregs and you never were.

Danish Crown in Denmark is leading the world with their slaughterhouse with glass walls. Their transparency is truly impressive. Also thanks to John Gregson of Waitrose and Jo Roberts and Dionne Parker of McDonald's.

Thank you to Temple Grandin for phoning me at 6 am her time and talking for two hours. I guess that is how you change the world, by working so damned hard.

The high street butcher is making a comeback thanks to the education of consumers and the hard work of farmers and quality independent butchers. Thank you to all those butchers who gave me advice during the writing of this book, especially Dave Lyall, who helped butcher my stag at such short notice.

I was invited shooting by some incredibly kind and generous people. Thanks in particular to Tosca Tindall, Dan Tindall, Fiammetta Rocco, Mhairi Morris, the ladies of Glad Rags and Cartridge Bags and The Shotgun and Chelsea Bun Club. Also gamekeepers and experts Richard Thomson, Sam Thompson, Kevin Ramshaw, William and Abigail Alldis, Chris Wheatley-Hubbard and Selena Barr. And ace 'roadkill recycler' Alison Brierley.

I'm also very grateful to my vegetarian and vegan friends. Everyone at Henderson's, and Hilary and Alberto of Sgaia Foods. Angus Buchanan-Smith and family for letting me share an extraordinary day and the whole team at Enroot Collective.

Understanding halal took the help of Ruby and Lutfi Radwan, Nadeem Adam, Said Toliss and family, Sean Wensley, Sameer Rahim and Nabeelah Jaffer.

The Virtues of the Table by Julian Baggini taught me 'to know how to eat is to know how to live'. Jonathan Safran-Foer's *Eating Animals* has also been a source of inspiration.

Thanks to the Kurt Vonnegut Trust for letting me use a quote from the great man and to Seamus MacNally, the National Trust Scotland warden in Torridon, for letting me use an extract from his father's poem featured in *Highland Deer Forest*.

All the team at *Scottish Field*: Richard Bath for commissioning yet another bonkers idea and Mark Duncan for making me look not-too-awful every month.

My stalkers and draggers Charlie Hill, Dan Fields and Ed Wainright-Lee. Not sure I could have gotten a 12 stone beast down the hill by myself.

Friends I have made over the years at the following charities or unions: the Humane Slaughter Association (HSA), Compassion in World Farming (CIWF), the National Farmers' Union (NFU), the Agriculture and Horticulture Development Board (AHDB) Beef and Lamb, British Poultry Council, the Soil Association, Meat Business Women, Friends of the Earth, Country Land and Business Association, the League Against Cruel Sports (LACS), the Royal Society for the Protection of Birds (RSPB), British Association for Shooting and Conservation (BASC), People for the Ethical Treatment of Animals (PETA), Game and Wildlife Conservation Trust (GWCT), National Trust, Countryside Alliance, Greenpeace, Linking Environment and Farming (LEAF), the Campaign to Protect Rural England (CPRE), WWF. Yes, I will put you all in the same sentence, even if it makes you feel uncomfortable, because it's good for you.

So many friends have gamely sourced, cooked, prepared or even just discussed unusual dishes: George Burgess, MJ and David Gray, Jenna Coull, Harriet Lowe, Jade Allen, Zoe Reid, Kirsten and Jonathan Bickford, and Hilary and Sarah Leverton Duncanson, to name a few.

My editor at Bloomsbury, Julie Bailey, and copy-editor Liz Drewitt have been calm and understanding throughout, getting their heads around a subject that is often complex. The vegan illustrator Samantha Goodlet has bravely watched me skin a deer and drawn some beautiful pictures. Thanks also to Sammy Cockhill for stuffing my rabbit and all the staff at Bloomsbury for sharing an office with taxidermy. I'll come and pick her up one day, I promise.

Jim Martin is the first person who looked me in the eye and said with complete confidence, 'You will write a book and I will publish it.' For that, you get this.

Thanks to Patrick Walsh and Carrie Plitt at Conville & Walsh for guidance throughout.

At the start of this book, I moved in with my friend Cal Flyn. She has proved to be a constant source of inspiration and support. Thank you for the advice, the laughter and the rabbit slow-cooked in brandy.

Finally friends and family: Grandma for stories. Hector William, my youngest brother, gave me my first lesson with a rifle and my first squirrel thighs. My big brother James has always gently nudged me in the right direction. Patrick, my wee bro, has been so clearly relieved he has nothing to do with it, it's kind of made me feel better. Anna and Clauds for sending recipes and advice. Loz for helping me with my website. Claire, the Tinsley girls, all the Edinburgh crowd, anyone who has put up with my weird eating habits and Luke for eating all the strange and wonderful food this year has produced. There is plenty more to come.

My father is the true ethical carnivore and this book is dedicated to him. I never found a prayer or a ritual I was comfortable with to say over the animals I killed. Nothing felt genuine. This book is a genuine thank you.

Further Reading

Here are just some of the many highly recommended books that fed into my resarch.

Anderson, Kip. 2015. *The Sustainability Secret*. Earth Aware Editions, San Rafael, California.

Baggini, Julian. The Virtues of the Table. Granta Books, London.

Cooney, Nick. 2014. *Veganomics*. Lantern Books, New York.

D'Silva, Joyce & Webster, John. 2010. *The Meat Crisis*. Routledge, Abingdon.

Ellis, Hattie. 2007. *Planet Chicken*. Sceptre, London.

Fairlie, Simon. 2010. *Meat: A Benign Extravagance*. Permanent Publications, Petersfield.

Harrison, Ruth. 1964. *Animal Machines*. Vincent Stuart Publishers Ltd, London.

Lymbery, Philip, and Isabel Oakeshott. 2014. *Farmageddon*. Bloomsbury, London.

MacNally, Lea. 1970. *Highland Deer Forest*. J. M. Dent & Sons, London.

Monbiot, George. 2013. *Feral*. Penguin, London.

Rebanks, James. 2015. *The Shepherd's Life*. Penguin, London.

Renton, Alex. 2013. *Planet Carnivore*. Guardian Books, London.

Safran Foer, Jonathan. 2009. *Eating Animals*. Little, Brown and Company, New York.

Walton, Izaak. 1653. *The Complete Angler*. The Bodley Head, London.

Wigan, Michael. 2013. *The Salmon: The Extraordinary Story of the King of Fish*. Harper Collins, London.

Young Lee, Paula. 2008. *Meat, Modernity and the Rise of the Slaughterhouse*. University of New Hampshire Press, New Hampshire.

Index